10 WAYS to Sell MORE Stuff, to MORE People, MORE Often, for MORE Money, and with MORE Efficiency

By T.J. Rohleder
"America's Blue Jeans Millionaire"

TABLE OF CONTENTS

INTRODUCTION

Hello there! **I'm T. J. Rohleder, President of M.O.R.E., Inc., America's leading direct marketing company.** In this book, I'm going to discuss the latest incarnation of our Ruthless Marketing System, which can help you make a fortune. I'm living proof of its effectiveness: **in the past 25 years, my company has made well over $100,000,000 in profits.** Sometimes, I literally have more money than I know what to do with!

Now, I realize that the term "ruthless" has some negative connotations in most people's imaginations. But we don't mean it as a bad thing—at least, not for you or your customers. So let me start by providing you with our definition of Ruthless Marketing:

Ruthless Marketing has nothing to do with ripping people off. **It's about maximizing your share of the sales and profits in your target marketplace, which requires a gentler, more personable strategy.** To do this, you must be able to re-sell to the largest possible number of customers again and again. You can't do that by souring them on you and your company. However, all ruthless marketers *do* have a few things in common: they're aggressive and they're relentless. To be a relentless marketer, you've got to develop the heart of the lion, the mind of the fox. **You've got to be bold and audacious, and a little bit cunning in order to seize the greatest opportunities. You've got to outcompete your competitors, and make their customers yours.** It's not about lying to people or cheating them—it's about mastering the art of getting the largest possible number of people in your market to give you the largest amount of their disposable income they can afford, in exchange for the tremendous value you have to offer them.

So rethink your definition of "ruthless." We could have called this the "Aggressive Marketing System" rather than the "Ruthless Marketing System." But it just didn't have the same flavor. Using the term "ruthless" in the title sounds more dramatic, doesn't it? And the truth is, it's more accurate—as you'll see in the following pages.

The Ruthless Marketing Mindset

One of my favorite books was written in the mid-1980s. It's called *Behind the Golden Arches* by John F. Love, and it's the story of the McDonald's restaurant chain. It's out of print, but you can still buy it secondhand on eBay—if you can find a copy I haven't already bought.

In Chapter 6, Love tells this story:

It was the early 1960s. Jack Roschman was standing in a Burger Chef he was about to open in Springfield, Ohio. It was to be one of more than a hundred Burger Chefs that Roschman would open in Ohio under his franchise for the entire state. But the opening in Springfield would never be forgotten.

A construction crew across the street was putting the finishing touches on a brand new McDonald's restaurant, and Roschman was intently watching the progress of the restaurant that would be his first head-to-head encounter with his archrival. He saw a man walking from McDonald's to his Burger Chef and he assumed it was the new McDonald's franchisee. It was actually Ralph Lanfor, McDonald's new area supervisor, and as he approached Roschman was preparing to exchange pleasantries and suggest that maybe the two new hamburger stores might provide each other emergency supplies of hamburgers and buns and other fast food supplies. He knew that McDonald's was gaining a reputation as not exactly the friendliest operator around. But nevertheless, he was not prepared for the greeting that he got. **And here was that greeting: "Hello, I'm the new McDonald's supervisor," Lanfor told Roschman, "and we're going to run you out of business."**

I first read that story years ago, and I've never gotten it out of my mind. Here was a man who thought it was all going to be about friendly competition, and sharing supplies when one or the other ran out—and McDonald's wasn't friendly at all. **They had this kill-or-be-killed attitude towards their competition, and still do.** They're loyal to their customers; but when it comes to their competition, McDonald's is very aggressive— and quite ruthless.

For me, "ruthless" means doing everything legally, morally, and ethically allowable to grow your business, regardless of what it means to your competition. So if it means that you gain a massive percentage of the market share and actually run a company out of town, or if a company goes bankrupt or belly up because you're better at attracting and serving the marketplace... well, that's just good business, and there's nothing wrong with it. All successful businesses think this same way.

Wal-Mart wouldn't care, for example, if Target went belly

up. They'd probably be dancing in the streets. McDonald's wouldn't shed a tear if Burger King went bankrupt, or if Wendy's went out of business. **They want more of the market share, so they can be more successful, serve more customers, and make more profits.** They can't worry too much about the health of other companies when they're watching their own bottom line.

Ruthless marketing is all about doing things that help you build your business bigger than the competition. I think more business owners should be treating business as a sport or as a game, keeping score with money. It's a competition—which is why we use that term for the other sellers in your market. **In order to compete effectively, you've got to aggressively make yourself known, and do something to distinguish you from the other players.** So ask yourself: what can I do differently? How can I be distinctive? If you're going to run the same type of Yellow Page ads right next to each other, or use the same door hangers or radio spots, then there's really not much competition there. You're going to get a few customers, they're going to get a few customers, and you'll both limp along.

That's not good enough. **You've got to leverage everything legally, morally, and ethically allowable to beat the competition—and you have to do it in your own unique style.** So you're obligated to try things your competition knows nothing about, to discover and implement new strategies, techniques, and ideas to help you grow your business and take a larger share of the market than your competition has. Ultimately, this gives you the opportunity to beat your competition, to serve more customers, and to make more money. If you're a true entrepreneur—if you're somebody who really wants to succeed in business—then this *must* be your goal! Sure, it's great to be nice and friendly to our neighbors and the people in our communities, but in business, that's a loser's strategy. **To succeed against your competition, you've got to be both ruthless and willing to think outside the box...** to even go beyond anything you've ever heard of anyone else doing.

That's what I'm going to teach you in this book, in the course of ten intensive modules. **I'll outline the strategies, methods, and techniques you can use to seize a major advantage—some people might even say an unfair advantage—over your competition.** I'll show you how you can take your business to the next level, and enjoy more success, more customers, and more profit than your current competition. In fact, these ideas can lift you to a completely different level, unlocking the success you've been struggling to find. So read each of these modules carefully, more than once. Implement the information you'll find in the Ruthless Marketing Program, because these techniques provide the tools you can use to transform your business and lifestyle.

Even as you treat this as a game, take it seriously—just as a professional athlete would. If you can't see doing that with a game, consider it a kind of war. In his book *Made In America*, the late Sam Walton (founder of Wal-Mart) discussed the fact that he got thrown out of more K-Mart stores than any other person in history, because he was always in there snooping around. Now, they didn't forcefully throw him out like a bouncer might toss a drunk out of a bar, but K-Mart security did often escort him out of their stores and tell him to get lost. Even so, he probably was in K-Mart stores more often than any person in their company. He was constantly checking out the competition, keeping himself in the game—or the war, if you prefer.

That kind of market research combines with the concept of

differentiating yourself to help you give your customers something they can't get anywhere else. That's the kind of proactive, offensive kind of thinking that distinguishes a ruthless marketer. **It's ruthless, it's aggressive—but it's honest and honorable.**

I'm glad you're reading this book right now, and I recommend that you read it repeatedly, and write notes in the margins, and stick Post-Its all over the place so you'll be able to return to the important points again and again. **But it's one thing to read about Ruthless Marketing; it's another thing to implement it.** As I lead you through these modules, it's important that you consistently think through how you can implement the strategies I'm telling you about. How can you put them into play to attract the greatest number of customers, and help make their lives better? **Because I guarantee, when you can do that and retain those people long term, you'll make all the money you'll ever want or need.**

Ready to learn how to make a million bucks? Let's get to it!

CHAPTER ONE:

On Being Ruthless, and Why It Matters

In true warfare, invaders like the Vikings and Spanish conquistadores who set out to conquer other countries would often figuratively—and sometimes literally—burn their ships when they got there, so there was no way out except to win. In business, this translates to total commitment. When I meet businesspeople (and I've met thousands over the years), I can always pick out the ones who are going to be successful by their high level of commitment—the fire in their belly and the look in their eyes that says, "I'm going to make this work!" Sometimes they fail; but then they get back up and get back in the race. **Ruthless Marketing requires that total commitment to making your product or company the best, so you can beat out your competition.**

Over the years, I've usually been in the forefront of this push to be the best. But it's easy get off track; there are times when you get a little lazy, and you're not putting forth the full effort you might otherwise. **When that happens, it doesn't take long to see that you're moving backwards.** You have to get back there and start pushing again; and as you do, it's very exciting to think about Sam Walton and what he did with Wal-Mart. Or consider Steve Jobs of Apple, and people like Fred Smith of FedEx or Jack Welch of the early edition of General Electric. **These people were passionate about their businesses, and were determined**

to make them successful. So don't misread the word "ruthless" here. I'm not talking about beating up the competition physically; I'm talking about using your brains and ingenuity to beat them fair and square in the marketplace.

Many marketers are far too passive... and many business people don't really think of themselves as marketers. They put themselves in a specific category, like plumber, dentist, electrician, attorney, or dry cleaner, and aren't aggressive enough about bringing themselves to the market's attention. **They have a specialty they're good at, so they've decided to turn it into a job—and that's basically all they've done.**

Put Marketing First

Here's a good example: my Marketing Director, Chris Lakey, has a man who does yard work for him. Whenever Chris needs some re-sodding or landscaping work, he's the guy Chris contacts. He's good at what he does—but he's a terrible marketer. Chris contacted him this past fall, right at the end of the season, asking him for a bid on some work he needed to have done before winter set in. Chris knew that he would be pushing it, but he also knew that the guy could do it if he got right on it. Well, a front moved in unexpectedly, bringing a hard freeze soon after Chris contacted him—and so the work couldn't be done until spring.

Well, as a good marketer, Chris figured that he would be first on the yardman's list as soon as spring came, given that he had a job lined up waiting for the weather to change. **But the man never called.** Chris could have called him to remind him about the work, but instead, he decided to do the work himself. So the yardman lost out on a profitable job, when all he had to do was call Chris and say, "Hey, are you ready for me to get started?"

Chris probably would have said yes, because he doesn't like yardwork that much. But the man never called. He's good at landscaping, but he's not good at marketing.

A ruthless marketer doesn't miss out on chances like that. **He's keeps track of his customers and is aggressive about reminding them when they need to do business with him.** But if you're a business owner and simply don't see yourself as a marketer, then you've completely missed the first part of the equation—and that's where I think a lot of businesses go wrong. *You have to start with the premise that you are a marketer,* **no matter what your business is.** If you don't see yourself as a marketer, then you'll never figure out how to be an aggressive marketer.

And you *have* **to be aggressive, because just as in any competition—game, war, or business—there are certain forces that are working against you.** I'm not trying to be dramatic here; it's a stone cold fact. The competition is fierce, whether direct or indirect. Even if people aren't deciding to buy the same products and services you offer from someone else, they do have to choose between buying either apples or oranges, if you will. Do they buy your moneymaking opportunity, or get a new hot tub? Should they buy your coaching service, or a spoiler for their Mustang, or a year's supply of steaks? There's only so much discretionary income to go around.

So you've got all this competition both inside and outside your marketplace—and some of your competitors are very aggressive marketers indeed. They're not just sitting around waiting for business to come to them; **they're out there doing everything possible to extract as much money as they can from the very same people you're chasing.** If they're smart—

and you bet they are—then once they get those customers, they'll try to do such a good job of serving them, and they'll be so ruthless in maintaining and building those relationships, that the customer's never going to want to go anywhere else. **If that happens, you're losing money that could and should be yours!**

That has to be your attitude here. From the get-go, you have to clearly perceive and understand all the different marketing forces working against you: the increased competition, some of whom are very, very aggressive, *and* the fact that your best prospects are trying very hard to hold onto every penny they can. **They're very skeptical, you see, and they're holding back all the time.**

Again, you have to look at this as warfare—you've got to be out to win, or what's the point? The way you win is by being aggressive, by being offensive, by being proactive, by differentiating yourself so you offer things nobody else possibly can, in ways that make people so happy they won't go anywhere else... *and* they'll tell their friends and family about you. You can't sit around waiting for people to find you and figure out on their own how special you are, and then be upset when they don't.

This is especially true if you're lucky enough to be in an area or industry where everyone else is doing just that. Sooner or later, someone who understands marketing will start building their business and taking customers away from everyone else. You need to be that person. **Start being proactive now, before someone else comes in and creates a huge business in a short time**—not necessarily because their business model is any better than anyone else's, but because they understand Ruthless Marketing. It's a lot easier to take the lead in creating a systematic marketing approach to bring in customers from other businesses than it is to try to catch up when you've already started losing customers.

Business conducted properly—ruthlessly—is a full contact sport you're playing to win, where you've got skin in the game and you're deeply committed. **No matter how often you get beat down, you need to get right back up again, and participate aggressively no matter what.** This puts you on a different philosophical path than when you just come to work and do the thing that the business does to make money. It requires a more strategic approach, and a bigger vision than the old nine-to-five work ethic. You've got to throw yourself into the game, let your emotions become involved, even have some fun. Because you know, this isn't "work" in a traditional sense, even though you may end up sweaty and bruised from the full-contact nature of the sport.

You've seen how hard athletes in those kinds of sports work. **But at the same time, they're also enjoying themselves, feeding that part of that human spirit that thrives on the best things that life has to offer.**

Boring = Bankrupt

My close colleagues and I work with many businesspeople in hundreds of different types of businesses. And the sad truth is, for most businesses—especially those in retail, for example—doing business is simply a matter of opening the doors and putting up the sign that says, "We're Open." Now, if you happen to have a nice little store in a hot spot downtown or in a major shopping center, you might actually make it just by having good products and being open for business. **But for 99% of the businesses out there, you need a lot more than that.**

If a restaurant's in a key location, then chances are they can make it—if the food is good. **But if you really want to squeeze out all the money that's available, you've got to market hard and aggressively.** You've got to use your head to get customers. Our mentor, Russ von Hoelscher, likes to tell a story about how 30 years ago, the gas lamp area of San Diego was all porno, massage parlors, hockshops, and soup kitchens. Now it's a beautiful place, with great boutiques and restaurants. Back then— when it was still third rate—there was an Italian restaurant down there called Sonny's that specialized in these wonderful hoagie sandwiches. They were just delicious, and the entire family put all their effort into making the business work. But they found themselves trapped in an area where all these sleazy businesses were opening up around them, and didn't know what to do.

Russ went in there often with his friends, and got to talking to the owners. They told him about their dilemma, and Russ said, "Look, just three blocks from here is a nice part of town. That's where all the insurance companies and the big banks are. If you want to get people to come down here to eat, make up a bunch of sandwiches, cut them up into small pieces, and send the girls up there with samples." And they said, "Well, they might not let us in." Russ replied, "Oh yeah, if you've got free food, they'll let you in!" So Sonny's started to do this, and within days they had hundreds of new people coming down to eat at this restaurant in the bad part of town.

Sometimes, all it takes to pump up the volume on your business is simple things like that. Russ currently works with a chiropractor in Pacific Beach who wanted to know how to get more business. He told her, "You're going to have to offer a consultation and evaluation, maybe even some free X-rays to get people to come in." And she said, "Oh my gosh, that costs so much money, Russ! I don't want to spend a whole bunch of money just trying to get a few new people!" Well, that's a mistake. Russ told her, **"Listen, it's not going to cost that much—and you'd better be willing to spend some money, because you've got to separate yourself from the competition.** All of them are in the Yellow Pages, and they're all saying the same things. **If you make a free offer, people will come in for that—and then you can try to sell them on more.** Many of them will buy; some won't." Well, she listened to Russ—and it worked like magic.

It's just a matter of changing your perspective to "No longer are we just open for business—now we're out to *get* the business! We're not just here to serve you. We're going to find you, bring you in here, and then we'll serve you even better." Ruthless marketing requires you to do whatever you have to (legally and morally) to attract and retain your customers. Now, there are a very few businesses that don't need to do this to survive. On the road from San Diego to Las Vegas, Russ tells me, there used to be a spot past Riverside on Highway 15 with a sign that read, "Last Call For Gas And Water—Next Gas 148 Miles." You don't want to run out of gas out in the middle of nowhere, so of course that was a draw. That business wasn't likely to suffer from lack of customers, even if they did no more business than that. Russ remembers driving that route once and his friend's wife seeing that sign and saying, "Do we have enough gas?" and he said, "Oh, about a half a tank; we can make it to Vegas, I'm pretty sure." And she said, "What do you mean, you're *pretty* sure? It's going to be 148 miles. Get into that station!"

Russ thought to himself at the time that this was one place that didn't need much of a unique selling position (USP), simply because it's 148 miles from anyone who can compete with it. **Most people coming up on it are going to stop and buy gas, even if they don't really need to.** But most of us don't have that luxury.

To get back to Russ's restaurant example: **most people are afraid to have to give away their product for free**—especially if, in the meantime, they expect to be broke and frustrated. But it's a simple idea, and illustrates well this whole concept of getting out there and kicking ass with some aggressive marketing. **It doesn't have to be complicated at all—and I believe that such simplicity is sometimes the key to success.** Sometimes Small hinges can swing big doors—but if you don't know what those small hinges are, then you can't implement them. So you end up spending thousands of dollars when the Yellow Pages guy comes by and has you sign the contract... and then you've got your same old, same old ad out there.

Measure by Measure

One of the great things about Ruthless Marketing is that, in addition to going above and beyond average marketing, **you don't necessarily have to spend a ton of money on it—despite what most business owners think.** Most people have been trained to believe they have to spend a fortune on advertising. Well, most people are using image advertising. Maybe they put their name on a park bench or do some radio advertising, but they're not really doing anything to attract buyers into their business—just reminding people they exist.

Doing Ruthless Marketing means doing more effective marketing. You can take the same marketing dollars you're already spending on image advertising, which doesn't produce much that you can gauge, and put it into techniques and strategies that won't just bring people into your business, but will also allow you to see the direct results of the marketing you're doing. **That way, you're not wasting money—you're using it effectively.** Now, you've got to do *some* advertising if you're a serious marketer; there's no getting around that. But you don't have to take the ad agency's word that this or that method will work great for you. They're just trying to sell ad space.

The methods I'll discuss in this publication will help you understand exactly how your marketing works, and how to tell whether it's working or not. Instead of being confused and frustrated about what's going on with your advertising, as so many business owners are, you can actually see how effective it is at a glance. Let's look again at Russ's restaurant example, because it's a great illustration of what happens when you're willing to give something away to attract business—and the results are obvious and easy to measure. **But in order to give something away, you have to be willing to spend money,** and many of the small business owners I've met are pretty tight-fisted. Well, frugality does make sense; flippantly spending money can get you in trouble. But so can being a tightwad. You've heard the old cliché, "You've got to spend money to make money." It's a cliché because it's true.

That simple decision to give away free sandwich samples to attract business cost the restaurant a significant amount of money. They could have sat there and done nothing instead... but if they had, people just a few blocks away wouldn't have had any idea of what they were missing, because this great sandwich shop was stuck in the middle of that unpalatable neighborhood. But those samples drew in a huge amount of business from the skyscrapers just a few blocks away, and **that business more than paid for their giveaway—especially since they netted some long-term**

customers.

Here's another example: once upon a time, a dry cleaning store decided to try to get more business by putting together a promotion where they would clean, for free, everything you could fit into a standard trash bag. For the people who did that, they made a second offer: next time, we'll do a bagful for half off. Well, that got a lot of people to come back. Then they did it *again*. **In the past, they'd found that if they could get someone to do business with them three times, they were likely to have a customer for life—unless they screwed something up royally.**

Most businesses would *never* do something like that, because frankly it would cost them a fortune. But ultimately, that dry cleaner attracted a lot of new, long-term business from that promotion, and made a lot of money they wouldn't have otherwise. **The lesson here is that you have to be willing to spend some money. You have to be willing to give something away—to do something to attract the business you're looking for.** That's the basis of Ruthless Marketing: implementing strategies for aggressively promoting your business, so you can acquire new customers and do more repeat business with your existing customers. One of the best ways to do that is to be willing to spend money. Otherwise, you'll never get the kind of customers you're looking for—even if, as in the example of Russ's sandwich shop, they are plenty of prospects right there in the local area. Sadly, until they gave away those free samples, most of the prospects had no idea that restaurant was there—and so Sonny's was struggling, barely making it.

Here's the thing: the awareness has to go in both directions. They need to be aware of you, and how well you can serve them, and *you* have to be constantly aware that all the money you want is out there waiting for you right now. It's in the pockets and purses and available lines of credit of thousands of potential prospective buyers—or even millions, if you're in a national marketplace. **All you have to do is find something to trip their triggers.** You have to be able to offer the thing they're looking for that they can't get anywhere else, or that they desire the most.

Another awareness that goes along with that is realizing this: with rare exceptions (stemming from certain legal or personal problems), no business ever went out of business because their sales and profits were too high. And where do sales and profits come from? Simple: **you just get enough people to give you enough money over a long enough period of time, with a high enough profit margin per transaction.** That's the whole secret, right there in a nutshell. To put yourself ahead of the crowd, to pierce the shell of your prospect's indifference, you have to pour your creativity into your marketing, and advance aggressively with it. Don't just run some standard ad the first time a salesman comes by to sell you one. Be offensive, proactive, and creative. Be willing to give away some sandwiches—however that happens to translate for your business.

This works everywhere, not just in the food service industry. **First you give, and then you receive.** It's a universal principle. **One of the things it does is kick in the power of reciprocity, which is the tendency for a person to do something nice for you if you do something nice for them.** If you give them a free sandwich sample or a free bag of dry cleaning and they like it, they may feel obliged to do something nice for you by buying whatever you're selling. **It makes them more open and receptive to your offer, especially if you present your giveaway with true sincerity.**

Be ruthless and take advantage of that tendency.

Important Questions

So ask yourself: where are my best customers? How can I prove to them that I have the goods they really want or need? Once you've answered those questions to your satisfaction, implement your solution on a small scale and see what happens. If the result is positive enough, roll it out aggressively, and get those Ruthless Marketing methods into play. **Because as the saying goes, you're either going out *for* business, or you're going out *of* business.** Those are your only two options. If you're not doing what it takes to get all the business available in your marketplace, then someone might as well stick a fork in you — because you're done.

Most business owners have no real understanding of how much money is being spent in their own marketplaces; there's probably a lot more available than they can even imagine. **As a marketer, you goal is to capture the biggest possible share of people's discretionary income — the money they can afford to spend.** It's up to them to determine how much that is, so don't assume you're depriving them of the rent or utilities money. By and large, people are smarter than that. Their discretionary income is the extra part of their income, above and beyond the basics, that they're going to end up spending on *something*, whether it's McDonald's milkshakes or the latest designer sneakers. Why shouldn't they spend that money on your products and services instead... especially when you can help them solve a problem or make more money?

Ruthless Marketing is not about depriving people of necessities. It's about getting the biggest share of your

---

marketplace's *disposable* income. That's it. Again, your mindset should be, **"If someone is going to spend a hundred dollars a month on things that aren't necessities, then why shouldn't they spend that money with me?"** This assumes you don't actually sell a necessity, of course. But generally, we're beyond things with razor-thin profit margins like underwear, shaving cream, and electricity. You want the money they can afford to spend otherwise—whether that's a hundred, a thousand, or ten thousand dollars per month.

Remember: in a free market economy like ours, both the buyer and the seller act in their own best interests. **It's up to the buyer to decide what their best interest is; yours is to aggressively market what you're selling.** So remember: don't let the negative connotations of the term "ruthless" slow you down. Your ability to profit depends entirely on your ability to sell your products and services, and you've got to beat out a lot of other people who are trying to do the same thing. While you don't want to be ruthless in any sense in your personal relationships, **"ruthless" isn't a dirty word in marketing. It's a** *necessity*— not only in terms of going out for all the business you can possibly capture, but also in terms of being the best you can be and dominating your competition.

Enlightened Selfishness

If I need or want to buy something, it's in my best interest to seek out that product or service. **I'm making a decision that the money in my pocket is less valuable than the thing I want to buy.** On the other side of the equation, you, as the business owner, know it's in your best interest to have your business make a profit. **That means you're offering me things I want to buy that you're willing to exchange for the money in my pocket.**

So that's a good deal for both of us. In both cases, we're making decisions based on what we feel is in our own best interests.

When you keep those things in mind, you realize that this isn't a strategy predicated on taking advantage of people or the situations they're in. **Instead, you just want to aggressively take advantage of and capitalize on the existing marketplace without doing anything immoral, illegal, or unethical.** When you get right down to basics, this is all just about people deciding to come together and do business.

One of the reasons that you, as a seller, have to proceed aggressively in the marketplace is the fact that having the best product or service is simply not good enough. A free marketplace is inherently unfair. Unless you've somehow arranged government protection for yourself (which is even more unfair, and of questionable morality to boot), **you can't just sit back, content in the knowledge that you have the very best product or service in the marketplace, and expect to come out on top.** It won't happen if you've got aggressive competitors. They might actually have the worst product in their particular niche, and still rake in the dough because they have a better marketing system in place. It's not good enough just to have the best product or service; you've got to do the best job at marketing.

That's what this Ruthless Marketing Program will teach you to do. To become the best marketer, you've got to be aggressive yourself. That sets up the playing field to your advantage. And the good news is, most business owners are too weak-minded and passive to take advantage of Ruthless Marketing; **so all you have to do is be a little more aggressive than they are, and you'll start to see amazing results.** And besides, as long as you have something that gives your prospects the biggest results they want

---

the most, then you're doing them a real disservice if you're *not* aggressive—that is, not trying to do everything possible to serve them in the highest possible way.

Think about that. You're not taking advantage of people by ruthlessly pushing ahead of the competition and marketing aggressively to your prospects. If you really do have the goods and you can deliver the results they want, then you're actually doing them a disservice if you don't do everything possible to get them to give you their money in exchange for those benefits you'll provide. **Ruthless Marketing goes beyond just beating the competition. It's rooted in an obligation to help as many people as you can as well as you can, with an excellent benefit that completely fulfils their needs.** You have to deliver real, solid value, and develop a mutually beneficial relationship in the process.

You're looking for a win-win situation. The marketer wins because he ends up with more customers, more money, and more success. The customers win because they've fulfilled a need or want in an effective, even spectacular way. Ideally, both sides will remain in that relationship that benefits them long-term, because now the marketer knows them better than ever and can better fulfill their needs, while the customer likes and trusts the marketer, and feels safe with them. That's one more of life's decisions that's easier to make. Everybody wins all around.

So don't worry about the negative connotations of the world "ruthless." The reality is, when you use the Ruthless Marketing techniques I'll teach you in this book, **you're just doing your best for both yourself and your clients, creating more success for everyone.** The only downside here is to those businesspeople who fail to understand that effective marketing—marketing that generates more income and more customers—is the key to long-term success for almost any business. **The people who ignore the chance to learn about this type of marketing, or refuse to implement these strategies and techniques to build their business, are going to be left by the wayside.** They're going to be hurting in good and bad economies alike, and are going to struggle forever for business. Don't be one of those people!

Sadly, most business people don't think that much about marketing; they think first about their product or service. They're restaurateurs, booksellers, electricians, plumbers, or insurance agents first. That's a wrong-headed attitude. First and always, they need to be marketers. **Marketing should never be secondary;** otherwise you put yourself at the mercy of the advertisers from the Yellow Pages or the radio or Val-Pak. Most businesspeople, especially those in service industries, do very poor advertising, consisting of little more than getting their name and number in front of people. They do very little to entice people to come to them as opposed to one of their competitors.

This doesn't mean you can't let others do your marketing for you; you just need to understand what good advertising looks like. That way, when you hire someone to help you with your marketing, you can look over their shoulder and determine—based on your studies and experience—whether they're doing the right thing. A plain name, address, and phone number isn't good enough. That's not going to make you much if any money, because everyone else is doing the same thing. **You need to develop a new perspective on what you are, and your role in the marketing of your business—and that's the goal of this Program.** I call it "Ruthless Marketing," **but what I'm really going to teach you is how to create the *greatest* marketing, campaigns that just beat the tar out of your competition.** Even if you don't involve yourself directly in the marketing—and I urge you to do so—at least you'll learn what good marketing looks like, so you'll be able to tell when the people you hire to do your marketing are on the right track.

A "Stupid" Idea

When I first got started back in 1985, I had a conventional carpet cleaning business with my buddy, Gary. We tried all kinds of things to make money; we really hustled. We knocked on thousands of doors, made lots of phone calls, gave away tons of free bids, did everything we possibly could—and it was all hit-and-miss. During the busy season, the six months of the year during the spring and fall, we did okay. But during the winter and summer months we practically starved to death. We listened to all kinds of advice from well-meaning people, and did what most small business owners do: **we followed the followers. We bought newspaper ads where we let other people write copy for us, we took out Yellow Pages ads... and it was all just a huge waste.**

Most people who sell advertising present themselves as if they understand everything about advertising and marketing... and they usually don't. These people are *not* experts in advertising or marketing; if they're experts at anything, it's in selling the display ads or broadcast spots on radio and TV. They're salespeople! I value my salespeople greatly, but I don't assume that just because somebody's a good salesperson they're also an expert at advertising. **These ad salespeople usually aren't—so they're misleading people, giving them the wrong advice just so they can make more sales.**

Personally, I feel it's a mistake to turn your marketing and advertising over to anybody else. **You've got to take charge of it, you've got to be responsible for it, and you've got to think outside the box.** It took me a while to figure this out, back when I was in the carpet cleaning business. For a couple of years, I beat my head against the wall, trying to do everything I could to drum up business. Then I had this one crazy idea that turned it around for me. I did a trade show, and because I had to have a show special, I came up with the idea of giving away three rooms of carpet cleaning absolutely free as part of a little contest.

There wasn't much to it: I had a handwritten flyer that read, "Win 3 Rooms of Carpet Cleaning Free," with 5 x 7 index cards that people could fill out with their contact information and drop into a little shoebox. That was it. When people came by the booth, my wife and I would say to them, "Hey, why not register to win three rooms of carpet cleaning?" A lot of people did, and later on we picked one and announced the winner. **But I had 50 or 60 leads left over, so I called those people back.** By then, having spent a couple of years in the business and talking to thousands of prospects in the process, I had my pitch down cold, and I knew what it took to talk about my services.

But I had never before experienced sales that came so quickly and easily. Within 90 minutes, I had two weeks booked solid. For the first week or two after that happened, I was in a state of shock, because I had never made that much money that quickly and easily before. Later we repeated it at other trade shows, and enjoyed similar success.

But you can only do so many of those home shows. So I came up with this silly idea of putting a little ballot box in a Mexican restaurant. Or at least, all my friends and family told me it was stupid and gimmicky, and acted like it was a joke at best. But this was a Mexican restaurant where you had to stand and wait for your food. I ate there all the time, so the owner knew me and let me put my ballot box there. **And sure enough, people registered.** I gave out a prize a month, and then called up everyone else and told them they'd won a consolation prize, conditional on them paying me to do a certain amount of carpet cleaning.

Well, even though all my friends told me it was a dumb idea, I still closed one out of three of those leads. I would give them their choice of several different things, and people just loved it! I closed those sales one after another—because the thing about it was, the only people who registered to win free carpet cleaning were the ones interested in getting their carpets cleaned anyway. With my little ballot box, I was getting people to raise their hand and say, "Yes, I'm interested!"

I turned that little carpet cleaning business into a moneymaking machine. Not long after that, my wife and I got involved in the direct response business. **We used a variation of that same simple strategy to generate millions of dollars in sales by offering people a free Report—something of value that only the most serious people raised their hands to ask for.** We converted a large percentage of those leads into sales, then we followed up and turned many of those people into long-term customers—and kept giving them more of what they bought from us the first time.

It all started when I did something unconventional, creative—and ultimately ruthless, in the positive, aggressive business sense. We didn't get a visit from a salesman saying, "Hi, I'm from the Acme Ballot Box Contest Company, and we want to put a ballot box contest together for you." It was just an idea I came up with on my own—a dumb little idea, according to my friends and family. Gimmicky. Stupid. "It might have worked in the home show, but it won't work anywhere else," they said. And yet I tried it anyway—and they were dead wrong. **If I'd listened to all those people and given up on the idea, there's no telling where I'd be today.**

You've got to learn how to ignore all the naysayers in your business, even (or maybe especially) the people who care about you, the ones who are honestly trying to help you. **That's part of being a ruthless marketer, too. It frees you to do the things you need to do, no matter how unconventional they may be,** to identify the small group of people who are serious enough about what you're offering that they'll raise their hands and say, "Yes, I'm interested." When you do that with a simple little system—no more complicated than my ballot box—you'll close a super-high percentage of sales. Once I started doing that with my carpet cleaning, I never had to do any cold calling again.

The Magic of Creative Thinking

"Free" is always a powerful incentive in marketing; that was part of what drove my success. People wanted that prize I offered. Now, obviously, most people wouldn't just randomly fill out the card and put it in the box; only the people who needed and could use carpet cleaning did that. And it works everywhere: trade shows, other people's businesses, and your own. Russ von Hoelscher once owned a chain of bookstores in California, and in each store he had a nice-sized box with fancy decorations and a sign on it that said, **"Drop your business card in here to win $50 worth of free books."** Prizes were awarded twice a month for each store. For those who didn't have business cards, he had paper and pen handy.

Once people did that, Russ would send them specials in the mail, telling them that they'd just received new books in their favorite categories, whether that was Harlequin Romance, mystery, or science fiction, pointing out that the store was having a sale offering 10-15% off. **Russ says that while it didn't bring in droves of people, it did bring people in, so it was well worth doing.** When you're in business, you have to constantly do things like that—constantly be thinking, "What can I do to make my business better and different?"

In the Introduction to this book, I gave you an example of Ruthless Marketing as practiced by McDonald's. Here's another fantastic McDonald's story. One day, one of Ray Kroc's vice-presidents was making the daily bank deposits for several stores in the Chicago area. Instead of going into the bank, he noticed that the bank now had a drive-thru teller. As he was trying it out, an idea hit him: ***Why can't fast food restaurants** also **have drive-thrus?** **And that was how the first restaurant chain drive-thru was born.*** The innovation gave McDonald's another ruthless edge over their competition. Now just about everyone does business that way. **It just goes to show that you've always got to keep thinking—and to be willing to adapt ideas from completely different marketplaces to your own.** That's how you beat the competition: by outthinking them.

And the great thing about it is that in many cases, your competition isn't thinking at all—they're just following the herd. I believe that unthinkingly handing money over to a sales rep for a billboard, sponsorship opportunity, or Yellow Pages ad is one of the real tragedies of marketing. Sure, it's easy. It's *too* easy. You write them a check, and it's all done for you. Maybe later you see the billboard or the Yellow Pages ad, but you don't know what's actually happening. There's no way to easily measure the response, unless you ask people how they heard about your business. They may be willing to tell you, if they remember; or they may not. In any case, that's how a lot of people in any industry do their marketing: blindly. **They don't actually know what's happening there. That's the unthinking way to do it.**

You're better off putting your brain to work and thinking outside the box. Instead of spending $5,000 on a billboard, try my little ballot box idea in a few locations, or adopt a marketing method that requires you to take action. **Make sure you can track it.** It does take time and effort, but you're going to see much greater results than you ever will from money you just hand off to someone else, for advertising you can't easily track.

If you're having trouble determining what might work for you, step back and look at the big picture. Examine the ways that the most successful businesses both inside and outside your industry are advertising, and what they do over and over again. They wouldn't repeat something if it didn't work. **Consider the things they do to make you want to respond, or request information and or ask for a free sample. Ask yourself, "How can I implement that in my business?"** You should be able to adapt it for your own use. Once you settle into that thoughtful marketing mindset, you're going to see tremendous things happening in your business that *wouldn't* happen if your marketing mindset was stuck on writing checks and handing them over to sales reps every quarter.

Be responsible for your own marketing; don't just give someone a check and think that's going to work wonders. It's fine to use those advertising methods if you're responsible for the design and offer, and can put together something that you're confident will attract people. Otherwise, it looks exactly like everything else and works no better than a business card. When the ads all look the same, why should people want to do business with you over anyone else? **Take charge of your marketing. Ruthless Marketing isn't passive; it's aggressive, and puts you in charge.**

While that may sound daunting at first, when you truly understand marketing and the principles that I teach about aggressive marketing, you'll understand the freedom Ruthless Marketing gives you. You'll see how much it can do for you and your business, and what kind of results you can achieve when you step up and take charge. **Because as I've mentioned before, very few other people are doing that... which is good news for you.** You can be just a beginner, taking baby steps towards this Ruthless Marketing mindset, and you'll *still* be head and shoulders above other people in your marketplace. Just reading this book puts you ahead of the crowd. That's part of what it means to be ruthless in the marketplace: **you put yourself in a position to succeed. Even though you don't have it all figured out yet, you're already far beyond where most of your competitors will be and, frankly, where they *want* to be.**

Because realize this: they like being lazy. It's easiest to sit there passively and hope you get enough customers to survive. But that's boring... and it doesn't work. Since you're reading this book, I'm guessing you're one of the few who refuses to take that for an answer. **You've come to the right place—welcome! I've got ten modules assembled here, packed with all the tips and secrets necessary to help you learn to put aggressive, Ruthless Marketing tactics into play for your business.**

Turn the page, and let's get start.

CHAPTER TWO:

Module #1: the USP

This version of the Ruthless Marketing System consists of a total of ten modules, but **it's important for you to understand that the first three comprise the foundation of the entire system. The other seven, while important, are built on top of that foundation.** We'll return to these foundation principles again and again; and if you're ever feeling lost as you build a marketing campaign, **these principles should be your touchstones,** always close at (mental) hand, always easy to understand and remember.

The first is the USP, which stands for your Unique Selling Position or Unique Selling Proposition (different marketers prefer different terms). No matter what you call it, **this is the method you use to separate yourself from your competitors, so you're doing something unique in the eyes of your target market.** You're still offering them the things that are most important to them, but in a different way from everyone else. This sets you apart from the rest of the crowd, both among direct and indirect prospects. So let's briefly look at precisely what a USP is, before I provide some guidance in creating one that will help you build your business.

Basically, a USP is a clear statement of the unique benefits that your customers get from doing business with you. It all boils down to a simple question: Why should anyone do business with you instead of every other alternative, including doing nothing? *Always* remember that "every other alternative" doesn't just include the competition in your market. It also includes DIY efforts on the part of the prospect; for example, they might buy one of those "For Dummies" books and figure it out themselves. They may decide to spend the money on a new armchair instead. And again, depending on how pressing the need, they may decide to do nothing for the time being. **Your USP needs to answer the question about why people should do business with you in a compelling way.**

Let's look at some examples. For years, Domino's Pizza had a great USP: **"You get fresh, hot pizza delivered to your door in 30 minutes or less... or it's free!"** That's a *huge* benefit. Hungry people don't want pizza in an hour or 90 minutes, after it's gone cold and disgusting. When you want pizza you want it now, and you want it hot. With the Domino's old USP, you'd get that pizza in 30 minutes or less, guaranteed—or it was free. That's simple and easy to remember: a great USP, summed up in one sentence.

Now, the interesting thing about this USP is that it doesn't say anything about great-tasting pizza. It doesn't say it's going to be the best pizza you've ever eaten. In fact, back in the day, I used to think Domino's was pretty nasty. But it was *fast*, and sometimes you're willing to exchange quality for speed. **That "fast or free" USP built Domino's into a major brand...** though eventually they had to give it up, because the government decided that forcing delivery people to get there within 30 minutes was dangerous.

There was a time when the U.S. Postal Service was the only game in town if you wanted to ship something long distance, and they often took their time doing it. Then FedEx appeared, with the USP that went, "When it absolutely, positively has to get there overnight." **Their USP leveraged the USPS's inability to provide overnight shipping, which soon built FedEx into a shipping industry leader.**

So ask yourself: how are you different from everyone else in the marketplace? How are you better? How are you positioned differently? What unique benefits do you offer your target market? And believe me: there's always *something* you can work with. If nothing immediately comes to mind, **then I've got a series of questions you can ask yourself to help you pin down your USP:**

1. *What does your target client really want?* You should have a thorough understanding of who your target client is: that is, the supreme, ultimate person you want to do business with. That will help you determine their desired end result when they do business with you.

2. *How do they want that end result?* Do they want it faster, do they want it easier, do they want it guaranteed—or all of the above?

3. *How can you deliver the end result the way they want it?* Do they want it delivered in person? Do they want it all done for them, or do they just want you to help them get started so they can go from there?

4. *What is the pain point in your marketplace?* What are people not getting? Even if there are a lot of other providers of your particular service or product in the marketplace, they may all be missing something. What is it?

5. *What can you add about your business that makes it*

unique? In some cases you don't even have to add it—you can just emphasize something when nobody else does. Back when Ivory Soap first came out, most soap was 99.4% pure or better... but they didn't bother to emphasize it as Ivory did.

Those five questions should give you some idea of what you can use to formulate a Unique Selling Position. **Some basic ideas off the top of my head include:**

- Offer a better than "risk-free" guarantee.

- Offer a stronger guarantee than your competitors, who often don't offer guarantees at all.

- Offer faster service.

- Offer a higher quality of service.

- Offer more advanced service, using more advanced technology.

- Give people easier, faster, and longer-lasting results.

One thing you should never use as the basis for your USP is "lowest prices." Let everybody else argue about and compete on price, while you compete on things that differentiate you from those competitors, and that attract a higher quality of clientele. Leave the "low price leader" business to Wal-Mart and Sam's Club. They have the size and resources to make it work... and even then, it's not easy. At one point, K-Mart was the low price leader among the big box stores—and then Wal-Mart found a way to go even lower. They developed a series of distribution centers around the country, so they had a better distribution network, and then they were smart enough to turn their distribution centers into Sam's Clubs. This move practically ran K-Mart out of business for a while.

Now, don't get me wrong; people love low prices. But for 99% of us, this approach does not work. **You get into a cutthroat, negative cycle, racing toward the bottom... and there will always be some psycho willing to go lower than you, even if it kills you both.** In the end you either have to give up and go out of business — or raise your prices again. Then you really have problems, because your customers have gotten used to the low prices, so they go shopping elsewhere.

While you're trying to determine your USP, keep the five questions I outlined earlier in mind at all times. Return to them repeatedly. Don't expect the answers to come suddenly; and even if some do, realize that immediate answers aren't necessarily the best. In a sense, it's good to be confused about those questions I've posed to you. After you've lived with them for a while, the answers will start appearing, and will very likely evolve over time. It may even take you months and years to figure out your true USP.

The best answers come when you intimately know your marketplace: especially who your customers are, what their biggest problems are, and what they're really searching for. The more you're exposed to all that, and the more thinking you do as a result, the better your answers will be. So while that can take a lot of time, don't let that scare you or turn you off. **You need to beat the competition by outthinking and outworking them, by offering prospects more value while doing things that make them feel good about doing business with you.**

Once again, beware of the low price trap. Too many businesses get involved in that, and it backfires.

Russ von Hoelscher tells me that there are plenty of barbershops in the San Diego and El Cajon, California area where he can pay $100 or more for a haircut if he wants (and he doesn't). Or he can go down the street about five blocks to a guy who has a sign up reading "$4.95 Haircuts." Now, that's a big spread! Russ goes somewhere that charges more than that $4.95, but well below the $100. The fact is, when a barber has to cut hair for $4.95, it's a real grind. And how sweet it is when you can build up a clientele where you can charge $100 for a haircut. **When you do that, you're not a barber; you're a hairstylist.** Well, Russ has tried out one of those $100 haircuts, and he found that the man he usually uses, who charges $20, does just as well.

Now, if you're going for that high price instead of the lowest one, I'm not going to knock you if you can sell it to enough people and keep them coming back. Some folks don't mind paying the premium price if they like what they're getting. **There's absolutely nothing wrong with having the highest price in your marketplace, or even the lowest price. But don't base your USP on either one.** Focusing on the price will *always* end up being a problem.

Your customers are naturally conditioned to look for the best deal, especially the lowest prices. This is something you can't really escape, **but you don't want to highlight it—or else your customers will start to look for it even more.** Remember, if they're your customers just because of low prices, they'll just as easily leave you. On the other hand, you can have the highest prices in town and have all the business you can handle, if you've got your USP set up right so that you separate yourself from everyone else, and offer great service and other advantages. **The idea is to develop a business model that shows people why it's worth spending more to get the very best.**

Avoid developing your USP around price, at least at first; find something else to focus on. There are all kinds of things you can do instead. You just have to be creative. **The most important thing here is tightly targeting your marketplace, so you know what they want.** If you have trouble determining what that is, instead of guessing, just ask them flat-out what they would really like from your business. Most business owners don't do this; they'd rather try to predict what their clients want. **But if you take some time to actually talk to your clients, you'll build a better USP.**

Of course, if you start a business in a field in which you were already a sincere, dedicated consumer, then you've got a built-in advantage. You'll already have a good idea of what your customers are like and what they want out of your business. I know from personal experience that it's easiest to deal with people who are like you in terms of mindset and goals, and the same is true for many of my colleagues. **We know our prospects' passions, hopes, and fears, because they were (and are) part of our own internal makeup.** This gives you a real advantage when developing your own USP.

Another thing to consider: how can you emphasize the high quality of your product or service? If you operate a French gourmet restaurant or a great steakhouse, you can tell people about the extraordinary care you take in choosing your food products: meats, vegetables, spices, and all. This concept translates to a thousand and one other industries. If you're offering high quality, then you need to explain to people exactly what the high quality *is*. Just having a simple slogan like "The best quality at a fair price" doesn't mean anything. People don't pay any attention to that kind of silliness. **You've got to go into detail to explain why and how you're offering the highest possible quality.**

Providing the best service is another USP builder. Going back to the restaurant example: you can emphasize how top-quality your chefs and wait staff are, and how your customers are going to get the best service and the best food in town at any price. **Too many people sell things but don't service them.** A business is so much more than a single sale to an individual. If you not only make the sale, but follow up with excellent service, that gives you a huge advantage over the competition. People are more likely to buy from you again if you make life easier and smoother for them. **Russ von Hoelscher recently told me about a business he saw in San Diego that advertises, "Buy it here and we'll assemble it!" Do you think that that helps them get business? You bet it does!** If they assemble your purchase, you don't have fight with it yourself. We're not all the handyman type... and even if you are, sometimes it's hard to follow the directions on these items.

Chris Lakey, my Marketing Director, has been dealing with a good example of this in his own household. Three of his six children are still quite young, and still like to play on a swing set. Well, the family has a fairly inexpensive swing set that's deteriorating and needs to be replaced. Chris keeps looking for online options and wrestling with them; he likes the way they look, and part of him keeps insisting he could put one together... but he's just not a handyman. He enjoys working with his hands, but he's not very good with assembly. **So he'd love for someone to have a USP that says, "Just buy it, and we'll come out and**

install it once it arrives."

Lacking that, he'll consider one he likes and then think, "Yeah... I'm not ready to buy it yet," because he's dreading that moment when all the boxes arrive, or he goes to the store to pick up the lumber and such... and it just sits in his backyard, with the kids asking, "When are you going to put it, Daddy? When are you going to put it up?" A website that promises assembly after the sale would be idea for Chris. **That's a perfect USP for people like him, especially if the company can also haul off the old item being replaced after the new one is up.** Appliance dealerships do that all the time.

Service before and after the sale is very important. If the customer knows when they make an expensive purchase that they can call you up if they have any problems, or if they need your help in figuring out how to add this attachment or change that, you're likely to acquire and retain more business, period. **Service is mostly a lost art — so if you have a business to which it could pertain, it's very smart to add it to your USP.**

Giving people lots of choices is also a good idea. Back when Coca-Cola was first invented in a drug store in Atlanta, Georgia (and there was still some cocaine in the mix, they say!) that was the only choice you had in terms of cola. Nowadays, even within the Coca-Cola brand you have regular Coke, Diet Coke, Cherry Coke, Lime Coke, etc. **More variety in the products you're selling will always be a big USP if you play it right.**

Another thing to consider as a USP is to offer long-term payments, if you can afford to. People love to buy stuff with no or very little money down, and then make payments over the long-term. Now, many of us can't operate that way, because we don't have enough money to finance it. But some companies will do that for you. Some furniture stores, for example, might say, "Come on in and buy this bedroom set for $1295, and even though it's summertime now, we won't start charging you till January of next year." That's a strong USP. Often you don't have to put any money down at all, and they won't even bill you for another six or eight months.

A while back, my colleague Jeff Gardner had Lasik eye surgery done. Now, this is not an inexpensive procedure, but the gentleman in the Dallas area who does the surgery runs a series of radio commercials about how you can have the surgery done for as little as $33 a month. **He doesn't claim the surgery itself is incredibly cheap, but he does offer an affordable payment.** That's been his ad for years. When Jeff went in to do his initial exam, he found that the doctor uses a sort of assembly-line set-up, where people come in and are prepped and interviewed by a team. He had to create this systematized process because that $33 a month pitch—that Unique Selling Position—is so hot that his office is constantly packed. He's done close to 100,000 Lasik procedures since he started in the business—apparently, more than any other eye surgeon in the entire world. **I truly believe his success is based upon that $33 a month pitch.** So this doctor has differentiated himself in this way, even though I'm sure there are other doctors who offer financing. You'd think they would realize the "hot" button is the $33 a month... but apparently they don't.

Maybe it's just that they don't want to feel like they're the "me too" person. More likely, they're thinking, "Hey, if they're coming to me... they're paying it all right now!" It seems that in many cases, professional people like doctors, dentists, and chiropractors don't want to offer anything free—not even a few

X-rays or a check-up so they can then sign up new clients. Often, those businesses are looking for any excuse to bill. If they could bill you for walking through the front door, they would. **They're certainly not in tune with the idea of giving something away, not even decent financing.** If they were just willing to give something away, they'd probably increase their sales and profits, and have happier customers in the end. But they're not in tune with the biggest problems that the customers are faced with—like the fact that they've got all these other bills every month they've got to pay. **When they hear the other surgeon's ads, their potential customers are thinking, "What the hell, I can afford $33 a month," and so that's where they go.**

Guarantees are also incredibly important. If you can tell someone, "We stand behind our product so strongly that if at any time you're unhappy with our product—six days from now, six months from now, six years from now—you can return it and we'll give your money back," then you've created an awesome USP. Again, most of us can't do that, because we sell things that probably won't hold up forever. **But it's wise to offer something fairly substantial to shore up your USP.**

Now, be careful here; don't fall into the trap of having a 10-day or 15-day guarantee, because that scares the hell out of people. They'll watch the calendar constantly, and return the product at the slightest sign of any problems. They're so focused on the narrow timeframe you've set that they don't even enjoy the benefits you tried to offer them in the first place. So if you're going to make a guarantee a part of a USP (and that's actually a great thing to do), the longer the better. **At the very least, use 60-to 90-day guarantees. Those build confidence with people.** The longer you can make that refund period, the more likely they are to be comfortable with it; there's no pressure. Even if it wasn't everything they thought it would be, they're not as inclined to want to return it if you offer a long guarantee period.

But if you put pressure on them with a short refund period, all you're doing is setting them up to return it even if they really didn't want to, because you made them focus on it. **So get the focus off of it. I recommend that you do use a guarantee as a selling tool,** but make sure it's long enough or grand enough to take away the pressure and make it easy for them to buy while, simultaneously, making it easy for them to get their money back if they're not happy.

Remember, a USP has to be built around serving the customer, and fulfilling their wants and needs. Knowing your marketplace well is a great USP, because you know the problems and the benefits of what you sell, you know what people are looking for, and you can converse with them very easily because they're a lot like you. **A Unique Selling Position can be something you actually add to your business, or it can be just something that already exists in your business already, but that you emphasize.** You might think, "Oh, everybody's got that, so it doesn't differentiate me." But if nobody *knows* that everybody's got it, then just by announcing that you've got it, you can differentiate yourself from everybody else in the market. Suddenly you've got a USP that makes you sound unique.

If you can't figure out how to differentiate yourself, then you've got to ask your customers the questions I outlined earlier. **Sometimes the customers won't know the answers you're looking for, but they *will* tell you the biggest problems they're faced with.** That's the one thing you can count on your customers always talking about. I've mentioned the company in San Diego that tells its customers, "If you buy it here, we'll assemble for you." That's because they had so many people like Chris Lakey who said, "Oh man, I'm not going to buy this crap because then I have to put it together!"

We sell information, because that's what people in our marketplace want. But at the same time, they don't want to buy just another information product, because it's likely to make them feel more confused. They already feel overloaded. They don't want go through the pain of learning anything new. **So we provide tools that make life super-easy for them. We give them all kinds of personal help, encouragement, and support.** We're not just dumping a bunch of ideas on them and then expecting them to figure it all out on their own, like so many other marketing consultants and coaches do. **We're right there helping them every step of the way.**

There are problems inherent in every product line, and a great USP includes elements that help you solve the problems that your competitors aren't solving. **When you get around to it, that's really why your business exists: to make a profit in your marketplace by solving some problem people are having.** If you're a restaurant, the problem is that people are hungry; they want something good to eat, in pleasant surroundings. But something like, "We have food!" isn't really a good USP, so you've got to come up with some way to convey the message that you've got what they want in a stylish way. Part of your struggle here is to craft that message into your USP.

If you run a car dealership, then you're selling to the marketplace of people who have a need for transportation. In this example, how you craft your USP depends on the problems that exist in the car-buying marketplace, and how you offer the best solution. That may be something related to vehicles, or it may

---

have nothing to do with the vehicles at all, but everything to do with the experience you provide while they're visiting. CarMax saying, "We'll buy your car even if you don't buy ours"—that's an excellent USP, because people are always worried about crappy trade deals when it comes time to get a new car. **CarMax makes an offer that's good for a week, and they keep that promise even if you buy elsewhere.** That takes all the pressure off you as the buyer.

Think about that while crafting or refining the USP for your business. **Never forget that people in your marketplace are looking for a solution to a problem they have.** Once you've determined what that problem is, it's just as important to figure out what they're willing to pay or do to get the benefit you're offering. **The bigger the benefit, the more they're willing to pay, or the bigger sacrifice they're willing to make.** If you sell a 50-cent candy bar, that's not a big sacrifice for someone who just wants a solution for their hunger; so the USP doesn't have to be too complex. But if you sell something that costs thousands of dollars, then you really need a strong USP that makes people realize they need to do business with you—because you're going to be asking them for a substantial expenditure on their part to receive the solution to their problem. The bigger your solution, the more grandiose your USP and the easier it is to get them to do business with you, because they're seeking out that benefit.

Another foundational principle of developing a USP is that you need to go into the game knowing how you want it to end. What's the end goal of your business model? What are you trying to accomplish in your marketplace? Who are you trying to attract as customers? As far as the last question goes, some people just think, "I want every customer who will come to me!" But that's the wrong approach. **You're looking for a very specific**

kind of buyer in your marketplace. You need to know who that is and what you're trying to accomplish with them over the lifetime of your relationship, so you can incorporate it into your USP and thereby convey that core message to your marketplace.

Let's use pizza as an example again. Pizza is one of those products that seems almost infinitely variable, so you've got plenty of room for USP development. Pizzas run the gamut from those gourmet pizzas with all kinds of weird stuff on them that you can find in fancy restaurants, through the really cheap delivery stuff and the frozen pies that you can buy in the supermarket and cook for yourself. If you own a pizza restaurant, what do you have to offer? Domino's old 30-minute guarantee was aimed at people who didn't care much about the quality of their pizza, but wanted it there fast. Well, if you're trying to reach that same marketplace but go at them with a message about how your product is really great, the very best they've ever tasted, but is delivery only or will take them two hours to get... then you'll completely miss the target market you're trying to sell to. You'll either have to readjust your aim to a different marketplace, or give your original target market exactly what it's looking for.

Here's another aspect you may want to incorporate into your USP: the free giveaway, so you can attract new customers in the first place. I've been doing things like this for decades now, and it works very well. Some people will come in just for the "free," but you'll end up selling to a certain percentage of the people who get the freebie. Some of those people you'll retain long-term—and that's where the big profit lies. This is the method I used to really rev up the sales in my old carpet cleaning business.

Recently, the restaurant chain International House of

Pancakes (IHOP) offered free pancakes for one day only. Of course, I wouldn't go no matter what on the free day, because I figured it would be a zoo! And I was right. My friend Russ von Hoelscher went there the day *after* they had free pancakes and talked to this very charming waitress who told him, "I don't want to go through that again! It was just hell. We had so many people here that they were waiting up to a half hour to get in to get the free pancakes." That's all they got, though: free pancakes.

Russ said, "Well, maybe some of them will return." And the waitress replied, "Oh heck, we made money. A lot of people sat down and had coffee with their pancakes, and a lot had eggs and bacon and other things, too." **Overall, it was a very profitable day; so as you can see, when implemented properly, this method can work like gangbusters.** Pancakes may seem like strange things to give away, but you have to work with what you have. What do you have in your business that *you* could give away free, just to attract people so you can then sell them other stuff? Be creative here; don't just give away something plain, the way dentists often give away toothbrushes. That's not especially thrilling, is it? Give away something that will really attract people's attention.

Another way to come up with ideas while crafting your USP is to borrow solutions from other industries. **Don't just stick with what other people are doing in your marketplace; adapt the best solutions from others,** the way McDonald's adapted the drive-thru bank teller idea to their restaurants. If you're in the restaurant industry, look at retailers and at dentistry or chiropractic, or something you think is completely unrelated, and study what they're doing. How are these businesses structured? What special things do they do for their clientele? What USPs do they have? **If you're careful and creative, you may be able to**

find some really cool ideas that no one in your industry has implemented yet. This is another great way to differentiate yourself from everybody else in your market, because a standard in one industry can be an innovation in another.

So stop just following your industry leader, and give some thought to how businesses in other marketplaces structure their USPs. **That way, you can cross-fertilize your own ideas with concepts and strategies that may never have occurred to you before.** Borrow them, work them into your business, and BAM— you've got a ready-made USP that's going to instantly separate you from everybody else.

So many business owners never really think these things through. They just do what everyone else does, working dirt-cheap and following the leader rather than designing their business around the customers. Ask yourself: Who do you really want to attract? What business do you really want to be in? **Start looking at what you can do to solve the big problems bothering your customers.**

So many people suffer from what some of us call "the Niagara syndrome." Instead of asking themselves tough questions and then trying to target the right people, they just drift along like they're in a rowboat—at the most rowing along very gently and basically going with the flow. But suddenly, they get swept up with the current and, somewhere down the road, they end up in a place they really don't want to be.

Don't get swept over the falls. **While constructing your USP, think hard about what you want out of your business, then really focus on the problems you can solve in your marketplace, and narrow what you get down into several key**

phrases. Throw in some of these other things I've discussed, like a refund guarantee, and make a list of the top things that are important to the kind of people you're trying to attract. That's how you start to come up with the core ideas that will then be boiled down into your USP.

Cautionary Tales

In this section, I'll share a few stories that illustrate some of the points I discussed earlier in the chapter. I'll begin by telling you how we created our Unique Selling Position here at M.O.R.E., Inc. My wife Eileen and I started our company back in 1988, with the help of Russ von Hoelscher. We decided from the beginning that we weren't going to pretend to be anything other than what we are. We're just regular people, you see. **Before we started that business, we were customers of our marketplace first, so we understood it thoroughly. Then we solved some problems the marketplace was faced with, and decided to share our solutions.**

When we began communicating with our marketplace, we immediately got very personal with our prospects. **We told our story honestly; we weren't afraid to just be ourselves.** This is something that I strongly believe that more marketers and business owners need to accept. Instead, they're afraid to express themselves in the fullest way. They're afraid of offending people. They build companies that are too corporate, too homogenized. **They don't realize that people want to do business with other people who are** *just like them* **— people who understand the fears, failures, and frustrations they're going through.**

We've generated millions of dollars because we went to the people in that marketplace and said, **"Hey, we're just like you**

are. We've gone through the same problems you're facing. We understand your pain. We understand your frustrations. We've been there." **And then we provided solutions for them.** People identified with that, and we built mutually beneficial relationships. **Ultimately, it's all about those relationships.** The better the emotional connection between you and your customers, the more likely you'll build relationships in which they honestly feel that you care about them, and that you're doing things to show them that you do—because you are. When you can demonstrate this, they'll be ready to do business with you for years. In the end, that's how you can keep charging premium prices for your products and services.

We've been doing this for more than 20 years with our marketing, coaching, and consulting businesses, and we've generated tens of millions of dollars in the process—but we're not coming at our clients like we're some kind of gurus, as if we're located way up at the top of a mountain and they should be lucky they're doing business with us. That kind of attitude is just a load of garbage. There are already too many of those people out there and, quite frankly, they're a turn-off rather than a turn-on. We're coming at our clients with the same USP that we built with our first business back in the late 1980s. **We know what it's like to be struggling small business owners, and this lets us make a direct connection with people.**

We're real; we're expressing ourselves fully. And sure, we're tooting our own horn in the process. But that's okay; a little self-promotion is absolutely essential to successful marketing.

There are so many nameless, faceless companies out there. Go on the Internet and start hopping around the websites in your marketplace, and you'll soon be wondering: Who are the people behind those sites? Where are they? We all want relationships with other people, not unfeeling companies. **So a big part of your USP—the thing that can completely separate you from the anonymous crowd—is the fact that there's a real face behind the company.** There's a personality there, somebody who really does care about the prospect and their problems. You want to help them, and they can see that.

This one little thing can make you stand out in a huge way. **In fact, it's the biggest advantage that a small business has over giant corporations, which just can't get very personal.** Sadly, too many small business owners forget this when the big companies come to town. Often, they're so cowed that they close up shop even before their business starts to deteriorate, because they just don't understand the concept that you can keep doing business despite someone else having lower prices, as long as you offer some good benefits to offset your prices. People *love* to do business with local businesses if everything is pretty much even, especially if you offer better service.

We've all dealt with a lot of service providers over the years, including plumbers and A/C people, and typically everybody just stomps in, does the work, and gets out. They're gruff and in a hurry. Everybody gets used to that type of service, so it really does set someone apart when they provide cheerful, people-oriented service in that field. My colleague Jeff Gardner once had a plumber who was super-nice, because the company had trained everybody in how to talk to people. So not only did you have to have plumbing skills to work for that company, but you also had to have people skills. They instructed the workers on what they expected in terms of addressing the customer, and how to talk to the customer and pinpoint their concerns. **They also built the relationship by taking care of the customer's house, and**

showing the customer respect as a person.

Many service people come into your house with muddy boots and dirty tools; but this plumber came in with clean tools, wearing a clean shirt, and always put little booties over his shoes before he came inside. Because of all that, Jeff used that company for years. When Jeff moved, he unfortunately moved to a place where that company didn't provide service—and he was heartbroken, because he really felt an emotional connection with them. If he could have, he would have done business with them for the next 20 years. **Building that relationship is key—and in and of itself, it can be a great USP simply because most people in the marketplace don't bother.**

A lot of restaurants are pretty much the same way. When you go in for a soup or a sandwich at lunch, you're just another person to them. **Wouldn't you prefer a restaurant where everyone is friendly, where they greet you by name and ask how you're doing?** Places like that go to extremes to show they're happy that you're there, which is perfect, because we all love to do business with people who treat us special.

It never ceases to amaze me how some small companies get started and immediately take on the look and feel of a big company—nameless, faceless, and homogenized. **That's foolish, because *people want relationships*.** They really, truly do. They want to know that somebody cares about them and their problems, and understands what they're going through. They want to know that somebody's going to be there for them, and will treat them with real respect, like Jeff's plumber. But instead, these little businesses try to pretend they're big... and that's not what most of the market wants.

In the last chapter of his book *Made in America*, Sam Walton made this point in a forceful way. The chapter was called "How to Compete with Wal-Mart," and it showed you how to do precisely that. I thought this was an awesome idea, even though he did it for purely personal reasons. You see, he absolutely hated the idea that when Wal-Mart came to town, all these little local businesses would just give up and shut down. People blamed Wal-Mart and Sam Walton for killing small town America... and many still do. But Sam Walton was a small businessman at heart himself, and as he pointed out, "There are only two things that we give our customers at Wal-Mart: great prices and great selection." Then he went on to say that people want a whole lot more than just that, which is very true. **His recommendation was to buy or lease space as close to Wal-Mart as possible, and start serving the hell out of the people he helped bring in.** Start giving them that personal touch, in the form of all the warm, friendly, intimate things no Wal-Mart can do. The best Wal-Mart can do is put that greeter by the door to say hi to you—the same person who's also making sure you're not stealing stuff as you're walking out. People want so much more than that. ***Never* forget that to succeed, you have to be a people person, offering something very special to your prospects.** USPs can be as different as day and night, depending on what you offer. Don't think there are just a few variations on the USP, or even 10 or 20 or 50 of them; there are thousands.

One of the most unique USPs I've ever heard of was used by my colleague and friend Russ von Hoelscher, back when he owned a Savoy Theatre in downtown San Diego more than 20 years ago. They played third-run movies, triple features—say, three science fiction thrillers or three John Wayne movies—and you could get in for a couple of dollars. There were a lot of theatres like that back then, because videos were uncommon, and you couldn't just go online and get movies on demand like you can now.

So Russ had plenty of competition—not just the first-run theatres downtown, but also all the second- and third-run movie houses where the proprietor could rent the movies cheap and then put a cheap price on them to get people to come through the door. Well, at the Savoy, Russ noticed that a lot of sailors would come in to watch the last feature, which would end around midnight or one o'clock in the morning. And then he realized what was happening: a lot of these sailors were lingering because they didn't want to go all the way back to their base, which was a good distance away. So he brought in more help and stayed open all night. Instead of having to get a cheap motel room or go all the way back to the base to sleep, they would come in and watch movies until they fell asleep. **Russ and his crew provided not just a motion picture experience, with action movies one after the other, but they also became a kind of hotel.** So put on your thinking cap. What can you offer that's different, unique, and special that no one else is offering?

Russ's example brings me back to the concept of looking at other industries and what they're doing. He took a movie theatre and turned it into a motel, filling a need unique to a segment of his clientele. So in addition to providing that personal touch that sets you apart from others, allowing you to develop profitable, long-term relationships, realize that there are all kinds of ideas out there in other marketplaces that you can tap—things they consider unremarkable and ordinary, yet are anything but to your market. **Often, you can adapt these ideas in a unique and special way that your marketplace will appreciate, because it fills a need or solves a problem they have.** Never feel like you're stuck only with what already exists in your marketplace, because to some extent your marketplace is probably stagnant, full of "me toos" all doing the same thing. If your USP sounds just like everybody else's, then none of you has a USP. **It has to be truly unique.**

Never assume, "There's nothing different about me." Even if that's true—and I doubt it is—then you have to *create* that difference. So start thinking about how to put together a Unique Selling Position that sets you apart from the crowd. Think deeply about what I've outlined in this chapter; read it over and over again if you have to. Be especially careful to consider the questions I asked at the beginning of the chapter. Then put the ideas they generate into play, to make your business so unique and interesting that your prospects have no choice but to choose you.

CHAPTER THREE:

Module #2:
Direct Response Marketing

Direct response marketing is a type of advertising in which you try to get your best prospective buyers, or your existing customers, to take a specific action that you can measure. Remember, most of your competitors aren't using this form of marketing. They're running image-based advertising, which basically amounts to giving people your business card information without telling you why they should ever bother to buy from you rather than your competition. Even those of your competitors who are using DRM have probably never mastered it, so they're making a lot of mistakes. **If you'll study this form of marketing and apply its principles aggressively, I promise you that you'll soon have an advantage over your competitors, and come to dominate your marketplace.**

In this module, I'll cover just a small part of what you can do with DRM, along with what shouldn't do. **One of the great things about DRM is that it works very well in conjunction with all the other things I discuss in each module of this book.** Now, realize that I'm only going to scratch the surface here. I can and have written whole books on the subject; so if DRM truly interests you, we have libraries full of other products and services that can help you dig deeper. Consider this module an overview — DRM 101, if you will.

Getting Serious

For most businesses, a pretty picture and a headline just don't cut the mustard. Business owners do their marketing this way because they see big companies like Coca-Cola just slap their names on things, and think that's the way it always works. Well, sure, it works for the big guys—but it can't work for the average marketer or business, because they simply don't have the money to do it right. Coca-Cola and the other mega-corps are spending millions, tens of millions, even *hundreds* of millions of dollars with their branding, which makes sense because you can get Coca-Cola almost everywhere. **They just want to keep that name in front of you all the time. But image advertizing just doesn't make sense for a small company.**

Your money is better spent doing DRM, for a variety of reasons. **First of all, you're going to be able to maximize your advertising dollars, simply because you can track the market response.** One of the big challenges with image advertising is that it's imprecise; the companies that use it don't really know what results they're getting from it. If you don't have any clue about where your results are coming from, then you end up wasting a lot of money. That's fine for Coke and Pepsi, but you need measureable results.

This is where direct response advertising comes in. It lets you track your marketing, so you can actually see where people are coming from. If you've tried different advertisements in the newspaper, TV, Internet, and direct mail, you can easily see which is generating the best results. **That allows you to focus your ad dollars on the most effective means of targeting your prospects, so you ultimately spend less money more effectively** than competitors who are just throwing money around willy-nilly.

Let's take a closer look at the two methods, because it's vital that you understand the difference between image advertising and direct response advertising. **Again, image advertising never asks the prospect to do anything in particular.** It's usually just a name and a picture; all it tries to do is implant that brand inside the brain of the individual... so, for instance, if you're thinking about insurance, you'll think GEICO and its little lizard.

But direct response is about getting the very best prospect to actively respond. It's designed to get them to pick up the phone and make an appointment, or to fill out an order form and fax it in, or to come directly into your business for whatever they're after. **Basically, you get them to raise their hand** and say, "Yes, I'm interested in doing business with you." That response might be to a no-cost offer—a free CD, booklet, or other information product. It can be a discounted offer, or a special test drive of the product. The idea is to get your targeted market to say, "Hey, that's something for me. I'm interested in that," and then come to you to get that offer... whatever the offer is.

At this point, you have more leeway than you would with image advertising. **You've narrowed your field considerably, so instead of diluting the impact of your advertising budget on a large, general audience, you can spend it more effectively on those relative few whom you know for a fact are interested.** You often end up being able to spend more money per client to convert them to sales, and then to long-term customers — especially if you have some idea of what the long-term value of your client is. You also have the ability to reach that target market through avenues that otherwise might have been closed off to you, due to limited funds.

In short, you have a greater ability to pinpoint your

market. You can tell where people are coming from, you can kill ads that don't work, and you take that money from those ads and put it into places where it *does* work. So if you're not using direct response advertising already, or if it comprises just part of your advertising efforts, then now is the time to focus on it wholeheartedly.

One of the best ways to learn how to use DRM in your own business is to study how other people deploy it successfully in theirs. So start paying attention to how it's being used in your marketplace—assuming it *is* being used. Watch infomercials, browse through magazines, and start becoming a student of DRM. **Adapt some of the ideas you see used most successfully, then start slowly implementing them in your own business.** Get rid of the concept of image advertising altogether. Don't just say, "Here I am, and here's what I do. Come see me if you're interested." **Instead, actively invite the prospect to do business with you.** Do something that makes them want to contact you directly, so you can capture their information and serve them more personally, with greater accuracy. That alone can turn your business completely around.

Most people can't get past this desire to emulate the big guys by using image advertising, in part because most industries don't train you in marketing at all. If you're a veterinarian, you might learn all the skills necessary to help and heal animals, but never learn marketing; so you end up being a great veterinarian, but a horrible marketer. Therefore, when you go out into the marketplace and try to promote your business, you assume that image advertising will work for you. After all, you're bombarded with it on TV and radio and in print, right? So you get a pretty picture and come up with a tag line and a slogan, and think it's going to drive business. You're confused when it doesn't, because after all, VISA and Coke are doing it. People in this position don't stop to think that they're playing on a completely different level than the huge multi-nationals.

Just because someone is a good plumber, veterinarian, or dentist, or they have a retail business of some kind, doesn't mean that these people necessarily know marketing. Sure, they understand their own profession, restaurant, or boutique, whatever the case may be; but to draw new customers in, they really do need help. That's why this Ruthless Marketing course is so important, if only to show you that just putting your ad out there in the newspaper or the Penny Saver, or even online, isn't enough. **Simply telling people who you are, what you do, and where to find you won't get the job done.** People aren't going to say, "Wow, this guy's business card motivates me to see him immediately."

It doesn't work that way. Basic information of that type has its value, and so does more straightforward image advertising; but at most levels of the game, that value is very limited. **You need to know the tricks of the trade to get people motivated to come to your store or your practice more often.** It's really not that hard, and you don't have to spend any more money than you do on image advertising. In fact, it usually costs much less.

And again, when you work with DRM, you get an immediate sense of what's working and what's not. **People who aren't using DRM are flying blind.** They're like John Wannamaker, the famous retail giant, who was once quoted as saying, "I know that 50% of every dollar I'm spending on advertising is being absolutely wasted... I just don't know which 50% it is!" That's more true today than it was a hundred years ago when Wannamaker said it.

People are spending a ton of money on advertising, even when they're flying blind. They know that if they don't advertise, they're not going to attract enough customers, and they're going to go broke. And yet they have no idea what's working and what's not! **But if you use the direct response methods I'll teach you in this program, and find a good role model to emulate, then you won't be flying blind anymore.** You'll be ahead of the game. You'll be able to track your advertising, and quantify how well every dollar you spend on it works—whether it's for ads on the radio or TV, or in the newspaper or direct mail. That gives you the kind of power most of your competitors simply don't have.

You can think of the dichotomy here as one between passive, dumb marketing and active, smart marketing. Image-based advertising is passive and dumb. The marketers are just trying to get you to recognize their brand; that's it. If you sell Coke, Dr. Pepper, or Pepsi, you're hoping that the next time they think, "I'm thirsty," they'll think of your product. If you have a car repair issue, you might think of AutoZone or Pep Boys first. These companies spend a lot of money on creating this kind of awareness, so you'll think of them whenever you have a particular want or need they can help you fill.

But it's hideously expensive. They spend millions of dollars on massive advertising campaigns, which is why you see their commercials everywhere. **Even so, they have no clue where their advertising is most effective; they just have this aggregate knowledge of whether their sales are up or down.** They can look at their total numbers, but can't tell you specifically what's working and what isn't.

The average small business owner doesn't have millions of dollars in ad money to spend. You can't even compete in that game, so it's foolish to try. The better approach is a DRM campaign, where you can account for every dollar, tracking it down to the penny, so you know exactly where your money is being spent and exactly where your income is coming from. **If something is working, you know exactly why it's working and where it's working.** If something isn't working, you know that, too. **This allows you to maintain accountability throughout the entire process,** so you can spend your money on the things you *know* are bringing you the most profit and return, and avoiding those things that aren't.

That being the case, why do so many small business people keep using image-based advertising? Simply because the people selling them advertising love it so much. And why is that? Because it can't be tracked. They're free to come up with the cutesy ideas, animals, and TV commercials that charm the business owner or their marketing department, then spend whatever money they think they need to without actually keeping track of whether it works or not. **There's no real accountability. As a result, the company doesn't know if they're getting any benefit from the money they're spending...** which is great for the advertising agencies, because heaven forbid, if the company knew what value they were *really* getting, they might not spend so much with that particular agency. So sure, advertising agencies love image advertising.

I've rarely seen a huge agency recommend DRM. I think they're usually scared to death to do so. **But I do know of one exception, and it involves GEICO's little lizard.** They're spending a mint on that little guy; in fact, they're one of the top three spenders on advertising in America now. They're right up there with Coke. Well, a recent business article pointed out that they finally came up with an idea made them more successful...

and it was the simplest idea I've ever heard of, something they should have been doing years ago. You see, they advertise on ABC, NBC, CBS, FOX News, CNN and other TV networks — and one fellow, bless him, did a great service to GEICO by coming up with the idea that rather than having everyone use the same phone number to call in their orders, **they'd advertise a different phone number for each network.** Now they can tell which network nets them the most customers, so this helps them decide where to put more advertising dollars.

Any DRM advertiser would have put this into place years ago; **we take the idea for granted. But the concept is alien to most large-scale marketers.** I find it amazing that GIECO has just recently put the idea into effect. We do this with every single ad... but when a traditional advertising agent recommends it, all of a sudden the client thinks he's a genius. Of course, the head of the agency probably said, "What the hell are you doing *that* for?"

Like I said earlier, I've always been amazed by how few local and regional businesses use DRM tactics and techniques. The ones that do are often the leaders in the industry, or the best stores in their area. It could simply be that one of the most important factors in DRM is copywriting ability; often, someone who's a good plumber or chiropractor can't do decent copywriting. Most of them don't know beans about it, so they turn to the traditional image-based advertizing as an easy way out — though it's expensive. **Well, I think it's critically important for local and regional business people to learn how to write copy, instead of just giving in and wasting money.** Even if they're going to have someone else write copy for them, at the very least they need to know what good copy looks like — or they could be taken to the cleaners.

A Few Suggestions

So let's look at some brief (but good) ideas that can help you learn what makes for good copy. **First, study the headline of any effective letter or ad. I like to use a good headline even in a letter, as long as it's used as powerfully as in an ad.** On the other hand, if you really want your letter to be personal and unlike typical advertising, then rather than use a headline, **put your great benefit in your opening paragraph instead.** Now, realize that what you perceive as the biggest and best benefit isn't necessarily what a particular prospect will see as the best benefit, which is why **it's important to include several other benefits along with it.** So we use a lot of bullets in DRM, to list as many benefits as possible. **I also think it's very important that you be specific about your benefits, explaining them as best you can in the space you have.**

Testimonials are important, too. People expect us to be all excited and gung-ho about our products or services, **so when *other* people make positive comments, that's a big bonus because it's coming from third parties.** And don't use initials, or otherwise hide who the person is. Get permission to use their real names and cities if you can. Telling folks that Mrs. T.F.T. from the Midwest thinks your product is the best thing since sliced pizza won't help, because it sounds bogus even if it's true. Make them sound like real people, and encourage your customers to offer testimonials. You can even bribe them a little, as long as you don't do it too blatantly.

Don't forget the call to action, by the way; so many people do, or just don't put it high on their list. **Whenever possible, offer some bonuses for people to "act now."** Bonuses don't have to cost much if they get people excited; people love freebies.

But if you do offer a bonus, you've got to pair it with a deadline. If you're a carpet cleaner, tell them, "This offer is only good for this month." If you're a restaurant, say, "My special offer is only good till such and such a date." If you have an air conditioning/heating service and you're offering a special deal on something that people need right now, tell them, "but it's only good for the next 20 days." Use as many deadlines as possible to motivate people to take action *right now*. **You don't want them to wait... or they might never take action.**

You also need to target the market very tightly. With few exceptions, you don't want to use the shotgun approach. If you're a carpet cleaner or a restaurant, or you have a brick-and-mortar store in a certain area, it's best to stick to a target radius of 4-5 miles from your establishment. But when you offer specialized services, or you've moved beyond the local or regional marketplace, then you want to try to get the largest possible customer base—local or otherwise—so in that case, "shotgunning" can work well.

And again, as I discussed in the USP module, **it's also very important to guarantee your products or services.** People are highly motivated to take advantage of offers where they feel they won't get burned. **The longer your guarantee is, the better.** Ten or 15 days is terrible. **Thirty days is a must; 90 days is better than 30.** If you can push it up to six months or a year, even better. Offer a strong guarantee, and show people you stand behind what you sell.

All these things are crucial to writing copy that sells. I've seen so many people fail with good products and services because their copy was badly written, just as I've seen people succeed with inferior products and services because the sales messages were so strong. Maybe that's not fair in the great scheme of things, but it's the way it is. Great copy can make up for inferior quality. **If you can match high quality with top-notch, well-targeted copy, you can make all the money you'll ever need.**

If you don't know where to start, then go back to the basics: study good direct response marketers who are already profiting by using these methods in their copy. **Examine the copy you see used repeatedly, because they wouldn't use it over and over if it weren't profitable.** And don't limit yourself to small-format direct response print or broadcast ads; study long-form direct mail as well. Get on the mailing lists of the leading marketers, and see how they're handling their copy. **If you really want a crash course, buy something from them and then study how they handle their follow-up marketing;** you'll probably get a lot of it.

You'll soon acquire an eye for what makes good marketing copy. Even if you can't necessarily describe what makes it special, as a Supreme Court judge once said about pornography, you'll know it when you see it. **Start what we call a "swipe file" containing examples of all the best marketing copy you find, whether in electronic or print versions.** Browse your swipe file occasionally, especially when you're looking for inspiration. **I'm not telling you to plagiarize** (that's unethical and illegal), but you can definitely use your swipe file for guidance, searching for general ideas and methods you can transfer to your own marketplace. **Even if you're not a copywriter, it's still a good idea to keep the swipe file, because you have to be able to recognize good copy when you see it.** Furthermore, it helps you stay on top of and in tune with what other people are doing in your marketplace in their attempts to reach the customers you're trying to reach.

A swipe file can be as simple as a folder or a notebook that you keep ads in. It may be a file cabinet, or a whole row of them. You can get pretty elaborate and fancy with them, if you want. **You can break them down by headlines, closes, envelopes, order forms, or a variety of other ways; whatever seems to work best for you.** Grab some little protective sleeves, and every time you get a letter that has some good sales copy on it, drop it in your swipe file so you can refer back to it. If you keep an electronic swipe file, then set it up in such a way that you can categorize and cross-reference it easily.

As with anything, recognizing good copy is difficult until, after long practice, it becomes easy. It's hard to define, except that, as I've pointed out, most people won't keep reusing copy that doesn't earn them money. **But once you've picked up on what makes a good piece of copy, you'll see it all over the place... and you'll look at things differently.** I often talk about getting on the other side of the cash register, where you stop looking at everything through a consumer lens and, instead, start seeing things from the business perspective. Suddenly, you'll pick up things you didn't before. Your eyes will clear and you'll more easily be able to tell the bad marketing from the good, and identify the differences between the two. **The ideas that work and those that don't become more obvious, without you having to test them yourself.** At that point, you can start implementing some of the things that work best for others in your own marketing.

It takes a while to find the right marketing "glasses" and get them adjusted to your vision. This isn't something you do in passing; it's a long-term process with a learning curve. But once you know what you're doing, it's like riding a bicycle. You'll never have to learn again, and even if you get rusty, it's easy to resharpen your skills. **Think of learning to craft and maintain your marketing as an ongoing self-education process.**

Again, don't limit yourself to your own field. **Keep your eyes open to what other people are doing in other industries, and even watch infomercials.** You can get lots of ideas for offers, pricing, benefits, and bonuses by watching your average infomercial. Keep the ads and letters that local auto dealers send out, or the brochures and cards you get from people in completely different industries that include interesting hooks, offers, USPs, or bonuses that you think or know you can use in some other form.

The swipe file is a shortcut method for writing copy that you should implement, and lean on, very early in your business. This is especially true if the whole idea of writing copy on top of running your business worries or overwhelms you. When you sit down to write your copy, have your swipe file near at hand, so you don't end up just staring at a blank computer screen and wandering how to get started. Instead, go through your file and pull out some pieces with great headlines, and others that have great benefits, and check how others present bonuses, make offers, and set pricing. **You can use them as models and inspiration for your own ideas, as long as you don't copy them word for word.**

When you get right down to it, the way you learn how to write great copy is to write good copy for a long time. **Give enough hours to anything, and you'll become an expert. Copywriting is really no different.** As your pieces get better, you'll get better responses, and you'll discover that writing copy really isn't that difficult—though it can, in fact, be very challenging. I happen to think that makes it fun, because if something's so easy you can do it with your eyes shut, then it soon gets boring. So rise to the challenge, because I guarantee you that the very first time that you write copy that causes hundreds of thousands or even millions of dollars to pour in—which is possible in some markets!—then you'll be hooked for life.

On top of studying advertising copy, study your supermarket tabloids and celebrity magazines. I know that sounds weird, but trust me: they do some of the best direct response-style headline writing out there. Why? **One reason is that they're not afraid of offending people.** Neither am I—at least, not anymore. In fact, a couple of the sales letters we've tested to sell this and similar programs used the term "Bullshit!" in the headline. Some of the letters we've tested said, "Enough of this bullshit!" Others said, "This is complete bullshit!" We used the term not because we wanted to offend people (although I'm sure that happened sometimes) but because we were trying to reach out to frustrated business owners who were unhappy with their marketing and advertising—and that's what *they* were saying. **They keep saying that every time something new comes along that promises to make them more money, because they've been hurt so often.** They've been ripped off, lied to, cheated, and abused by advertising salespeople who really don't understand DRM and probably wouldn't care if they did.

Don't be afraid to be totally outrageous. **Take it as an article of faith that it doesn't matter who you offend; it just matters who you sell to.** Besides, sometimes you have to be willing to offend some people in order to really shake 'em up. That said, don't swear just for the sake of swearing. You're not a sixth-grader. We use the term "bullshit" because that's what the advertising people with the Money Mailers, Val-Paks, and Penny Savers are handing you. You don't get decent results with that BS because they're giving you business card ads that *don't work.*

To make our point to most folks, we have to cut right through the disappointment and skepticism they feel. We know how to make people millions of dollars; we've done it. **So we want to slice right through the crap and say, "If you're ready to learn, we're ready to teach you how to get away from all that other BS."**

DRM is *vital* to the average business owner, because it allows you to compete with all those corporate giants who are willing to spend millions on huge image ad campaigns. The big guys blanket the marketplace with sales messages, knowing that only some of it's going to stick, and hoping that what does will increase their name recognition and therefore their profits. You can't afford to do that, so you have to focus on targeted sales messages. **Direct response gets your message to the right kinds of people—those who are most likely to become your long-term customers.** You spend less money in the process. The money you do spend is targeted and accountable, and in the end you can reach all the people you needed to reach in your marketplace anyway.

So ask yourself: which is the smarter approach? Spending millions of dollars to blanket an entire city or county with your ads, hoping you're reaching some people who are going to do business with you, but knowing that you're mostly not—or, spending less money targeting the people you know are most likely to be interested in what you have to offer? The answer's obvious, isn't it? **DRM has so many advantages over the traditional method of throwing it against the wall and seeing what sticks.**

Meet, Convert, Upgrade, Expand

Here at M.O.R.E., we're passionate about DRM, and we use a four-prong strategy for maximizing profitability that offers an excellent good summary of how to approach the field. It's called "Meet, Convert, Upgrade, and Expand."

The "Meet" portion of this formula involves identifying the right prospects—the people most likely to want to do business with you. Who are they, and how do you go about meeting them? **Two-step marketing is probably the best way.** You deploy your message via direct mail or some other direct response method, either online or off. It naturally attracts the right kind of people, who identify themselves by raising their hands and asking for more information or whatever you're offering for low or no cost.

The second part of the formula is to "Convert" the largest possible number of those prospects into first-time buyers. You need to make it as easy as possible for them to do business with you. Now, there are a whole lot of people in your marketplace who *might* be interested in what you have to sell, but they're never going to be your customers. **So you need to focus on the ones you think represent the best possibilities, and on converting as many as possible into actual customers.**

The third step is "Upgrading" them. Once you've converted them, you want to make them a bigger and better offer. **Try to get them to step up the amount of business they're doing with you.** Maybe your initial sale was a low-cost sale just to break the ice—to build rapport with them, to get them to take a baby step toward becoming your best customer. **The upgrade comes when you get them to do more business with you,**

taking your relationship to the next level where they're so excited about your offerings that they're eager to trade their money for what you're selling.

The final step is to "Expand," extending the relationship with the customer for as long as possible. This requires staying in touch with them, offering them related products and services, and otherwise building the bond that makes them want to do business with you over all your competitors—the bond makes them look to you first for the products and services they need, based on why they became your customer in the first place. **This process of expanding your relationship with people you've already met, converted, and upgraded can become a lifelong mission as you keep that fire going.** Just like any good relationship, you have to communicate on a regular basis and keep the relationship strong, so they'll remain your customers.

It works the same way whether you have a brick-and-mortar store, or you're working with an email or mail order list. **If you don't constantly communicate with them, they'll forget they did business with you and move on to other things.** But if you're always there for them, then they'll remember you for what you've done for them, and they'll be there for you when you have new products or upgrades or other things to offer them.

Once you've got that formula in place, your goal should be to keep repeating those four things over and over again. Part of the process of constantly meeting new prospects may involve a new customer acquisition campaign where you mail out so many pieces of mail on a weekly basis, attracting new people, then converting them, upgrading them, expanding them and expanding the relationship. **Do it right, and the whole thing can work like a well-oiled machine that practically prints money.**

That's how good direct response marketing works: Meet, convert, upgrade, expand.

In some ways, it's very simple; and yet it can get quite complicated as well. **You've got to set up systems to capture your customers' names and addresses, their email addresses, and their telephone numbers, so you can make special offers to them.** If you have a retail store, you can do this by having people drop a business card or some kind of slip including their contact information into a container, in return for the chance to win something free once a week or once a month. This works no matter what your business is, and it gets you tons of contacts that you know are interested in what you have to offer, or they wouldn't have given you their contact info in the first place.

So capture, and then communicate. **The communication really is key. It's amazing how even simple communications really can build that relationship.** Here's a little story that illustrates that. Once upon a time, there was an auto salesman named Joe Girard. He was pretty well known for what he did; in fact, he was literally the top salesman in the world for a while. The *Guinness Book of World Records* honored him for selling more cars than any single person in history, a feat that hasn't been broken yet, and *12 times* he achieved the annual ranking for top vehicle sales in the world. In his best year, he sold 1,425 retail vehicles.

His secret was greeting cards. He'd capture the contact information of the people he did business with, and then stay in contact with them. Every single month, he'd send all his clients a greeting card: Valentine's Day, Christmas, their birthdays, and all. He didn't include any big sales presentation or huge offer. Inside the card it basically just said, "I like you," and he'd sign it personally. **At one point, he sent out 13,000 greeting cards every month.** It took two assistants, which he paid for out of his own pocket, to keep track of and send those cards out. There wasn't any automated system at the time.

That was his secret weapon. Think about that: no fancy copywriting, no amazing offers, just the power of communication. Now imagine if you did something like that. Imagine how your clients and customers would respond to you contacting them on a regular basis, making them amazing offers—offers that made them want to come back and do business with you and keep that relationship alive. **All you have to do is capture that information, and use it.** Don't just let it sit idle on your computer or in your files. Put it to work. Some companies do collect this information, and then don't use it. Have you ever had to give a clerk your address and phone number, and then never heard from the store? Sure, they immediately know who you are and what they did for you last time you were there when they type in your phone number... but they don't send you any offers.

Don't make that mistake. **Get into the habit of communicating with your customers on a regular basis—because virtually nobody else does it.** When you do, you're going to stand head and shoulders above your competition, even if you use the simplest type of communication possible.

The Hand

Now that you've got that in mind, I'm going to give you another formula. There are all kinds of them in this business, and it's always good to know as many as you can. I call this one "The Hand," and **I got it from studying Bill Graham, the world's greatest rock-and-roll promoter** (*not* Billy Graham, the famous

---

evangelist). If you like reading interesting biographies, then check out *Bill Graham Presents...* to learn more about this innovative marketing system

Sadly, Bill Graham has been dead for many years now, but he left behind an amazing legacy in the rock-and-roll world. One of the reasons why he was the greatest promoter ever was because he always applied "The Hand" to all his concerts and promotions. No matter how big they were, **he focused on the five things that were the most essential—and of course, he knew everything there was to know about each one of those things.** Here's my version of The Hand as it applies to direct response marketing:

1. You get the right offer...

2. To the right person...

3. Through the right media...

4. With the right hook...

5. With the right tie-in.

First things first. **You have to realize what we marketers sell is not necessarily products and services, but *offers*, especially in the direct response field.** An offer isn't just the product or service; it's that plus all the other things you combine with it, including the price, the guarantee, the bonuses, and all the benefits.

Then you've got to get it to the right person; I've already talked about this somewhat. **Who is your #1 target?** Who are you really looking for? What's it going to take to reach that person? To reduce it to a bumper sticker jingle, your job is to attract the best and repel the rest. Chant that a few times, and you'll remember it.

Getting it to the right person requires you to use the right media. Personally, I love direct mail, and I've produced whole books and audio programs about it. But direct mail is expensive, so maybe that's not the route for you. Maybe you should use radio instead, or put an ad in a newspaper or a regional magazine or even on TV. **Whatever medium you choose, test it carefully, and make sure that it *is* the right one for you.** Pay close attention to which of your tests are more successful than the others—which is part of the big secret that I'm trying to pound you over the head with here.

The fourth "finger" of the Hand is using the right hook (and I'm not talking boxing here). **Find something that grabs people and pulls them in.** In the music business, a hook is part of a song you can't get out of your head. You keep singing it over and over again. It's catchy. In good writing, it's the first line—it sets up such a great interest in what happens next that you just have to keep on reading. **In DRM, good offers are like that. They grab your attention and stay right there in your head.** You know, the richest person in this business that I've ever spent good, quality time with came to our first seminar back in 1990. On that occasion, **he told me that as long as something sounds good, he'll go with it.** That was his whole thing: that it *sounds* good. That's what the right hook does for you.

Usually, a hook sounds right to a prospect only when you really understand them—and that's often a result of you yourself starting out as a customer in that market. You know the hopes and fears of the prospect—their absolute mindset, and what they aspire to. **When you understand what the customer is** thinking—and you'd better—this helps shape your hook to match your customer base. If you open an Italian restaurant, hopefully you've been to many Italian restaurants before, so you know the exact type of food that your customers want and expect. This works in all aspects of all businesses.

Last but not least, there's the right tie-in. Your offer has to tie in with the things you want to sell them in the future. This correlates directly with the fourth point of my earlier formula, which was to expand. You're trying to build long-term relationships with customers, because that's where your real profit lies.

True Education

Using either of the above formulas successfully requires some advanced thought, and you won't get everything perfect right away. But the more you think these things through, the more successful you'll become. You don't need an expensive education to make it work. I've known plenty of people who've gone to school to supposedly learn business skills, but somehow, they never learn any of the elements of either of the formulas I've outlined here. They launch their businesses, and before long, they're thinking of their clients or customers in completely the wrong way—a negative way. They don't respect the people who come to them for help, and in some cases, they don't even like them. Business becomes difficult for them, because they've put up a barrier between themselves and their prospects.

They never bother to understand their customers, or try to see things from their side of the cash register. Their attitude is, "I'm the service provider, and I'm doing you a favor. You need to bow down to me." Well, *they* need to put themselves in the shoes of their prospects and customers if they expect to make money. The Soup Nazi on *Seinfeld* may be funny, but in real life, that kind of attitude will kill your business.

You can't afford an elitist attitude unless you have absolutely no competitors, or you're already at the top of the game—and even when that's the case, you can slip if circumstances change. Just ask the original AT&T in the U.S., or TelMex in Mexico. **So to succeed in the long term, you need to understand the problems of the people who come to you, and where they're coming from in the first place.** Otherwise, why should they select you over everybody else?

When I tell you that you should step into their shoes and become a customer, I mean that literally. Instead of staying holed up in your own castle of a business, go out and use other people's services. If you run an Italian restaurant, visit other Italian restaurants and see what they're like. If you're a bookseller, go to other bookstores. If you're a mechanic, go to other mechanics. **Learn from them—both what to do, and what not to.** On top of all that, try to talk to people who use those other people's services, so you can get a more well rounded perspective.

You really have to connect in that way, because taking some vague idea and trying to come up with the right hook for the right target without intimately knowing the marketplace will result in many more mistakes than if you're a client yourself, and otherwise connect with people who use the services and products you want to provide.

Ultimately, following the right formulas and doing the right things always leads back to knowing your customer. You

---

need to know what they want the most, what keeps them up at night, what makes them keel over in pain, what problems they require solutions to. **If you don't know your customers, you're never going to be able to craft the right offer or the right hook, or you'll never get the timing right—or even be able to produce something as basic as the right product or service.** It's through that knowledge that you gain your ability to create all of those right situations and scenarios.

Again, it's best if you start by knowing your marketplace because you're already a customer. If you don't have that, that's not to say you can't be successful at it; but it may take you longer. **You have to begin by thinking about things exclusively from your customers' perspective.** Don't just guess what they want, or what you think they should want, or try to make them want what you have. Learn what they *really* want, so you can fill their needs. Get to know them. Spend a lot of time talking to them. Do surveys, or just watch closely enough to see what they're buying in your marketplace. In DRM, that's fairly easy. **All you need to do is study the available mailing lists, and then you can purchase those lists and offer the people on them something similar to what they bought before—something familiar, but with a new twist.**

If you don't start with a working knowledge of who the prospects are in your marketplace, then nothing's going to work right, no matter what formula you use.

Direct response marketing is an exciting way to reach out, touch your prospects, and draw them in. **It can give you a real competitive advantage over all of your competition, and it can allow you to spend less money and make more money.** It can make you very, very wealthy, because you can track it and quantify it and see what's working. That way, you can concentrate your marketing in the most effective venues.

DRM works wonderfully well with almost every other form of marketing. It works best when used in conjunction with everything else I'm going to share in this book—including the material in the next module, in which I'll discuss front-end and back-end marketing systems.

.

CHAPTER FOUR:

Module #3: Front-End and Back-End Marketing Systems

In this chapter, **I'll discuss the power of a good marketing system.** As you know, marketing consists of all of the things you do to attract and retain the largest possible number of the best prospects in your market. Marketing strategies fall into two basic categories: front-end and back-end. **Front-end marketing brings in new customers, people who have never done business with you before. Back-end systems follow up with existing customers, getting them to come back and do more business with you.**

These systems can be built so they can pretty much run themselves. They do require a little maintenance, but a well-planned, well-balanced system can do all of the grunt work for you, allowing you to focus on those few things that you can do best to bring in the most money. It all works just like a money machine, printing all the ready cash you'll ever want or need.

S-Y-S-T-E-M

Systems are central to building any scalable business. **Think of the word "SYSTEM" as an acronym for "Saves You Some Time, Energy and Money."** That's exactly what a good marketing system does. A lot of business owners lose track of this fact. They'll run out and do a lot of marketing, have a grand opening, and bring in some clients—and then they'll get busy managing the employees and business, forgetting about the marketing until they suddenly realize that no new people are coming in, and their income is shrinking. **If you can systematize your marketing so that you're both bringing in new customers and capturing new business from your existing customers, you'll have predictability in your business.** Instead of there being high highs and low lows—peaks and valleys—your business will consistently grow over time. You'll also have the ability to duplicate your business. If you have dreams of having multiple locations or maybe even franchising, you definitely have to create workable marketing systems first.

One of the best moneymaking systems in the world is McDonald's. It's been polished so well that high school kids can run it, and mostly do. That's what I mean when I emphasize the importance of good marketing systems. You want a marketing system in place that will consistently and constantly generate new clients, and another that lets you go back to those clients you've already brought in and make more money. **The first is a front-end system; the second is back-end. Let's look into the differences between them.**

Back to Front

Front-end systems can consist of numerous components, including advertisements, commercials, referral programs, and more. Whatever the case, **the ideal is to attract new customers as automatically as possible, so you can focus your time on where the *real* money is in your business.** This is the spot where most business owners fall short—not because they don't do enough, but because they do too much. When you spend 90% of your time focused on new business generation, what happens to the clients you've already done business with? Some people just ignore them, and ultimately forget they exist. To be blunt, that's stupid. Imagine what would happen if a restaurant tried that. **Your repeat customers are where your big money is—always.**

You've already done the hard part of attracting them; and having transacted business with you, they already know and trust you. **So if you're not offering new deals to your existing customers, you're sabotaging yourself.** You have an opportunity to sell to them repeatedly for huge profits, since you don't have to lay out the money to bring them in; you've already hooked them. That's why savvy marketers are sometimes willing to go hundreds or even thousands of dollars into the hole to acquire a new customer. **Once they know you're trustworthy and offer top-quality products and services, you can sell them high-end offers and bundles.**

So it's very important to realize that even as you're developing front-end marketing systems, you also need to spend a lot of time developing your back-end systems. *Always* **go back to your loyal fans, and focus on making them that next great offer.** First, brainstorm what that next offer will be, and then the next and the next, and find a way to systematize making these offers.

This can be done very inexpensively and easily by having staff members send out mailers and postcards, or by doing other simple types of marketing. It can also go very high-tech. I've seen marketing systems with automated tele-seminars and webinars, with database programs that capture the client's information and contain certain triggers, so that a day or two later they'll get a thank you card. Then, in 7-14 days, they'll get a new offer in the mail, an automated phone call, or an invitation to an event. **Without doing a thing after the basic set-up, you** can grow your business with automation—again, so you can worry less about your marketing and more about working on your business.

Scaling the Heights

Once you've got a front-end marketing system automatically bringing in a consistent number of new customers, and you've got the back-end converting them to long-term clients, you have the opportunity to spend more money on your marketing so you can bring in even *more* clients. **Now your business is scalable; now you can take it to the next level, and blow the competition out of the water. That's what this module is really all about: doing something that most other businesses aren't.** I'd say that 80-90% of businesses aren't systematized like this. Now, it does take a little time to set up all this, but it's definitely worth the effort due to the huge ROI.

Here's a quick story about how my colleague Jeff Gardner did this in his business. A few years back, Jeff was selling a $1,000 product and knew that very few new clients would plop down the full amount right away. Before they did that, they needed to know who he was—to connect with him and develop some trust first. So he came up with a $10 information product to sell on the front-end. He used marketing copy he wrote once and then placed multiple times to generate leads and sales for that report. Whenever someone purchased it, his database captured their information and then automatically sent out the product, along with the $1,000 offer.

Jeff promoted that $10 offer like crazy... even though every sale cost him about $20. **But you see, many of the people who got the $10 product upgraded to the $1,000 offer on the back-**

end—and about 80% of *that* **offer was pure profit.** That system generated $2.5 million in sales over a two-year period. **Once Jeff set it up, he just placed more advertising.** More people bought the $10 product, more people upgraded, and the system just kept chugging along, grinding out profit.

Look for the opportunity to do this in your own business. Create a front-end marketing system and a complimentary back-end marketing system, and set them up in such a way that they operate mostly automatically, so you can save yourself some time, energy, and money (remember the acronym, SYSTEM). In this business, we often talk about "the funnel"—the upside-down pyramid where we draw in prospects, and keep qualifying them repeatedly until we end up with the cream of the crop: the few customers who stay with us and really support our business. **Arranging complimentary front- and back-end marketing systems makes this process a lot easier to establish and automate.**

In Jeff's case example, the people who gave him $10 were willing to do so because it's an insignificant amount of money they were willing to gamble with. He was an unknown, so most of them weren't willing to risk $1,000 immediately—but they had no problem giving him $10. That pre-qualified them, since people who aren't willing to spend $10 will never spend $1,000. **It's a simple process, but very effective for separating the tire-kickers from the serious buyers.**

That lets you spend more money on converting them to serious buyers, thus achieving a higher conversion rate. Like Jeff, I'd rather have 100 really awesome prospects that cost me $10-20 each than 1,000 free curiosity seekers. So I try to get prospects to raise their hand one way or another. The $10 Jeff was charging defrayed the cost somewhat; but really, the intention was to pre-qualify the buyer. **Most experienced marketers try to set their front-end price low, so that even if the prospect hates what you sent them, they haven't risked much.** That's why Jeff's offer was so successful.

Of course, what you *really* want is for them to take that back-end offer, so it's critical that you over-deliver on that $10 deal. When they get it, they've got to think, "Oh my goodness, this is worth $50 or $100—if not more!" If you can do that on the front-end, they're going to think, "If this 10-buck deal is worth *that* much, then the $1,000 deal has got to be worth much more than they're asking."

Marketers use this strategy constantly. For example, restaurants might have special offers just to bring people in and get them hooked. But what I *don't* see them doing often enough is grabbing the customer's contact information and then going back to them with more special offers—for Valentine's Day or their birthday, for example. In that sense, they're leaving a lot of money on the table. If you're in the restaurant business and someone has a phenomenal time, and then you don't contact them and remind them of your business with special offers designed just for them... then it's up in the air. They might come back if they think of you, or they might not. **You've got to make sure you tie your front-end and back-end together to make sure they do.**

Companies that do this properly, that take the time to figure out both sides of the coin, are doing themselves a huge favor. But so often, a business focuses on bringing in new customers and then forgets about you once you *are* a customer. You've probably seen offers like that; DirecTV springs to mind for me. My

Marketing Director, Chris Lakey, has had DirecTV before, but he's not a customer now. Well, at the moment, they're going all out to make him become a customer again. They still have his email address from when he was a customer and now they're treating him like a brand new client.

Back when he *was* a customer, they never made him new offers that might have profited them more; once a customer, he was a customer, and that was it. And when Chris was a customer, the initial offer he responded to was *not* the same one he lived under after his initial offer period was over. The price goes up tremendously later, the deals aren't nearly as good, and they just don't treat you as well. They're going all out to get new customers, but blow off their existing ones—which is why they have a lot of customer service complaints and unhappy ex-customers.

Ross von Hoelscher went through something similar with AT&T. He was with them for a long time, and the prices they guaranteed him just kept going up and up, until finally he switched to Cox Communications. As soon as he did, AT&T offered him just about everything including the moon to come back, bending over backward to regain his business. Well, why didn't they just offer him great deals when they had him for a customer for many years? Because the whole thrust of their business model is, "We want new business, and the hell with the ones we have already. They're already in the fold." But those in the fold can get *out* of the fold nowadays. AT&T is no longer a monopoly, but apparently, they've never gotten that through their thick corporate skull.

Clearly, there must be differences between what you do to attract a new customer and what you do to serve an existing customer; but you need to attend to both sides of the

equation. It's not enough to spend all of your emphasis on attracting new customers. Quite the opposite; you should spend more time servicing *existing* customers. That said, it's not enough to serve your existing customers without also attracting new customers, because existing customers do fall away over time, no matter how well you treat them. Some pass away, some move away, and some just leave your marketplace. **So a good, effective marketing system takes both front-end and back-end into account; and the best sustain themselves automatically, working hand-in-hand.**

We have what we call our "Chip Off the Block Offers," where we sell or give people a small part of a larger offer before trying to upsell them on the full package. This is very like Jeff Gardner's $10 front-end package that upsold a $1,000 package—it all runs smoothly and automatically, letting people qualify themselves before stimulating their interest in the high-dollar item.

For many years, Ross von Hoelscher ran a book distributorship (which I eventually bought from him). He offered a variety of books, mostly his own through his Profit Ideas company. He ran ads in all the business opportunity publications, usually full-page ads selling an introductory book for one dollar. But it wasn't a cheap little book: it was a 140- or 150-pager that others might charge $10-$20 for. The idea was to get people to realize, "Hey, if I can get this great book for one dollar, and it's worth at least 10 times that, then I should be able make money with the other books Profit Ideas offers."

That was the basis of Ross's front-end strategy. **You bring people in cheaply, you take good care of them, and eventually they become customers.** Just because someone comes into your business to look around, or even to spend some money, doesn't mean they're instantly a customer. They're a first-timer, possibly a tire-kicker. When someone comes back a couple of times, they've made the transition to a buyer. But it takes even more than that to turn them into a *real* customer. **The key here is their long-term value.** What is that customer worth over a year? How about over their lifetime?

I'm fond of looking at this question from the restaurant angle. If you have a diner who comes in about once a week, say 50 times a year, then you can multiply the profit from an average one-time visit times 50. That's going to reach into the hundreds of dollars, if not more. Obviously, that person is meaningful to your long-term success. So at the same time you're going after the new customers with your 2-for-1 coupons and Internet specials, remember that the guy who comes to your restaurant 50 times a year is already a golden customer. You'd better have some specials for him, too. You'd better have the manager come along and slip him a complimentary slice of strawberry shortcake every once in a while.

You *have* to do things like this, no matter what kind of business you own. It doesn't matter if you're cleaning carpets, dry cleaning, or selling diamond rings. **Realize that you *must* recognize your existing customers and value them above the people you haven't yet sold to, or you're going to lose them.** People have plenty of choices nowadays; if you don't provide little extras or, worse, if you seem to punish them with higher prices just because they're loyal to you, they'll *stop* being loyal to you. So figure out how to take care of the people you depend on for a living month after month, year after year.

The Newsletter Angle

It doesn't take a lot to make people feel special, like you're paying them attention and catering to their needs. **A newsletter can be a valuable tool in this sense.** It keeps you in touch with customers at least several times a year—sometimes monthly, even weekly. **It gives them news about your company or the industry in general, informs them about special offers or sales, and provides a caring, personal touch.** Some newsletters go out free to customers; some require a subscription fee, especially if you're selling valuable information. Some marketers toss in a free subscription as a bonus when you make any sizable purchase, which is also a good idea.

Something like this could work for restaurants, for plumbers, for construction contractors, for booksellers, and for many other businesses. If you're not putting out at least an email newsletter now, consider doing so. **Keep in touch with the people you want to do business with, and eventually they *will* do business with you again.**

I'm reminded of a little newsletter a realtor kept sending Russ von Hoelscher for years, every couple of months; and in the months she didn't send a newsletter, she'd send some scratch pads or a pen, and Russ thought, "God, this woman is sending so much stuff to me, and I don't have any need for her business!" Ah, but when he eventually decided to sell his home in San Diego, he called her up—and she ended up making a commission of thousands of dollars. She was persistent, and it didn't cost her much to send those memo pads and pens and that two-page newsletter—but it kept her in touch with Russ. Eventually it profited her, even though Russ never thought he'd use her services.

So keep that in mind. **Stay aggressively in touch with people you want to do business with.** Don't give up; and realize you may have to wait a while and spend some real money before you recoup that investment—and possibly much more. It's super easy to do, and **it builds a relationship with your clients so they start to know you, like you, and trust you, which is crucial in any business.** It also gives you the opportunity to make special offers directly to them. The reason they're getting that newsletter or other contact is because they're a client, whether they've done business with you once or 14 times before. Now you have the opportunity to go back and make them offers and package deals that bring in new business. Whereas many companies wonder, "What am I going to have to do *this* month to bring in business?", you already know you're going to be sending out a newsletter intended to bring in a flow of new business. That's a great feeling to have as a business owner.

Newsletters, then, can become elements of an effective marketing system, especially on the back-end. They're simple enough. Russ von Hoelscher produces a little newsletter every other month, and he knows he's got to collect a few items to include here and there every few days. That's become part of his routine. Through that newsletter, he builds relationships with his clients, and promotes all kinds of offers, products, and services that endear him to them. If you decide to follow Russ's lead, try to figure out what it's going to take to create a great customer experience that encourages people to come back for more.

Seamless Success

Unfortunately, many small business owners are afraid of spending money before they make money, or else they want to bill for everything they do—like an attorney, every minute has to be billable. The concept of sending out a free newsletter or giving something away sounds alien, even crazy to them. **But it *works*.**

Chris Lakey and his wife went out of town for the weekend for their last anniversary, and at their hotel's restaurant one morning, just happened to mention they were there celebrating their anniversary. A few minutes later, as they were sitting at their table, the woman they'd been talking to five minutes before brought them drinks and said, "Congratulations—these are on the house." Something as simple as that made a *great* impression. Chris tells me he really enjoyed his experience at the hotel, and was impressed by their attempt to go above and beyond.

Sure, the hotel spent a little money on those free drinks—but that tiny expenditure made a great impression. Now Chris is more likely to refer or recommend that hotel to others, or even go back there himself the next time he's in the area. How does that apply to front-end and back-end marketing systems? Well, it's all part of a strategy to build relationships with existing customers. **Such relationships facilitate more back-end business, and can pay off with new referrals as well.** So don't think of things like this as expenses, because ultimately, they make you money.

And don't think for one second that the hotel's response to Chris's anniversary wasn't systematized as part of their business process. It's probably even in their handbook, because sadly, a lot of employees these days just can't think for themselves. That's not intended as a judgment call, it's just an observation. They're so busy thinking about what they're going to do over the weekend or after they get off work that they don't have their minds on the fine details of the job. But at the hotel Chris visited, they're trained to respond to birthdays, anniversaries, and other special events as part of their company's marketing system. **Excellent customer service doesn't happen by accident; it's all part of a systematic business process.**

Your income depends on getting people to spend money with you, and the best way to do that is to serve them in the highest possible way from every angle you can think of. Spontaneity is uneven; systematizing your approach to customer service always works best, both on the front- and back-end. Most businesses do one or the other with varying levels of success, but have no system to do both seamlessly; and so they suffer.

Suppose they're great at drawing people into their system, but terrible at maintaining relationships with existing customers. It's like having a bucket with a hole in it, because even as you fill your system with new customers, others are dropping out in droves. You can have people gushing in like a fire hose, but you still won't make much money if the bucket's bottom is rusted through. **Succeeding at one side of the equation doesn't mean squat if you can't succeed on the other side as well.** And let me remind you: even the best "buckets" aren't watertight. People die, move away, leave the market, stop spending money — so even if you're great at retention, you still need to be great at attraction. Otherwise, your existing business will eventually dry up.

That's what I'm *really* trying to tell you here. **It's not a good front-end marketing system *or* a good back-end system that matters, it's both, working together.** It's just a smarter way to make money. You can have one without the other, but they're incomplete and at odds if that's the case — and you'll inevitably hemorrhage red ink.

Let's reconsider Jeff Gardner's $10 offer from earlier in the chapter. Often, that offer cost him $20 (or more) to fulfill. But he didn't look at it as losing money, because the back-end profits were huge; he sold so many $1,000 follow-ups that the front-end losses just didn't matter. That should be your approach. It's not necessarily about spending less money on the front-end; cheapness doesn't translate easily into profits in good marketing schemes. You may very well end up spending more money than you make on the front-end... which is what stops many small businesses in their tracks. **But don't ever think of it as a loss! This is a smarter way to spend your money.** If you can perfect your front-end/back-end marketing system, you don't have to worry about how much money you're spending—within reason, of course.

You have to let the numbers tell you what to do, so keep a sharp eye on profit-and-loss. Track those down to the penny, and be efficient about it; make sure all expenditures are accounted for. Now, if you can figure out a way to make a profit on the front-end of a promotion, then of course you should. But the back-end is generally where you make the profit, as you convert your leads into repeat customers.

The DRM Angle

Most traditional advertising is just image advertising; all it does is remind people you exist. That's fine for AT&T and Coca-Cola, but it's a hit-and-miss prospect for most of us. If you're advertising in multiple ways, you have no way of knowing where your income is coming from—which means you have no idea what's working best. If you can't figure that much out, how do you know what to cut back on or expand on? **Direct response-based front-end and back-end marketing systems allow you to be more accountable to the advertising that's working for you.**

That's why I prefer these kinds of systems, because you can account for everything. **You can see what's working and what isn't, based on each method's "dollar score," so you can spend your money more wisely.** You can actually spend less money on advertising but make greater profits. That's one of the strengths of good combined front-end/back-end marketing systems. On the other hand, once you see that higher profit ratio, you'll probably want to spend more money on the front-end, because you know you can make more. For the sake of simplicity, imagine knowing that for every dollar you spend on marketing, you'll get two back. In other words, suppose you invested $1,000 and got a return of $2,000—not in a matter of years, but in a few months.

That's an excellent ROI. If you knew that would happen consistently as long as you kept tracking everything carefully, you'd be motivated to not only keep up with your tracking but to invest more, wouldn't you? How much money would you spend then?

The truth is, the one-time cost of your advertising is immaterial, whether you're talking about a $500 ad or a $50,000 commercial. **All that matters is ROI. How much money are you making from that advertising—today, next week, next month, or next year, in long-term customer value?** Whatever the case, direct response marketing gives you the ability to track those numbers, so you can know if your system is profitable or not.

I encourage you to reread the previous chapter on direct response marketing for a better understanding of this issue. As I outlined there, DRM is not only the most powerful form of marketing on the planet, but it can also be one of the most expensive if you do it right. **Good DRM is nothing less than good salesmanship... and you don't tell your salesmen to shut**

up after 10 minutes. If you've got a quality prospect, you tell them to keep trying until they secure the sale.

Because that's the whole point here: you do whatever you can to get the sale. Doing a complete selling job can be *very* expensive—which is why I say that most marketers don't spend nearly enough on marketing. **They're pennywise and dollar foolish, and miss out on money that could and should be theirs.** So be thoughtful and careful when you build your overall marketing systems—and **don't give up on your prospects too soon, especially on the back-end, or you've just wasted your efforts, time, and money.**

This brings up the concept of follow-up, an integral part of back-end marketing. Now, whether it's no-cost or low-cost, lead generation is designed to do one thing: get people to raise their hands and express interest in what you have to offer. **That's when you send them the first round of information. Once they have it, you follow-up in an attempt to get them to purchase the initial package you're offering.** Here at M.O.R.E., Inc., we might spend 4-8 weeks, possibly more, just sending out reminders that someone hasn't bought yet. Then the lead might get a call from one of our client service representatives, asking if they have any questions about the offer.

Once they make that initial purchase, the secondary sequence goes into effect. **We let them know we have additional, related services or products they can purchase if they're interested.** This is an entirely separate but extensive follow-up campaign to someone who has already become a customer, having been pre-qualified by their earlier actions. We've narrowed the field, and now they're on our general client list. They'll keep getting offers until it's no longer profitable for us to keep following up with them.

It's not enough just to invite people to do business with you once; **you have to consistently remind them that they haven't done business with you, that there's still an offer on the table.** It may take several tries or more to get them to respond. Most people have very busy lives. They've got a lot going on, and they're evaluating product offers from other companies as well as yours. There are all kinds of things in front of them.

That's why you have to constantly remind them they still need to respond to your offer. You do that with follow-up marketing. If your primary method is DRM, as ours is, you send them follow-up postcards in the mail, or even larger direct mail packages that invite them to do more business with you. If you're an online marketer, you can create an e-mail sequence to remind them. Auto responders are big these days, although some people find them cold and distant, since it's basically a robot communicating with them. It has to be done just right, or it won't be effective. **In any case, you do need to keep following up, whether on- or off-line or even by phone.** If you have a sales team, you can call them. You can use tele-seminars or conference calls to try to convert leads into sales.

All these things represent actions intended to convert leads into customers; because if you don't take some kind of massive action, you'll miss out on money that should be yours. It's as simple as that. You might have a hot campaign that shows promise, but you can't maximize your profits if you give up on prospects too early. **So don't neglect the long-term follow-up marketing, because it helps you convert the largest number of prospects to customers, and then customers into repeat customers.**

Reward Everyone

Special discounts or other deals to draw people in are so common in front-end marketing that most marketers don't think twice about offering them as a means of boosting sales. But once you're a customer, it's like some of them stop valuing you—which is ridiculous. I've told you already about how AT&T and DirectTV do this; and the really ironic thing is that they're willing to spend a fortune and accept huge losses to try to lure you back once their apathy has driven you off. It would be easier if they'd just offer you special deals while you're already a customer, rather than trying to bleed you white.

This works for *any* business, from DRM specialists to chiropractors to dog boutiques. If you have a brick-and-mortar store, create a special day or evening when customers can come to your business, by invitation only, and receive a big discount or a special arrangement for their future business. If you have a service business, offer a special service at a price just for them. One jewelry store I know of has its best customers in for a special evening of wine and cheese occasionally, then presents its special offers to them; sometimes, the offer is simply that they'll get first crack at a new product.

Treat people special, and you'll keep their business. They go where they're welcome and stay where they're appreciated. And realize that this, too, can be systematized. Just put it on your calendar and add a "tickler" to remind you when it's coming up. You can do things like this every month, or every few months—your choice. It can easily become an integral part of your marketing system.

No More Cold Calls!

One big advantage of a good front-end/back-end system is that once you've got it in place and working correctly, you never have to make cold calls again. I started my first carpet-cleaning business in December 1985 with a friend. We didn't have any money and knew nothing about marketing; all we knew how to do was walk up and down Main Street, knocking on doors and giving away bids. Then we'd get phone numbers and call people up. We'd also try to get referrals; it was all about personal selling.

If you've ever done that, you know it's all hit-and-miss. Every month we'd knock on thousands of doors and call hundreds of people, mostly ending up talking to folks who had no real interest at the time in carpet and upholstery cleaning. We got doors slammed in our face and got hung up on. Once, a man came to the door with a gun. He didn't aim it at me, but he answered the door and the gun was right there in his hand. It scared the crap out of me, and I told him, "Whoa, I'm just a carpet cleaner, man! I'm not here to rob you."

My first actual marketing system was crude by my current standards, **but it *was* a system.** My wife Eileen and I went to a home show, set up a table, and noticed everyone around us had home show specials. We decided we needed one too, so we grabbed a shoebox and put a little pad of paper beside it. When people came by, we said, "Hey we're giving away three rooms of carpet cleaning absolutely free after the show. Why not put your name and phone number in the box?"

A lot of people said, "No thank you," and just walked past us. But those who were interested in getting free carpet cleaning dropped their contact info in the box. **We walked away from that show with 50-60 leads, from which we chose a winner right away.** Then I called everyone else who had signed up for our contest and offered a consolation prize. It was conditional: if they had us in to clean three rooms, we'd add a protective Scotchgard coating, or we'd clean a chair for free, or do an extra room for free.

It was the easiest business I had done up to that point. I converted one lead out of every three; I was only on the phone for a few minutes, and I walked away with a couple of weeks' worth of work, just booked up solid. During those weeks, I was in a state of shock. I couldn't believe how well it had worked, and I wanted to do it again.

There wasn't a home show that I could go to every month, so I took that little ballot box and put it on the checkout counter of this little Mexican restaurant I used to frequent, along with a handmade sign that said "Win Three Rooms of Carpet Cleaning Free—Register Here." It worked like a charm. While people were waiting for their food, they saw my little sign. If they were interested in carpet cleaning, they filled out my form; otherwise, they ignored it. I came by and picked up the leads every week, then announced a winner. Afterward, I called up the rest and sure enough, just like with that home show, I closed about a third of my sales. It was a great little system that got people to come to me instead of me going to them.

That shift of perspective—from me chasing them to them chasing me—made all the difference in the world for my business. No longer was I wasting time with people who had no interest in carpet cleaning. **The only people who filled out the form _were_ interested, so they were pre-qualified.** Even though I initiated the contest, in their minds they chose me, because they chose to participate. Every week after that I was booked solid. And of course, every night I'd call a few of my old customers back and make a pitch for additional work.

Today, I would create something a lot more sophisticated that would work automatically and would bring in a lot more business, so I could keep more than just one carpet cleaning truck on the road... but back then, I was in heaven. I no longer had to deal with the misery of cold calling. When you have great prospects who are coming to you on a regular basis and you know they're interested in what you have, that changes the dynamics of the entire game, shifting it all in your favor.

Many of us start on a small scale like that, just out of necessity. Back when he was first beginning his mail order business 30 years ago, our mentor Russ von Hoelscher sent little personal notes to the people who made inquiries. They hadn't invented Post-It notes yet, so he'd write a little note on a 3 x 5 card: "Dear Betty: Thanks for your inquiry. This program will help you make money." He did that repeatedly, and it worked very well. But as he got bigger, he thought, "Well gee, I'm not going to sit there and write thousands of these notes." So he came up with a more automatic way to respond.

Some of the things you come up with purely out of necessity work beautifully on a small scale. Sometimes they're not scalable, though; for example, I don't use the ballot box method much these days, because it doesn't fit my business plan. But when you can, take that information you receive and find a way to use it on a larger scale.

Russ still talks about how excited he was at the beginning of

---

his mail order business, just to think that people all over the nation would be sending him $10 or $15 for a book. It was like Christmas every day, and that's the kind of feeling that encourages you to keep thinking of new ways to reach out to our customers. Now, sometimes when you get larger, you get a little too blasé about business and let things take care of themselves. **Instead, stay proactive; think of ways you can reach out and touch somebody, because if you do that, your business will flourish.**

And don't assume you have to pile on the high-tech to make this work. The methods I've just discussed are quite low-tech, and still very effective. Recently, Jeff Gardner was telling me about an independently-owned gym in his area who attracts more business the exact way I used to attract it in the early days: with a ballot box system. He goes around to small businesses in the area and says, "Hey, I'll give the owner a free membership if you let me put this ballot box offering a free trial membership and guest memberships here on your counter."

Those little boxes are transparent, so there's some social proof working there: people can see that others have put their information in the boxes, which encourages them to do the same. Sure enough, he empties it out on a regular basis—and suddenly he's got invitations to contact people and invite them to come in for their free membership or free session, as the case may be. He then upsells them on special discount packages for six months, 12 months or two years. That system just keeps working; and because it worked so well in the local barbecue place, he put one into the Mexican restaurant and the burger joint, and lots of other restaurants in the area. Then he started branching out, putting them in other independently owned stores. **So as you can see, you don't have to do search engine optimization and social media marketing and all the high-tech stuff just because it's**

available. Don't forget the simple, off-line marketing methods. They can generate tons of leads, and they can keep generating money for years to come.

And again, try to keep that passion and the excitement flowing. Just thinking back on the ballot box system I stumbled upon, I can still feel the excitement I felt when I realized what I had. It was a simple idea that worked wonderfully well, and it was easy to maintain that excitement because it did.

Your strategy should be simple, no matter what the media you use to implement it. **Use the DRM strategies I've outlined in this module to target a group of people who are most likely to be your customers.** Get them to self-qualify by raising their own hands to express interest in what you have to offer. Follow up with them, turn them into customers, and then hone your back-end strategies to fill out the system. **Work hard to build the relationship required to succeed long-term.**

This strategy works no matter whether you're using it on the Internet or via snail mail, or advertising in publications, on TV and radio, even in the Yellow Pages. Whatever you're doing, your goal is to attract prospects and then work to convert those prospects into customers, so you can keep doing more and more business with them.

That's really how simple it is.

CHAPTER FIVE:

Module #4: Direct Mail Marketing

In this module, I'll introduce you to what I believe is the most exciting marketing method in the world: direct mail. We love direct mail here at M.O.R.E., Inc., and we believe almost anything can be sold to almost anyone via direct mail. **It's made us more money than all the other marketing methods we've tried combined.** Of course, you have to do it right; there are plenty of people out there making terrible mistakes with direct mail, and when they don't get the results they want, it sours them completely on the process.

Well, they shouldn't blame it on direct mail; it's their own fault for not understanding the medium. **Now, I'll admit that direct mail is probably the most expensive kind of marketing you can do,** other than having a live sales representative go out there and knock on doors for you. **But it's also very effective if you do it right, and can make you a tremendous amount of money.**

Most of my close colleagues also use direct mail, and have similarly come to love it over the years, especially after having experienced other methods of marketing. **For example, Jeff Gardner—who got an early start with marketing—fell in love with direct mail after an early experience when he *didn't* use it.** Back when he was a teenager, he saw an infomercial for a product called the Super Shammy (I believe they call it "Sham-WOW!" nowadays). This is one of those products that does the rounds every 10-15 years: an orange cloth that can soak up Coca-

Cola through a carpet and do all kinds of other magical stuff. Jeff thought, "Wow! If I could get a few hundred of those and take them down to the local flea market, I'd be rich!" because obviously they were selling like hotcakes.

And that's exactly what he did. He held a garage sale, made a few hundred dollars, and ordered his product from the Super Shammy wholesaler in China. His parents thought he'd gone insane, and he says that looking back, he can't blame them. He put his cloths in his pickup and drove them down to the flea market one weekend, set up shop, and waited for the hordes to descend. Well, he sold two or three Shammys to the hordes, and that was it. He went home with 99% of them in this big package, thinking, **"OK, how do I do this *right*?"**

Obviously, flea marketing selling wasn't the best idea. He couldn't go from flea market to flea market selling two or three cloths a day; there just wasn't enough money in it. That's when Jeff stumbled onto direct mail. During the same time period, he'd been buying a lot of different opportunities through the mail and subscribing to home business magazines—and suddenly his mailbox was filled with letters about various books or courses that could show him how to profitably work from home. **Basically, they all revealed the secrets of using direct mail.**

So he started doing DRM very inexpensively, and began to see some money come in. Not a huge amount, of course, because he was brand-new and didn't really know what he was doing—but it was a lot better than the response he'd had gotten at the flea market. **Over time, he got to be a better copywriter, made better offers, and since then, he's generated millions of dollars using direct mail.**

One of the reasons why direct mail is so effective is because you have the opportunity to target your market. In the town where Jeff set up his table at the flea market, there were probably tons of people interested in the Super Shammy — but he wasn't targeting them. He was setting up in one spot, hoping that the people who wanted his product would somehow find him. **Direct mail lets you tighten your focus, making your offer directly to people who are more likely to want what you have.** You have the opportunity to buy or rent mailing lists of people who have a specific interest in the kind of product or service you're selling. **Usually these are people who have previously bought something similar, or who fit a certain demographic.** That lets you cut down on marketing waste, because you can directly target those who are most likely to buy from you. It's a more efficient way to market. Plus, mail really demands attention — especially nowadays.

When I first got started in the business, direct mail was all there was. With the advent of the Internet and the rising costs of printing and postage, marketers moved onto the 'Net in a big way — so ironically, folks who still focus on direct mail are getting more attention now because there's less junk in the mailbox. Think about that before you decide to "save money" with an email blast.

One of the key reasons why I think **every business should be involved in direct mail is that it gives you a unique opportunity to package up your best sales message and leverage the U.S.P.S. to put it in front of hundreds, thousands, tens of thousands, even hundreds of thousands of potential buyers at a time.** Every package is like a little salesman — except that those salesmen never get tired, bored, or depressed. No one slams doors in their faces. They never have problems at home, or demand pay raises, or just up and quit like a human salesperson or telemarketer can. They're never late to work—and they can work every day of the week. You don't have to train these little salesmen, either. Their motivation never runs out, and they never get sick!

That's not to say that direct mail entirely replaces a good sales team. But here's the thing: you don't have to waste people on door-knocking or cold-calling when you use direct mail. You never even hear it when people say no; they just toss your package in the recycling bin or the trash can and move on. You only hear from the people who are truly interested—if not pure "yeses," at least a mix of "yeses" and "maybes." Direct mail lets people qualify themselves—and goes out rain or shine no matter what it's feeling like.

When you get right down to it, **direct mail combines all the advantages of your best sales rep on his or her best day ever with the reach and power of the postal system.** You can duplicate this sales pitch as many times as you like, as long as it keeps working. You can mail your sales letter, month after month, year after year, to thousands and thousands of people. Sure, it's expensive—but **direct mail gives you the opportunity to maximize your sales at a decent cost, and gets the consistent results you need over time.** It's scalable; as you make more money, you can mail out more little salesman, and the more money you make the more you can mail at once. There are huge benefits to doing direct mail. Is it any surprise I absolutely love it?

Setting the Hook

One of the chief lessons of direct mail marketing—of any direct response marketing, really—is that you have to make your prospects a compelling offer. **No matter how fascinating the product, no matter how much they need it, you have to really sell it, painting a vivid word picture that draws them in.** But that's achievable—and it's certainly a skill that you can learn. I know this to be true because I've done it myself.

People new to direct mail sometimes get worried about writing their sales copy, and that's understandable, even justifiable. They say, "I've never done this before; I'm not really a writer. I don't know how to write copy." Well, the truth is that while learning to write great copy is important, you can be a so-so copywriter and still make money as you hone your copywriting skills. **Just pair your copy with the most irresistible, awesome offer you can find.** Rosser Reeves, one of the pioneers of television advertising, once said, "A gifted product is mightier than a gifted pen." Bill Bernbach, another great advertiser, echoed that when he said, "The magic is in the product, not in the copywriter's pen."

Advertising doesn't create a product advantage. It can only convey it. No matter how skillful you are, you can't invent a product advantage that doesn't exist. So I recommend that you find or create a great product or service, then focus on making a compelling offer that people in your target market will drool over—something they just won't be able to turn down. Now, to accomplish that **you might have to go a bit crazy and do something like create a guarantee that nobody else in your market would even dream of offering;** but believe me, it's worth it when you start pulling in new long-term clients.

When I started in the business, I certainly wasn't a master copywriter; but the one thing I knew was that offers that excited me would probably excite my market. So I tried to craft the most irresistible and compelling offers I could. Even though I look back on that copy and laugh at it today, it pulled in hundreds of thousands, and in some cases millions, of dollars. The same thing is true for many of my colleagues. **So do a lot of brainstorming, and jump right in there with the best, hottest offer you think is most likely to attract your target market—and I think you're going to see some great results.**

Thank You, Internet

Which brings me back to the biggest reason there's less direct mail now than there's been in the past century: the Internet. It's a wonderful medium for exchanging information, which makes it a wonderful advertising medium. But it doesn't work for everyone, and I say that as a person who's made millions via the Internet. **For me, the 'Net just doesn't work to the degree that direct mail does. But I do appreciate all the folks who've gone the online advertising route to save money—because it's opened the gateway for greater direct mail profits for me!**

I've already pointed out how expensive direct mail is, in terms of postage and printing rates. But if you do it right, you can capitalize on it like *nothing* else. You don't even have to do it on a nationwide basis. I know that some of you reading this will be carpet cleaners (as I once was) or doctors, chiropractors, electricians, or plumbers. Such businesspeople tend to be local, or regional at best. They just want to capture the most business they can from the city or town they live in. Well, that's fine—mailing list companies have everybody on their lists. You yourself are on the lists of just about every company you've ever done business with, and they've probably sold that list to someone. You may be on other lists because you're a homeowner or just because you're alive. If you have a hobby—computers, photography, fishing, hunting, whatever it is—you're on a list.

So anyone who goes the direct mail route can define a particular list to use by subject or region. If you own a dealership for expensive cars, you can drill down to the names of locals at a specific economic level—say, those who are making at least $100,000 a year. There *will* be a list for that. Direct mail opens up all kinds of vistas for profits, allowing you to do business on a local basis, on a nationwide basis, or even a worldwide basis—and so the potential is absolutely fantastic.

Although the U.S. Postal Service is loaded down with bureaucracy, it's generally very reliable. **Your sales letters go out and hit your target prospects with your message almost without fail.** If they don't want to hear it, they just ignore it; and that piece of mail isn't going to be annoyed or mad because someone slammed the door on it. **And really, it's cheaper to send mail than to send a salesman out on the road, isn't it?**

Salesmanship in an Envelope

While you can use something as simple as a postcard to drive sales, **one of the greatest advantages of direct mail is that the venue lets you address your prospect's objections and explain your benefits at length, without resulting to a real, live salesperson.** Oh, you can still have sales people like we do, as long as your little direct mail salesmen help you pre-qualify the prospects your flesh-and-blood salespeople talk to. In fact, it works great as a way to generate leads for your front-end marketing system, as I discussed in the previous chapter.

We did a consultation for a gentleman recently who showed us his direct mail package, and his offer was basically, "Call for an appointment." He's a financial advisor, and by his own admission, he's trying to catch what he calls "the whales." A whale is somebody with lots of money to invest who's already working with one or two other financial advisors. Yet the language he's using isn't the right kind of bait for a whale; at best, it's a minnow, which is so small that a whale's never even going to notice it. **"Call for an appointment" is anemic. All it means to them is that you're going to try to sell them something. They don't want to be sold anything; they want to choose to buy.**

In a case like this, you've got to find some intermediate step; something that doesn't take them too far too fast. Making them a special offer that eases them along a little right now can help you ease them right into a big sale later on.

Direct mail is perfect for this. It's the epitome of salesmanship without all the negatives that go with it. When you put your little salesmen in an envelope, you've (ideally) already dealt in advance with all the objections to your offer—anything that might cause them not to buy. **All their questions should be pre-answered,** if not in the initial sales material then in the additional literature you send in the follow-up phase. By the time people come to you, they're mostly pre-sold, and definitely highly qualified.

Authenticity Attracts

The biggest mistake I see people making with direct mail (besides not presenting an irresistible offer) is that they make their copy too "salesy". **They try to appeal to the entire marketplace at once, and you can't do that if you want to make a significant number of sales.** Everything gets too homogenized and boring; in their attempt to appeal to everyone, they appeal to no one. You have to realize that you're *not* talking to the entire market or the entire world (even if, ideally, that *is* your market). **You're actually talking to an individual; that's who will get your sales letter, not some idealized Joe Average.**

So address your copy to the individual prospect. Talk to one person about how your product, service, or offering will benefit them. If your offer goes to someone who doesn't fit your profile, then they'll toss it; fine. But when it fits, it *really* fits, and that immediately increases your chance of making the sale.

So be authentic, and really care about their experience; try to see it all through *their* eyes. In doing that, you can write some truly amazing copy. I've seen people whose first drafts are very "old school salesy." They look almost like something a 1960's car salesman would use. I tell them, "Strip all that slick stuff away, and **just pretend you're telling a friend how great your product is.** Pretend you're sitting across the table from the one person who represents your ultimate target. They've got a name, so use it (at least in your mind), and envision that person as fully as possible."

Once you've fixed that image in your head, **write your copy as if you were talking to that individual.** Even if doesn't end up being what some people would consider amazing copy, it's still going to be very authentic. **It gets the benefits across and sells a lot better than something that's flashy but empty.** It's got that one-on-one communication feel.

That's the key here. If you've got an irresistible offer and you explain it to somebody as another human being, that's going to build some trust; they're going to be excited about the offer. It doesn't matter whether you've studied direct mail and copywriting for only a couple of weeks or for ten years—**all that matters is how you get the message across about your irresistible offer.**

Right on Target

The most important element of any direct mail campaign is, unsurprisingly, the copy; and the only way you can get that right is to *know who your target market is.* You have to know everything possible about the person you want to reach. That's fairly easy if you've specialized in a specific market for a while, or if you yourself come from your target market. But if you're venturing out of your market or your area of expertise, you need to do some targeted market research first. Without it, it's hard to say who might need plumbing or dental work right now, or who needs a new financial product.

In cases like this, you do have to think in terms of a specific customer, especially if yours is a service business. Most of the people in your target market may not need your services today; they may not need them for another week, month, or six months. But someday, they *will* need it. So when you craft that copy, talk to them on an individual basis as much as possible. **No sales letter should be written for a mob...** though it's amazing to me how many people actually do write letters that begin with, "To all my customers" or something similar. No! **Make it an individualized letter, where you're talking one-to-one.**

In addition to knowing what your target wants (or probably will want), you've got to think about the appeal that works best for them. What service or product do you have that's going to turn them on? How can you get them really excited? **You have to out-punch and out-think the competition. You have to**

differentiate your offerings from everyone else's. What can you offer in addition to your products and service, such as better service and follow-up after the sale?

Then you have to pour on as many potential benefits as you can think of—because what you think of as the #1 benefit may be #10 on someone else's list, or vice-versa. Just include everything you can; because if nothing else, outlining the benefits and exactly what they can do for the prospect helps to answer any objections they may have. **Toward the end, tell people the action you want them to take**—whether to call a certain number, to come into your store, or send for a free sample—and sweeten the deal. Offer a bonus of some kind. It can be a cut rate on a certain service, or a small physical gift. Finally, it's good to know what the competition is doing, so you can try to do it better.

All those things should go into your copy, and you should introduce it with an eye-catching headline. Even letters that are meant to look personal in nature should have a headline, because a headline will jump out at people—especially if it contains what you think is the biggest and best benefit you have to offer. Later on, you can use bullets to list other benefits, just in case you missed the mark with some people with the headline. At the very least, though, it should tempt them into reading.

The Call to Action

Direct mail can work wonders, whether you use it with 100,000 people or just a few hundred at a time. But don't be like so many people, and write genuinely great one-on-one personalized copy... and then flub one of the final steps: the call to action. **A great offer with ideal reasons to try it out is one thing; but then you have to explicitly invite the prospect to**

take action. Too often, when I review the flawed systems of other people, I see them get to the closing and just say, "Well, thanks for your time," and that's it.

My friend and colleague Jeff Gardner used to be afraid to ask for the sale. Like me, he's a people pleaser—so when he'd get to the end of his sales letter, he wouldn't push too hard. But you absolutely have to provide the prospect with very specific directions on how to respond; and luckily, he learned that early on. **You see, one of the best things about the direct mail business—above and beyond the incredible money!—is that it's a no-rejection business.** Very few people who get your offer are likely to take the time to write a letter telling you to bug off. They just toss the offer. Even if they rip it up before they do, what do you care? You'll never know. **With direct mail, you see only the results, the profits, and the response.** On the other hand, selling door-to-door is a high-rejection strategy. People may even call you names and slam doors in your face.

Never be afraid to actually ask for the sale, and to get very specific about what action the prospect should take. You might tell people, "Pick up the phone and dial this number. If the line is busy, make sure you call back." You can really push them on ordering: "Order right now! Do not put this down, or you're likely to forget about it until it's too late!" Even if you make an irresistible offer, even if you know all of your benefits hit their hot buttons, you have to make sure that when it comes time to ask for the action, you do so in a strong way. *Always* **encourage prospects to take action. Give them a strong reason to do so.** If you don't, even if they're interested they're going to lay it aside, thinking they'll come back to it later... and unfortunately, many people never do.

Here's a real-life example that Jeff recently experienced during a conversation with his oldest daughter. She was going to attend a party about 45 minutes from home, and she was waffling over whether or not to ask the friend who was giving her a ride to the party for a ride back as well. Well, Jeff certainly didn't want to make an hour-and-a-half round trip, so he encouraged her to stop waffling and just ask. She hemmed and hawed, because her friend hadn't offered yet, and she didn't want to ask, so Jeff said to her, "You know, it's probably not a big deal. You just need to ask." He tells his kids all the time that there's never any harm in asking; the worst thing someone can do is tell you no. And it turned out that her friend *did* offer her a ride home when she asked.

This concept is especially important in marketing. You always have to ask for the sale. If the answer is no, fine; but you're much less likely to make the sale if you don't just come right out and ask for it. There are other things distracting your prospects, so you have to urge them to act immediately, and you also have to give them the instructions on how you want them to follow through and complete the purchase. Tell them it's a Limited Time Offer, if that is indeed the case. Or try this, which I think Jeff Gardner was the first to do: suggest they send their order form by FedEx, because it might not get there in time if they send it by regular mail. Create a sense of urgency in your prospects.

Most people read a sales letter as if they're reading it aloud—in their own voice and tone. **Ideally, they'll sell themselves as they read your offer, so when you tell them what to do, in their minds they're telling *themselves* what to do.** "I need to pick up the phone and call. I need to respond now. I need to get into the store because the sale ends today," or whatever the case may be for your specific offer. By telling them exactly what actions you want them to take, they're reaffirming their need to follow through and complete the purchase. I can't stress the importance of this step enough.

Again, what we're talking about is salesmanship here. This isn't advertising; don't think of it like that. **Think of it as a way of duplicating multiple times what a good salesperson does.** A really good professional salesperson has spent years, in some cases decades, learning how to overcome rejection and answer objections. It doesn't bother them to hear the word no after a while. Remember this little saying: *A great direct mail letter is not afraid of the word no.* It doesn't even have to develop that thick skin that good human salespeople do... or, in some cases, fail to do. **A great direct mail letter never hesitates to ask for the sale in a direct, forceful, relentless way.** It lets you become the most aggressive sales person on the planet.

Don't worry about offending people. Worry that you're not selling hard enough.

A Formula for Wealth

All this becomes formulaic when you've done it as often as my colleagues and I have, regardless of the offer—whether it's for a health program, or precious metals, or for information of some kind. That's why we can help people who've never written copy before make money doing so, no matter what kind of business they run. You've already encountered a number of our formulas in this book's other modules. **In this case, you start by determining who your likely buyers will be, then narrow down your target market before you start mailing.** To some degree, your efforts will be hit and miss, but you can certainly use specific criteria to increase your likelihood of scoring a sale.

Let's say, for example, that you're in the carpet cleaning business. Well, you're probably not going to make much money if you're mailing into parts of town where most people have hardwood floors, or areas where the homes or apartments are rundown and people are driving old cars. Go for the more prosperous areas, and you'll be more likely to make a sale. If you're using a shotgun approach, then at least market to people you feel can afford your offers.

Once you've decided on your target market, start putting together your sales letter just as I've outlined above, with a big, bold headline. **Stress a wide variety of benefits and keep the copy tight... though I recommend you repeat yourself often, because people usually have to be told something more than once before it sinks in.** Then make sure your copy is easy to read. Read it to yourself out loud. It's amazing how you can write a sales letter that you think is great, but when you try to read it, it just doesn't seem quite right — and then you read it out loud and realize that you've *really* screwed it up here and there, and have to make changes before it goes out. **Reading your copy aloud will always help.**

Along the way, make it as personalized as you can. Make the message clear, talking to your reader as if you understand what their problems and desires are. In fact, you'd better understand those things at an almost instinctive level. Now, what you emphasize will depend on your business; in some businesses you just want to focus on their fears and problems, while in others you may want to focus on specific needs, or their greed, or their desire for success. Sometimes they just need to get rid of a mess, so you tell them, "Look, you've got a real mess there. We've got the solution, and we're going to come in there and clean up your mess like it never even happened." **Toward the end of the copy,**

ask for the sale as quickly as possible, and give them a reason to take action immediately.

So yes, what I'm teaching you in this chapter is a formula—**but it's a formula that works no matter what you sell.** And there's nothing wrong with a formula; a formula is nothing less than a recipe. Would you complain because Rachel Ray taught you a recipe for *coq au vin* instead of telling you to guestimate your way through the process? Of course not! Recipes are proven formulas for culinary success. And as with culinary recipes, your direct mail recipe allows leeway for experimentation. **In fact, you'll always do better if you test the fine points, because eventually you'll find something that works best for your particular situation and marketplace.**

Direct Mail Is Here to Stay!

I heard the funniest thing recently. I've heard similar things before, but this statement struck me as especially funny—and revealing. I purchased some software from a self-anointed Internet marketing expert, because I believe education in your chosen field never ends. I was watching an instructional video on how to use his software and what it would do for me, and he made a statement that his programs would work great with direct mail—because direct mail is becoming popular again.

When I heard him say that, I laughed out loud. I've heard comments like that a lot since the beginning of the Internet Age, as marketers flooded the Internet because of the cost benefits it offers. **Those benefits are quite real, and I'm definitely in favor of Internet marketing as a tool in the sales arsenal.**

However, over the years people have lost sight of the fact

that direct mail has *always* been a great way to reach customers and prospects. So when I hear things like "direct mail is back" or "direct mail is coming back," **I laugh, because *direct mail never left*.** People just made the mistake of following the shiny new thing and left it forgotten in the dust. It's been an effective means of marketing for 100 years or more, and that didn't stop in the early 1990s just because most people shifted to Internet marketing. **In fact, their doing so was beneficial to those of us who didn't abandon direct mail!**

Years ago, my wife and I were part of a group of sharp marketers who got together four times a year; Jeff Gardner was also a member for a while. There were about 20 of us at any given time, including a number of Internet marketing gurus. This was when the Internet was really taking off—the mid to late 1990s. Now, Eileen and I never pretend that we're anything we're not: we've always admitted that we're average people from a small town in Kansas... and these people were *laughing* at us because we mailed millions of direct mail pieces a year. They weren't even laughing at us behind our backs; they were brazen and egotistical enough to laugh in our face.

These individuals thought we were a bunch of dumb-ass hicks who didn't know jack, just because we were still using direct mail in our campaigns. In their minds, their marketing techniques were superior to ours; they thought we were doing it the stupid way, even while we were making millions of dollars annually. Well, I had the last laugh. When I saw the same two guys five or six years later, they were pushing the latest, greatest way to make money on the Internet: using direct mail to drive traffic to your website! I laughed my ass off when I realized they were selling the idea of using postcards and small direct mail packages to drive web traffic as being the most awesome DRM method ever.

So other folks have finally realized that they can cross their online sales methods with direct mail to produce some truly interesting hybrids. But let me repeat: direct mail never went away. **Smart marketers have been using direct mail the entire time the Internet has been popular, to make billions of dollars in total.** In fact, let's be realistic; direct mail is probably a big part why the post office still exists. Given cheap long distance and email, post office revenues are circling the drain—but direct mail continues to be a big part of their business. Direct mail's not a zombie, resurrected from the dead—it was never dead in the first place!

Don't Give Up

Now, direct mail isn't perfect; and that's one of the reasons why so many people dislike it as a marketing method. I often talk to small businesses about it, and over and over I hear, "Yeah, I tried that once and it didn't work." So they stopped using it. **Yet it's a proven model that brings in billions of dollars a year for a wide range of companies.**

What doesn't work is *bad* direct mail. In order to cash-in, you have to determine what good direct mail is, and then put it into play. It really can work for almost any business, though I suppose there are a handful of business models exempt from that statement. There's no absolute in business, or in life at all. But the simple fact is that most businesses *can* find a way to successfully implement direct mail marketing.

The problem that plagues many direct mail efforts is that the copy is worthless junk. Either it's an ungrammatical, poorly written mess, or too neat and clean to be believable. Often that translates to "boring," and bored people don't buy. As I mentioned earlier, we recently consulted with an investment specialist. He showed us his direct mail copy, and it was utterly bland. There was no headline, the font was all the same size, there was no bolding or italicizing, or even paragraph indents. It was the cleanest, neatest copy you can imagine... and it was hard for me to even look at because it was so boring.

Talk about homogenization; this was horrible work. It lacked any personality, it was created to not offend anyone, and while it's very professional, it just looks too neat. **There's no involvement, nothing to engage you, nothing of any serious worth.** That's the kind of thing people are talking about when they say, "I tried it and it didn't work."

This isn't the only example where I've looked at direct mail pieces that just didn't work for someone; some of the awful stuff I've seen makes me think, "Why in the name of God would anyone ever respond to this? There's no *there* there. There's no feeling of connection at all." Look: if you do direct mail the right way, you're going to see some big results, because so many people are either using it poorly or not at all. **You have to use the formula. You have to reach out and touch people's hearts with it, not just put a bunch of words on a piece of paper and send it to them.**

Your sales material must be real and raw. It needs to include your emotions and be filled with personality, not a sterile sameness. You need to do something completely separate from what everybody else is doing, something that attracts attention and actually keeps it. You may have the best product in the world and never be able to sell a single item if your copy is so boring no one ever reads past the first paragraph—while purveyors of true crap are making money hand over fist because they know how to write sales copy properly.

So while you're applying all the other elements of our formula to your sales copy, make sure your work is non-homogenized, *not* neat and tidy. **Write it as well as you can, but do off-the-wall things that grab the prospect's attention and make your pieces stand out, and you *will* make money.**

Here's another thing to consider: you can't be too cheap when it comes to incorporating direct mail into your strategy. Sometimes people get all hung up on mailing postcards or little one-page flyers, thinking, "It's going to be real cheap to get this in the mail," which is true. **But brevity can lose you customers, because you can't really address their objections in a page or two.** In one sense, you have to think about marketing as actually buying customers—and you know the truth in the old saying "you get what you pay for." **You have to avoid spending too little, because what you're doing with your marketing is investing in future profits.** It takes money to bring in a high-quality lead you can convert into a lifelong customer.

In some situations, it makes sense to buy those customers at an initial loss; but remember from Chapter 4 that this works only when your marketing system is designed to make it up on the back-end. That's where nearly all your profits come from anyhow. **So if you're cheap when implementing direct mail, you may fail that way, too.** I'm going to just say this flat out: if direct mail doesn't work for you, you're doing it wrong. When done right, it can be very profitable indeed.

One of Jeff Gardner's most successful sales letters, for

example—one which generated over $1 million in sales—was a 32-page long-form piece that came in a 9-x-12 inch envelope and had multiple inserts, including a one dollar bill glued to the top of the sales letter. It did a phenomenal job, but was very expensive to mail. Still, Jeff knew that in order to get people's attention and to really get them to read the letter, he needed to go to those lengths. Because he did, people responded. **So don't go the cheapest route, because sometimes that can kill an offer that might otherwise put you on the map.**

Pile A, Pile B

While you should avoid making your mail too neat and corporate, you should avoid making it look like junk mail, too. I get direct mail from pizza places, car dealerships, and a number of other sources, and they *all* look like junk mail. If you model your direct mail after junk mail, people are going to throw it in the trash. Most people sort their mail into piles—the A-pile and the B-pile. **The A-pile consists of personal letters, important bills, and interesting offers—stuff you've got to open up. The B-pile goes in the garbage: junk mail, cheesy coupons, and the like.**

The ones that crack me up are these offers for 10-20% off. C'mon, now; is that *all?* Those aren't good offers. They go straight in the trash. What you need is for your mail to look like it belongs in the A-pile mail, like a card from a family member or a bill or an official piece of mail. **If you can't even get your direct mail piece opened up, it doesn't matter how irresistible your offer is, or how perfect your sales copy is or how authentic you are.** *Nothing else matters if you can't get your offer into the A-pile.* You've got to make sure from the very beginning that it doesn't look like trash. **If you can get your copy in the A-pile,** *then* **you can let your copy do the rest of the job for you.**

The Proof is in the Paying

Here at M.O.R.E., Inc., we mail 30,000-40,000 new customer acquisition pieces every week, 52 weeks a year. We used to slow down around Christmas time, until we realized that the fewer people there are in the mail stream, the better we can compete— and therefore, the more money we can make. So now we let our competitors take Christmas off and keep moving forward.

Nothing is more important to successful direct mail strategies than the mailing list, so we always mail our offer to people who have shown through their actions that they're very interested in the kinds of things we sell. In other words, they've either purchased or inquired about a similar type of product in the past; we just buy a list of their names from a broker, and go from there.

I've already told you that you have to spend more money if you want to make more money with direct mail, and really, that's true with almost all facets of business. One of my favorite quotes came from a man who's still a household name: the phenomenal marketer P.T. Barnum. We've all heard of the circus that still bears his name, but Barnum was only in the circus business during the last few decades of his life. He had a rich entrepreneurial life otherwise; there are plenty of good biographies about him out there, and I would advise you to read his story. Now, remember my mention of the financial advisor who was after whales, but was using minnows for bait? **That concept comes directly from P.T. Barnum, a century ago: "Most people are trying to catch a whale by using a minnow as bait."** When I first read that quote, it hit me like a bolt out of the blue. What a perfect analogy for what so many people do wrong in the direct mail world!

To the financial advisor Chris Lakey and I were consulting with recently, a whale is anyone who has $100,000-$250,000 or more to invest and is already investing with other people. His job is to get their attention and try to get them hooked on *his* financial products, so they'll drop some of the stuff they're already doing. But his direct mail package was wimpy; it did a terrible job of selling, especially to the "whales." Yet it was still getting him some results, which I find a bit shocking.

We advised him to practice what we preached; we told him, "You've got to do something to shake people up — something bold, audacious, and different." That's what we do with our own current customer acquisition offer, which is different from what 95% of our competitors are doing. We mail a little booklet to leads; as I write this it's 32 pages long, but we're testing a 48-page version. If that works, we have plans of increasing it in increments of 16 pages. **As the saying goes, the more you tell, the more you sell; that's a basic principle of salesmanship.** Therefore, a good direct mail package should tell quite a lot. You're trying to get the best qualified prospective buyers to raise their hands, which is why we send out this 32-page booklet (along with an 8.5 x 11" order form, a cover letter, and a return envelope).

That's our entire direct mail package, and it goes to new prospects inside a colorful little window envelope. We're trying to blow people away; we're trying to shock them so they pay attention. Everybody else is mailing small sales letters and wimpy little postcards; but we're putting it out there with a nice-looking booklet. **We're disguising our sales message that way so, at**

---

first glance, it looks as valuable as it actually is. Right from the get-go, we're surprising people. It pitches a free offer, too. Respondents send for an information package which includes a two-hour audio program plus a 50-page report. That report is just another sales letter. It goes into more detail answering objections, it does a better job of expanding on all of the various benefits, and it goes on and on. Some people see that and say, "Oh my God, you guys are being wasteful idiots! Who's going to read a 50-page letter?"

Well, first of all, most people *don't* read it from cover to cover—and we don't expect them to. But we're trying to sell, which means you have to prove your point as completely as possible. **We're trying to prove that what we have for them is far more valuable than the money we're asking in exchange.** That's why we're delivering a long-format letter that answers every possible objection—not to mention that two-hour audio program. We're selling a product we're asking thousands of dollars for, and in our market, that's a lot of money to get right off the bat. That's why we have to go above and beyond.

We follow up with a sequence where we send out as many as 10-12 different pieces in as little as 4-6 weeks, so we're really putting the pressure on. Plus we've got salespeople following up on those leads, trying to build rapport as well. That's our entire system. It does a complete job of selling, which is our ultimate goal.

Ultimately, though, THE most profitable form of direct mail is the kind we send to our existing customers. When you run a business, you've got to capture the names and addresses of your customers and then market like crazy to them. It amazes me how many flower shops, bookstores, beauty shops, and other local businesses miss the boat on this one. They might see someone walk in the door and say, "Hey, Don, nice to see you," but they don't know Don's last name or his address or anything else about him.

Don't make that mistake yourself! **Capture the names of your customers, and then do regular mailings to them.** At the very least, put a fishbowl up there and let people toss in their business card. Now, 90% of those customers won't have a business card, so include some card stock and a pen, so they can print out their name, address, and phone number and drop it into the bowl. If you own a bookstore, offer a premium like $50 worth of free books if they win your monthly drawing; and make regular offers even to those who don't win. If they're a science fiction fan, tell them when the latest stock comes in and offer a nice discount. **Always keep in touch with your existing customers on a regular basis. Those mailings can be the most profitable of all.**

The Tip of The Iceberg

As I round out this chapter and module, I want you to realize this: **what I've covered here just scratches the direct mail surface.** It's enough to give you a tiny taste of the subject. **You can spend your entire life learning everything you can about direct mail, and still not know it all.**

In particular, pay close attention to the companies that are making tremendous amounts of money with direct mail; keep a swipe file containing their best, most profitable sales copy. **Look for formulas to act as shortcuts to success.** Don't be afraid to invest more money in programs, seminars, tele-seminars, webinars, or other training materials on direct mail, because the topic can make you a fortune. **The cash you spend on it really is an investment—one that can have a huge ROI down the road, simply by giving you a tremendous competitive advantage over everyone else in your market.**

CHAPTER SIX:

Module #5: Takeaway Selling

In this module, I'll discuss a rather conceptual sales method that must be used in conjunction with other methods, including some of those I've included in this book's other modules. It's related to some of these sale methods, too. **It's generally known as takeaway selling, and in a general sense involves doing the opposite of what most marketers do.** They chase the prospects so hard that they lose most of the power in the relationship. Neediness isn't exactly an attractor factor in business. **On the other hand, takeaway encourages them to chase *you*, rather than you chasing *them*.**

In simple terms, takeaway selling limits the supply of a product or service in order to increase its value. It's a proven fact that scarcity boosts sales, based on that age-old law of supply and demand; the smaller the supply, the greater the demand. You can enforce scarcity artificially, and many businesses do. It's just human nature to value scarce things highly. Once upon a time, aluminum was worth more than gold, because it was so hard to extract from ore—even though it's one of the most common elements in the Earth's crust.

You can apply the supply and demand principle to just about anything. There was once a study in which scientists asked people to rate chocolate chip cookies. They put 10 cookies in one jar and two cookies in another jar. Now, these were the same chocolate chip cookies, but the subjects were told that they were *different* cookies, and they needed to rate each type separately. The cookies from the two-cookie jars received the higher ratings—just because they were made to seem scarcer than the others.

So the scientists thought, "We showed them jars in which cookies were already scarce. What if we do another experiment, and start by showing them a jar that's just packed full of cookies—and then during our discussion of the process we switch the larger jar of cookies for one that just has a few, showing that they're going away?" Well, it turns out that the few cookies left after they switched out the jars received higher ratings than any other cookies, just because they were obviously running short.

We tend to value scarce resources, and things that are in high demand versus things we can get anywhere at any time for low prices. Leverage that aspect of human psychology by pointing out that supplies of a specific service or product are limited—and ensure that they really are. Reveal that you only have so many spaces left in your consulting calendar, or a set number of discounts available. That will drive a perception of a large demand for those resources, one in which people will want to compete for them. **You've created a sense of urgency, which increases conversions from leads to buyers.** All active marketers have seen this strategy work.

In fact, one of the best examples I can think of is a video of an amazing presentation by speaker Robert Allen. It's among the best I've seen. Robert created an absolutely irresistible offer for the hundreds of people at this live event. **He kept adding value, and adding value, and adding value.** If he would have then said at the end of the presentation, "Anybody and everybody in this room can have what I've just offered," then he would have failed to create a sense of urgency... and he wouldn't have sold nearly as much as he actually did. Ah, but he understood this principle quite well. He told his listeners, "Look: there are hundreds of you in this room, and I can't take on everybody, because I'm doing a lot of personal consultation. You're coming to my house, you see, and I only have X number of spots." The "X" was a very low number compared to the number of people in the room—say, a tenth of the total.

Instantly, that created scarcity. **Automatically people valued his offer even more, even after he'd already created an immense value in their eyes.** And *then* he said, "Okay, I've got a handful of dollar bills. Each represents *one* space, so if you want one of these spaces, you need to come up to the front and grab one of these bills." Well, people started getting up out of their chairs... But here's the interesting thing. When people started jumping out of their seats, more people got up out of *their* seats, and they ended up mobbing the guy, grabbing for those dollar bills and almost overwhelming him. People were pushing other people away, actually shoving them down to the floor. **It was mass hysteria, based on takeaway selling.**

Having seen that quite a while back, Jeff always makes sure he includes scarcity in all his orders, and I include both scarcity and urgency in many of mine too, because they're obviously so powerful. **They add to the value of the offer you're already making. So: make sure that you too add it the mix.**

This module goes step-by-step through exactly how to use this strategy of scarcity. But before we get moving on that, I wanted to impress upon you just how powerful it is, and how just by adding scarcity to a hot offer you already have, you immediately increase the value and the rate at which you turn your prospects into buyers. Robert Allen uses that technique powerfully to get people excited. He tells them, "Hey, I wish I could take everyone here to my house, but my wife won't allow it. She makes sandwiches for us and we have such a great time, and learn so much, but the only way I can do it is if I limit it to 25 or 30 people." Now, in his Las Vegas seminars, he'll have so many people sign up that he says, "Okay, looks like we're going to have it next weekend, too, and the weekend after that, and so on."

Often hundreds of people sign up for his consultations, and he charges a very good price—at least $1,000 for the weekend, sometimes more. Russ von Hoelscher spoke at one of his seminars in San Diego, and saw Robert use that technique right from the beginning. It works like magic—and you should keep that very much in mind, because it's a very good illustration of how people want something that they perceive as special. **They want something scarce, something exclusive, something most people can't get. They want special treatment, period.**

Remember: if something is readily available, it's probably going to be in low demand. That's just how people are. If gold were as common as copper, it would just be a useful metal in electronics and dentistry. The opposite is also true: something that's scarce and rare creates high demand, as long as it's an item that would be in demand at all. In primitive cultures, certain types of rocks were expensive and highly prized because they were rare and could be chipped into wonderful tools. Remember the movie *Waterworld*? Soil was highly prized because there wasn't much of it to be found. **Well, the idea behind takeaway selling is to make it so that you tightly control the supply of your product or service, and the supply is indeed low.**

Using a more modern version of the valuable rocks example,

there's a big difference between a piece of chert you can pick up on many a street or pull out of a streambed, and those slightly greasy, really hard crystals we call diamonds. Diamonds are rocks, too, and yet the diamond is in much greater demand than chert, and has a higher value because it's so rare. Even low-grade diamond, bort, is worth much more than plain rocks, just as an abrasive. **So you can sell rocks, or you can sell diamonds.** Which do you think is more worthwhile? Do I even have to answer that?

Diamonds are just carbon molecules in a special configuration. They're closely akin to coal that hasn't been subjected to enormous heat and temperature. Takeaway selling involves mastering the art of making diamonds of your own, whether out of "coal" or something more valuable. **Whatever it is, you make it scarcer to push up the price.** Do it right, and you can receive any price you ask for, and people will clamor to get what you're offering—just like the folks were stampeding Robert Allen in that presentation I discussed earlier.

Speaking of diamonds: according to an article I once read, there was a time in the 1800's when diamonds didn't have much value at all. According to the article, this idea that there's a shortage of diamonds is complete nonsense. There are plenty of diamonds, but the industry restricts mining to limit the supply and therefore keep the price up. DeBeers has basically created the entire industry out of whole cloth; but then again, that's true of many industries.

I love the idea that you can create scarcity artificially and thereby build value. **It gives you more power in the buyer/seller equation.** Handle it right, and you can make an offer so irresistible that it's difficult, if not impossible, for qualified prospects to say

---

no. You have more power to do that than you might imagine; marketers are doing it all the time, with the diamond industry being just one excellent example. I've done it myself. We've had people stampede the stage to acquire a limited offer.

But what if you're a solo operator or entrepreneur, and you *are* the product? It still works. You can do things to increase your own value, increasing the perception that you're not just a cheap date, so people will be more than happy to stand in line with money in hand. **Why don't more marketers use this concept?** Well, I think it goes against what most business owners want and expect when they enter the field. They want an incredible amount of business, not a small amount of insanely profitable business... mostly because they haven't thought the matter through.

The last thing on their mind is saying something like, "No, I'm sorry; you may not be able to do business with me." That goes right against their instincts and everything they've been taught. But there's only so much you to go around—so you *have* to use scarcity, at least until you've established yourself. **As a corollary, you also have to charge premium prices even as you say, "There's a limited number, and *this* is the limit."** You might actually end up turning people away; people in high demand often do.

You can see why a normal business owner would say, "Why would I want to do *that*? I want as many customers as possible!" That's justifiable in a scalable business where you can hire more people and delegate authority. **But the reality is that you can create a form of scarcity where you turn very few people away just by increasing the prospect's response rate.** That's really what takeaway selling is all about. It's not about turning people off or away. **It's about increasing response speed and**

getting them off the fence. This strategy can get you all the business you'd normally get, faster and more efficiently.

Which reminds me of another interesting use of the rare, the scarce, the unique, and the exclusive. If you like lobster, well, you're probably going to pay through the nose to get it. Even in seaport towns, a good lobster dinner may cost you $35 or more. Ah, but let's back up to 100 years ago, where there was a prison in the state of Maine, practically on the beach. Fishermen could bring in all the lobster they wanted, because they were so easy to get — so the prison decided to serve the inmates lobster every day. Maybe they liked it at first, but it wasn't long before they started complaining about it as "cruel and unusual punishment," and actually got a judge to rule that the prison had to start varying their diet. **That just goes to show that what's plentiful isn't held in high esteem, especially if it's forced down your throat every day.**

Most businesses don't offer unique services or products. A wine store might have some 100-year-old bottles on hand, but most don't. Ditto for every other industry you can name — which reveals a marketplace gap you can capitalize on. Think about your situation and what your market wants, and try to put together at least one premium service or product for your very best customers. **There are plenty of people out there looking for something different — not *too* different, not enough to be weird, but different enough to add some spice to life.** They want something that says they're special, and they'll pay big money for it.

Try to think of something exclusive, because people love being one of the few and the proud. When Russ von Hoelscher offers his coaching program, he sets a rule that he'll accept no more than 25 people at one time. To be fair, he tells me that this is partly because he doesn't want to deal with too many phone calls or too much client interaction. But people are clamoring for his services, so by setting a limit, he can charge more money—enough to offset any losses suffered due to not taking on more clients.

At a seminar Russ helped promote in San Diego many years ago, Art Linkletter was the keynote speaker—a marvelous man who, sadly, is no longer with us. After the event, as a fellow named Vince Spargaloni and Ross were having lunch with him, Art said, "You forgot to do one thing that more and more people who promote seminars are doing that would've been good for you and good for me." Ross asked Mr. Linkletter, "What's that, Art?" And he said, "You should sell the first two rows of the seminar for a special price."

Now, this was in a big venue, a sports arena, so that made sense. Then Linkletter said, "Give them a pass to come backstage, and I'll tell some stories and talk to them individually. Instead of just charging $20 for the seminar, you can charge $75—and I'll split the money with you. It's too late now, but in the future, that's what you should do. **In Anaheim we did that, and we had 100 people pay $75. It was an extra $3,750 for me, and an extra $3,750 for the promoter."**

Always look for something exclusive to do. **Look for the limited offer, or put a time limit on a special offer so people know it isn't open for all time.** They've got to take advantage of it by June 1st or September 10th or whatever; and you have to hold them to it! Don't tell everyone you're going to have a special sale that then lasts forever.

The Personal Touch

In an earlier chapter, I briefly mentioned a jewelry store in El Cajon, California which did something special for a while that worked quite well for them. They would have special nights—I believe it was on the first and third Tuesdays of every month—in which they would host a wine and cheese party for their very best customers, during which they would show off their new creations. **This was by invitation only, and that was the key: they made people feel special.** Something like this tells them, "You're important to us, and we want to treat you right." People just love to be treated extra-special.

Exclusivity can pay off big. **When you make someone feel like one of the special few, they're often willing to pay top dollar to get an item.** In any group of customers or clients, in fact, you'll have a certain percentage (and it might be a small percentage) who will happily pay you to make a fuss over them, whether in the form of exclusive services, exclusive products, or exclusive events nobody else has access to. **We call these items "slack adjusters," because they help take up the slack in your income stream.**

These can be high-priced items that are very high profit, therefore covering a lot of your advertising costs and putting a lot of money in your pocket. Quite a few marketers in the information industry offer exclusive "Masterminds" as slack adjusters. They might have a high-end Mastermind group with only 15 seats that gets together four times a year. That automatically creates a built-in scarcity. Some of these information marketers have tens of thousands of customers, and if they offer only 15 seats in their Mastermind, they're able to charge top dollar.

My wife Eileen and I were once in a Mastermind group that allowed 12 to 15 members at a time. Back then, we paid as much as $7,800 per year to be members—and then we had to pay airfare, hotel, and all the rest on top of that. Over the years, those dollar figures have gone up and up. **Nowadays, this Mastermind's fee is $30,000 per year.** You might think, "Holy cow! Who in the world would pay $30,000 per year for something like that?" Well, guess what? This marketer still has a full group. His 15 or so mastermind members (out of his tens of thousands of customers) feel that $30,000 per year is affordable to them, if only because they want to feel exclusive. I assure you: whenever someone drops out, they have no trouble filling that hole.

Believe me, the marketer who sells this Mastermind makes them feel very exclusive, because he makes sure to let everybody know they're part of a very special group. If they go to any of his other events, they have special nametags with a special color that indicates they're part of his Mastermind. **He really plays up their desire to be recognized special individuals.**

If you can do things like that to create some exclusivity around your scarce item, you have the opportunity to charge *very* high prices for that item.

I think that's one of the greatest benefits of having unique products. Now, there are a lot of products out there that you can resell; if you're looking to get started in business, you can easily push products that other people developed or invented. You can become an affiliate for all types of items, many quite good and profitable. **The only problem is, if people can get the products from anybody, not only is the price going to be low because there's high availability, it's going to be a lot harder for you to compete.** For example, if someone can go to Wal-Mart and pick up a specific product, why buy it from you? And there's probably a Wal-Mart around the corner from their house.

The way you combat that is to invent something as unique as possible that instantly creates scarcity. Even if you're selling one of those common products, you can combine it with other items to create a unique and interesting package deal. That way, when they do business with you they see that they're not only getting the widget they can also buy at Wal-Mart, but your deal also comes with bonuses only available through you. That's another way to create scarcity and make people want to do business with you.

Finally, packaging offers you the benefit of not only being able to create your own scarcity, but also of attaching a higher ticket price. Earlier, I mentioned the platinum group I was part of. The fact that there were only a few of them made it very exclusive, so they could demand a higher price for that group.

Here's another example. There are any number of books available that discuss marketing. Some of them are even useful. Now, a lot of those books contain the exact same information that the author sells through exclusive coaching programs—and yet a coaching program can sell for a *lot* more than a $30 book. Why is that? **Usually because a coaching program is more exclusive.** That's about it. Books are essentially in unlimited supply, especially when you consider public libraries and digital e-books. Most publishers do limit print runs, but usually, if there's enough of a demand, they'll print more to meet that demand.

The problem is, **the price is capped on a book—whereas that same information can be delivered in a different package** by way of a coaching program, a workshop, or some other kind of

---

hands-on method for thousands of dollars—even though it's the same information. And why not, if it's potentially worth millions?

The point here is that you can easily take information that wasn't scarce to begin with, and create scarcity that increases demand just because you've limited the number of people who can get involved. All you have to do is say, "This is exclusive. We're charging $10,000 for this, and we only have room for 10 people." Even if it's something people could get very cheaply by doing their own research, you can do this if you position yourself properly. There are several reasons this works, among them the fact that it would force the buyer to do the work himself instead of just paying someone to reveal the secret. Besides, most people don't value things that come cheaply, no matter how potentially profitable they may be.

A similar method of takeaway selling would be to tell people, "You can get my book and have all my main secrets for $30. My book is available at any bookstore everywhere. But if you want me personally, if you want the coaching where I work with you one-on-one, it's going to cost. It's an extra-special deal, because I'm going to invite you to my house, you're going to spend the weekend with me, and my wife's going to cook you a great meal."

That sort of approach drives a unique form of scarcity. **Price and demand go up because you can only have so many slots like that.** It's takeaway selling, because you're taking away the opportunity to be a part of the deal by limiting the number of people who can participate—even when the reality is that someone might offer that information for a lot less elsewhere. If someone wants this exclusive package, they'll have to jump through some hoops and pay a lot for it, to show they're serious.

Otherwise, they're going to miss out on a truly sweet deal—the chance of a lifetime. **It's up to you to create the perception of value. Remember, if everyone can have it, nobody will want it.**

Here's one of my favorite stories about the late Peter McWilliams. In his catalog he offered one book that was much smaller than most of his other books; he was famous for writing these giant 600-800 page volumes. But he had this one book that was maybe 170 pages long, and he made sure to point that out clearly in his copy. He sold the book for $99, even though it cost him just a few dollars to produce. He called it the world's most expensive book. The title was *Self Publishing Self Taught*.

As small as this book was, it contained the very best of the best of the insider secrets that had helped him sell millions of copies of his self-published books. Because I wanted to learn those secrets, I gladly spent my $99—and I've read that book many times since, because damn it, I spent $99 for it! I've got a lot of other books that I've barely skimmed through that cost much less... but that $99 book I've read multiple times, because he created an expectation of great value via exclusivity.

Why don't more people do things like this? I believe it all comes down to the simple fact that most people are so encumbered by their businesses, so bogged down, that they're just trying to stay open. **They're working hard, not realizing that in order to really succeed you have to take a little time to think—and the best thing you can think about is marketing.** Most people who run businesses aren't marketing masters or pros. They don't give a lot of thought to marketing beyond location, product selection, and a Yellow Pages or newspaper ad now and then—and then wonder why people don't come through that door in droves.

Well, folks, we're past the days when you could just hang up a shingle and get all the business you needed, if in fact those days ever existed. Most businesspeople just don't think much about what they have to do to market effectively. That's one of the things I hope this book will change for you.

I want to stimulate you to start thinking about not just being in business, but also about what you can do to create *more* business. **Business owners who create new products and services on a continual basis always have the upper hand against the people who just say, "I'm open for business.** If people want what I have to offer, let them come." That's a terrible attitude! You've got to do things to lure them in; you've got to do creative things to make them *want* to do business with you. **Make special offers that they find so enticing they'd have to be foolish not to take advantage of them.** Sure, it's a lot of work. But my philosophy is that it's a lot of fun, too; after all, who doesn't like money? When something is truly enjoyable, it's not work in the traditional sense.

If You've Got It, Flaunt It

Let me re-emphasize that takeaway selling hits hard on a core economic principle, one that everyone understands: **supply and demand.** Now, I'm talking about real laissez-faire economics, not the manufactured economics that governments tend to get involved with. They can limit sales of certain products, or just print money as if it solves all the world's problems instead of causing more.

Needless to say, you do generally have enough room in your market to take advantage of this method—even though it flies in the face of what you seem to experience in the marketplace.

Think about how most marketers promote their products or services. **In many cases, business owners want you to think there's plenty of whatever they have available.** "Come and get it! We've got plenty!" They want you to feel there's an endless supply of what they're offering, and you can get it very easily through them. They like to pretend there's no scarcity at all. Why? Heaven knows.

Recently, Chris Lakey was looking for firewood for his little backyard fire pit. He likes to occasionally sit out on the back deck, put a fire on, and roast hotdogs and have s'mores, even when it's warm out. Well, firewood is readily available in the middle of winter; you can go to any store and a lot of gas stations, and they'll have all the firewood you can buy. But try to buy firewood when it's warm out. It's not easily available. Why? Because there's not much demand for it.

Chris went all over town looking for firewood for his fire pit, and everywhere he went he got the same story. "It's not winter." So Chris asked, "Have you ever heard of fire pits? People need firewood for their fire pits. I just want a little bundle." They sell the perfect little bundles for three or four bucks—in the winter. Well, Chris had pretty much exhausted all of his resources, but the last place he called told him they had three boxes of firewood. So he bought them; and because of scarcity, they cost him $10 a box.

That's how you should handle it: make it scarce, not overwhelmingly available. Chris bought way more than he needed at a high price so that he'd have enough to last for a while. There wasn't any supply, so the price went way up—and Chris was willing to pay that. The business that had the firewood didn't intend to use takeaway selling *per se*, even though they should have; they just told him what they had in stock and he happened to know from his own research that there wasn't any in town anywhere else, unless he special-ordered it from someone who went out and chopped their own wood.

As you can see, sometimes businesses accidentally create scarcity like that. The government does, too. You may remember that a few years back, our government ran a program called Cash for Clunkers. I think explaining it can help you understand a little more about the theory of supply and demand.

By their rules, a "clunker" is defined as any non-"green" car built 10+ years ago. Some of these cars run quite well, but might get poor gas mileage due to a big V8 engine or something similar. They're still good cars, the kind that people buy when they need a good low-end first car or because they just like older cars. Well, if you agreed to take the government your clunker, they'd give you so much off one of the new models. They were trying to stimulate the economy, and in the process half a million cars were turned in—and they destroyed them. They *intentionally* destroyed cars that often worked just fine. That sharply limited the supply of cheap, entry-level cars in the range of $5,000 or less.

And what happened as a result? The price of the cheap cars still available went way up. Ostensibly, the government was trying to help the very people who look for those kinds of cars, but they hurt them instead. We're still feeling the effects of that crash in the auto marketplace today. Ultimately, the Cash for Clunkers debacle was *not* a good thing for the economy. The government should have promptly sold those cars to people who needed them! This is a clear example of what happens when you artificially lower the availability of an item still in demand: you make the price go up.

Takeaway selling consists of anything you can do to get the supply, or the perceived supply, as low as possible so that you can get the price as high as possible. That's all you're really trying to do, and there are many ways you can do it. You can do things that are real, like saying, "I've only got five of these, and once they're gone they're gone." Alternately, you can do things so that they're perceived as scarce, saying things like, "The deadline for this offer is next Tuesday, so you need to get involved now or else you're going to miss out." There are many different things you can do to limit something people want, so that they want it even more. Unleash your imagination!

Profitable Positivity

Now, the purpose of any type of takeaway selling is *not* to make it seem like you're desperate to get the prospect's business, but exactly the opposite. **You have to pretend you don't need their money.** Some well known marketers just come right out and say things like, "Whether you take advantage of this offer or not, I'm eating steak tonight. Your move." Even if you're not that blunt, **takeaway selling implies you're not worried about selling or inventory issues.** You'll have no problem moving this inventory, so your prices are high. You've only got a few available—if they don't buy them, someone else will. **You never want it to seem like you're desperate. Ever.**

That's one of the more important takeaways from this module—pun certainly intended. **Do things to make it so that people want what you have, and they *know* that there's only a small number of them, so they end up pursuing you.** They're trying to do whatever it takes to be one of the people who gets what you have to offer—unaware or not caring that they've let you take full control of the buyer/seller relationship.

Here's another positive outcome of using takeaway selling: you usually end up with fewer customers, which means you can spend more quality time with each, making them *happier* customers. Happy customers don't cause much trouble; and in any case, you'll find that the people willing to pay the most for your services and products tend to be more willing to take you seriously than the cheapskates (though this is by no means universal). Promoting a coaching program with 10-20 participants gives you more time with each person than if you charged half the price and worked with twice as many people. It balances pricewise, but you can actually serve your customers better by using this method.

And here's something to consider: **when you set a limit and a commensurate high price, you should tell people why.** This is especially true when you're publishing digital information, because let's face it: you can have an unlimited number of e-books. There's no scarcity of electrons; so if you tell people you're offering only X number of copies, tell them why. **Provide a compelling reason why your supply is low and the demand is high, something that rings true with your prospect.**

Earlier, I discussed Robert Allen's tactic of taking only 20-25 people into his consulting groups. He said it was because his wife only wanted a certain number of people in the house to cook for. That resonated with people; they understood instinctively why there was this set number, and why the supply was low. People responded because the scarcity was real. So don't just make up a number; **come up with a reason why you're using that number or why your product or service is otherwise scarce, and be sure to make a point of it in your marketing.**

This is why everyone in direct response marketing—

though not so much in local business—**adds a timeline to their marketing.** "Offer good for the next 10 days," or "If you want to save $100, you must act within the next seven days." Now, often that's an artificial distinction that's easy to see through, assuming the marketer even holds to it. But you can also give them a simple reason like, "We only printed up so many of these." That's not the world's best reason, but it is a reason. Or you can use something that's absolutely true: "If you order this book in the next 10 days we'll also give you a six-month subscription to our newsletter." Just make sure it *is* true.

Now you've made a very special offer by admitting, at least implicitly, "There's a reason why I'm making this available for just the next 10 or 15 days. I don't want to give away my newsletter free; but if you buy this manual today, or if you buy this product today, I *will* throw it in absolutely free, so act now." That's something all merchants should learn. **We call it bundling. So think in terms of selling multiple products as a unit.** You'll find you can often get more money for a group of products than you can for them individually. Plus, if they really fit together, you're offering true value.

Remember the old saying, "Perception is reality." **But remember, too, that you're the one who creates the perception in marketing.** It's up to you to do the kinds of things I've outlined in this chapter; and if you do it well, you can influence reality more than you might realize.

Sitting on a Shelf

I mentioned earlier that if you're an entrepreneur selling a service of some kind, or if you have a very small company, you or your company *are* the product. **I think you should think about**

you or your company as a product like any other on a shelf.
With that in mind, I'm going to give you the fastest, simplest, and easiest way you can use the power of takeaway selling to promote yourself or your company.

Here it is: you have to become an expert, the absolute authority on your particular type of product; or at least create the perception that you are. **And it's fair to do so, because if you know more about your field than the prospect, then you *are* an expert.**

You have to elevate yourself in the minds of the prospective buyers in your market as someone they really want to do business with. There are all kinds of ways to do that. In Module #8, we're going to talk about the power of information selling. There's probably no better way I know of to start promoting yourself as an expert. Write some books, or have some ghostwritten for you. Conduct some seminars or workshops. **Put yourself on the line, educating people on all the reasons why they should be spending money with you.** In some cases, you can tell them literally everything you know.

Now, you might say, "Why in the world would I do that?" **Simply because it works—sometimes because you make it all look so hard that the prospects would rather pay you big bucks to do it than tackle it themselves.** A good example of this is the financial advisor I wrote about in the previous module, who's after the "whales" in his market. Chris Lakey gave him an idea that I'm going to outline for you now, one he was very receptive to. You see, a lot of these people he's looking for feel that, with the advent of the Internet, they just don't need financial advisors anymore. Hell, they'll just work through the 'Net; it's powerful, they're smart, and they'll figure it all out themselves.

That's one of the biggest objections he's hit with, over and over again: "I don't need you. I can do my own research. I can buy my own financial products."

So one of the suggestions Chris gave him was to start producing information products telling people *everything* he knew about investing—to go over all of the details, just overloading them with information. That's part of the whole expert strategy here: you tell them exactly what they can do, assuming they're willing to do so, and you don't pull any punches. **You prove immediately that you're the expert, and then offer to do it all for them once they see how hard it is.** Finally they just say, "Go ahead and take care of it for me. Here's the fee." You have their respect now. **And you *must* earn their respect; you can't expect to get it automatically.**

When you create information products, books, tapes, audio CDs, seminars, workshops, and the like, you're earning respect. Freelance copywriters and consultants use this technique often. They produce books that basically tell people everything they know... and then some. **They complicate the hell out of it so much that people finally say, "Here's a blank check. Do it for me."**

Instead of doing something like cold calling, you're building yourself up as an expert, thus increasing the prospect's perception of value. They know an expert doesn't cold call his prospects. Oh, you might have someone call them on your behalf, but you're not doing it yourself. **In fact, your marketing should be designed so people call *you*.** They're chasing you now. Why don't more people do this? The same old reason: it takes a lot of work. They think about having to create or publish this expert information, and they think, "Good God, I don't want to do all that."

They never bother to consider the fact that what they're doing already obviously isn't working for them. They're not getting the results they want, or they wouldn't be unhappy. Here's a way they can spend a concentrated, focused period creating materials that would elevate them to the status of an expert in a way that could pay off for years. **They're not thinking through to the fact that you can spend six months or a year working hard at developing all this, and then get paid for life.**

Another positive result here is that when you create your expert materials to establish yourself as an authority, you end up with something that's uniquely yours, which you don't have to share with anyone. **That's another form of scarcity.** While you can do it, it's hard to take something that already exists and come up with an angle that gives you that edge. There's no way you can convince someone that you have scarcity when they know they can get your product from everyone and his dog—and probably not just now but next week, next month, even next year. You don't want to have to deal with that kind of disadvantage.

By making yourself an expert, you're in a position to name your price and terms, and you control the supply completely. We've even done promotions where we've smashed the master CD we used to make our copies with a sledgehammer, destroying it forever. **You control *everything* once you control the product. If you're relying on someone else's product, you have no such control.** That's why it's important to come up with packages that are uniquely yours, whether they're information products or widgets that you create or invent. No matter what it is, it's *yours*: You control all the variables.

In the News Today...

Tap into the media if you can. If you're the owner of a restaurant, for example, you can court the media to get them into your restaurant, enjoying your food. Then you can get some free plugs. Or, you can donate dinners to various functions, and make substantial donations during charity or pledge drives. If you're Pete the Plumber, offer some tips on what people should do to ensure their pipes don't burst in the winter.

One of the great ways to position yourself as an expert, and also to work with the media, is to give the media just what it wants. One of the challenges of creating a newspaper, radio program, TV program, and even online news is that you chew through a huge amount of content. You *always* need something to fill up the space or airtime. **So if you contact the media, you become the go-to guy in your field when they need a particular type of content.** You're not just pushing yourself, you're trying to give them news; and you're likely to find they contact you and make you an expert in your field.

Whatever your field, look for trends. What are the talking heads talking about? What studies were just released? What polls have come out? Which holidays are coming up? How can you give advice and information in your field to the media, so they have something to report on? **If you can do all that, they'll seek you out as an expert.**

Jeff Gardner chose his financial advisor after he saw him on TV. He thought, "If NBC trusts this guy enough to give financial information on the news, then I want to be doing business with him!" He was a great financial advisor. Now, he probably wasn't better than others Jeff might have chosen, but he got a huge amount of business just from the fact that NBC tapped him whenever something noteworthy appeared in the financial news. Markets were up, markets were down, people were talking about investments, or the Baby Boomers were aging—and he was on TV talking about what they should do with their retirement funds. The TV station loved his work—"Thank goodness we got another five to fifteen minutes filled up!"

So think about that. In addition to positioning yourself as an expert, you get a lot of free advertising that way!

CHAPTER SEVEN:

Module #6: Lead Generation

In this module, we'll take a closer look at the sheer power of lead generation marketing. This is the first step in the multistep marketing process (sometimes known as Two-Step Marketing), and it's all about generating the best-qualified prospective buyers—those who are the most serious about buying whatever it is that you're selling. **These are the people who stand the greatest chance of becoming your best customers.** What can you do to get the largest number of those people to raise their hands and express an interest in you? How do you then turn those leads into customers?

Let's start with what my friend and colleague Jeff Gardner calls **"the instant lead monetization strategy."** This is a way for you to very quickly turn leads into buyers so you can cover some of your front-end costs—maybe even all of them—and put yourself into profit territory when you're generating leads for your business.

Here's how the strategy works: offer something free or for a very low cost to your target market. I covered this to some extent back in Chapter 3. Pitch a free report or booklet, maybe a free sample, or a "chip off the block" for a very low cost. **One reason to charge a little bit of money is to filter out the freebie-seekers and tire-kickers.** If you seriously want to get people interested in your business, **you have to make them a low-risk offer that triggers a response, so you can capture their information (whether online or off) so you can use it in**

future marketing.

The challenge is that you can easily spend yourself into a hole generating leads. It can then take weeks, and months, and sometimes even years to recoup your expenses, depending on how much money you spent "buying" the lead. The instant lead monetization strategy speeds up this process. **As soon as someone requests that free or low-cost item, make the prospect an irresistible offer.** This is a powerful method, because if the numbers work out right, you can increase your marketing efforts commensurately. **If you know you'll get $2 back for every $1 you put into generating leads, how many days consecutively can you keep doing that? Indefinitely, right?**

Here's a real-life example of a company that uses the instant lead monetization strategy very successfully. **One author gives away his book online, but asks people to pay $6.95 to cover shipping and handling.** The book costs much more than that to produce — believe me — but he's just charging shipping and handling. This is a book that you'd otherwise have to purchase at Amazon.com for $15.50 plus shipping if you want a hardback; even if you want a digital version for your Kindle, it'll still cost $12.99. So getting the hardback for just $6.95 for shipping and handling is a great deal.

When you purchase that book, you immediately get taken to a page where the author appears on a video and makes an irresistible offer. This author normally holds four-day live events on the topic covered in the book, and of course the book isn't going to be able to cover all the information he'd be able to cover in such an event. Because he *does* cover so much information during this event, he charges quite a bit: $1,000-$2,000 per ticket. That doesn't include the costs for hotel, food, airfare, etc. necessary to attend, which would bring it up to $1,500-$3,000 total.

However, on this follow-up page, he offers the complete unedited videos from his latest event—all four days—for only $197! Now, that's an incredible deal, and it's incredibly easy to buy. All you have to do is click a "Buy Now" button, and that $197 charge will be added to the credit card you just used to pay for the shipping and handling of the book. I'm sure he hooks a high percentage of the people who want that $7 book with the follow-up offer. **So while the author probably loses $5-10 shipping out each book, he immediately recoups that loss with his video sales**—which cost absolutely nothing to send because they're delivered over the Internet. Oh, sure; he invested a little money to have the sessions filmed, and he pays a small monthly price to host the videos online, but otherwise that $197 product is pure profit.

Of course, not everyone takes the up-sell; but let's say 10% do. Let's run some numbers, assuming he gives away 1,000 books. Let's assume his out-of-pocket cost is five dollars per book. That's $5,000 that he's spent to generate 1,000 new leads. And remember, these are good leads because these are people who took out their credit cards and paid a minimum of $6.95 for S&H. **These aren't just looky-loos.**

If just 100 of those people (10%) click the "Buy Now" button and purchase his $197 product, then he's made $19,700 on that irresistible offer. Subtracting the cost of those 1,000 books ($5,000), he's still made $14,700—and he still has his 1,000 leads. **Heck, even if only 5% (50) of those people take the up-sell, he'll still make $4,850 and add 1,000 leads to his mailing list.** Now he can go back to those leads and sell tickets to his live events and other product, training, and consulting offers.

Because he's making money immediately by offering that up-sell, he can afford to scale up his marketing and generate even *more* leads. Using a strategy like this one, you can actually make sizable amounts of cash while generating leads instead of losing money. When that's true, you have the opportunity to out-market your competition, because you know you're going to make many times more money back. **This is a killer strategy you should put into practice in your business.**

Putting Your Best Foot Forward

This idea of giving away something for free or low cost in anticipation of high returns has almost a spiritual basis. The person who gets it has warm feelings about you, and is likely to become a customer if they like what you have. **Just be sure that whatever you give away is something appropriate to your market, while simultaneously being something of high value.** If someone gets some cheesy trinket from you, you've lost the whole show. Your goal should be to make them say, "Wow! If this was free, can you imagine what I'll get from this company when I *do* have to pay?"

This is especially true when you're making a first impression. I realize that your natural inclination is to think, "I need to hold back the good stuff, so I'm not out too much money. I don't want to give away my best secret for nothing. I want people to pay for that." And maybe there's a line there that you *do* have to find; but I'd definitely err on the side of generosity. **Somehow, you have to balance the difference between giving away the farm and holding everything back. Most marketers make the mistake of giving away worthless items.** That's a mistake simply because people see it and say, "It's obvious there's nothing worthwhile here. Why should I want to *pay* for anything they produce?"

Ah, but on the other hand, if you give away something extremely valuable right off the bat, the recipient is blown away and they think, "If this is what I get for free, the stuff I have to pay for must be unbelievable!" The choice is obvious: put your best foot forward. **Give away your best information and your best ideas, and you'll gain trust with the customer. Your relationship will become more solid.** They'll feel like they trust you more. You delivered more than they expected, because you gave them your very best up front. That will come back to you in the way of additional orders, additional revenue, as more and more of those people trust you and decide that what you have must be valuable indeed if you're willing to give away all this good stuff for free or for a low cost.

Never forget this simple fact: the market (whatever your market may be) is overhyped and oversaturated. The average consumer has more choices now than ever before; the customer is no longer king, but a dictator. We're all used to having things our way (thank you, Burger King). The average consumer is better educated than ever before, too, and is somewhat jaded and skeptical. **They feel like they've heard it all, so you have to do something that goes above and beyond right from the start—or why bother?**

Consider the book I used in my earlier example, which the author was giving away for $6.95. It sold on Amazon for $15.50 plus S&H in the hardcover version. That kind of offer has credibility to it. We're using a similar lead generation system here at M.O.R.E., Inc., where we take some of my books that are sold on Amazon and (because we're the publishers) we're able to give them away for a very small S&H fee. We do it for the same reason the other author I mentioned does it: **it blows the prospect's mind. That guarantees a high conversion rate,** especially when combined with the fact that only the people who want that book to begin with are going to pay the S&H fee. **They're self-qualifying, which offers you the opportunity to obtain even more money from them if you can tie in an irresistible upsale.**

It was easy for that first author's self-qualified prospects to make the connection between his value-priced book and the video collection he offered for just $197, when it usually takes up to $3,000 to acquire that material in person. **It's an enormous, overwhelming value—something that a substantial percentage of his self-qualifiers just couldn't say no to.** There's a guarantee built in, too, so it all just made sense.

Don't Stumble!

Now, be careful here. Even if what you're giving away is insanely valuable and people absolutely love it, you can overdo it with the low-cost lead generation strategy. Years ago, my wife Eileen and I bought a company from Russ Von Hoelscher, and with that company came half-a-dozen products that were selling quite well, along with a full-page ad Russ had written that had worked very successfully for years. It gave away a 120-page book for just one dollar. Well, we were brand-new in the business at the time and I was young, dumb, and cocky; and so I thought, "I'll stop asking for that dollar, and I'll bet we'll get a lot more leads and make a lot more money!"

Russ tried to tell me that would be a disastrous mistake, but we didn't listen... until our lack of profits proved him right. **Most offers require some sort of qualifier, depending on the marketplace.** The qualifier in that case was the dollar. Such a simple little thing, but it separated the serious prospects from the tire-kickers. Russ gave away hundreds of thousands of books for a dollar over the years in order to sell many, many more than that. Other dealers probably would have charged $9.95, $11.95, or more for that book.

Now, Russ once made a terrible mistake himself—which is probably why he knew better than to just give away certain products. *Parade* magazine had a section in it where you could advertise absolutely free. Well, *Parade* goes to 30 million people in hundreds of newspapers around the country every Sunday... so Russ thought this was an astounding opportunity. **What they did was charge a quarter for every lead they got you.** Russ thought, "Wow, what a deal!" and jumped at the chance.

He was part of a half-page ad that included about 25 companies. Some had information on sewing, fishing and hunting, shirts and ties—all sorts of things. Russ's was the only business opportunity ad, and it was a disaster. Not at first, though—he thought he'd hit the jackpot, because he got over 12,000 responses. *Parade* magazine sent him a huge number of names from people who had asked for the free book he was offering... and of course, *Parade* wanted their 25 cents per name. **So Russ sent out his 12,000+ free books—and got almost no subsequent orders.** He was out over $3,000 just for the leads, not including the cost of the books, which drove the loss much higher.

That taught him a lesson that he didn't forget. **Sometimes you *need* a qualifier, even if it's a measly dollar.** Why? Because when a person takes the time to fold up a dollar bill or write out a check for a dollar and sends it to you, they've made some extra effort... and that makes all the difference.

In addition to Russ's own marketing efforts, he's also worked with a wide variety of clients. Here's a good example he once told me about: there were two partners up in Seattle who were offering a real estate course—not to investors, but to new agents who had just gotten their licenses. When they came to Russ they were doing OK, but not great. Well, they showed Russ their course, which consisted of eight cassette tapes and a booklet which they sold for $149. Russ said, "Look, let's send out some postcards first."

This was before most people were even using postcards for business, so they were cautious. He explained, "Let's send a postcard to new agents that says, 'We have a great course on how to make big money as a real estate agent. We want to prove to you how great it is, so we'll send you a cassette tape that explains the whole course. Even if you don't buy the course, you're going to get some great ideas to work with. All you have to do is send us your name and address, and we'll send you the tape.'"

Then Russ worked with them to create that cassette. Their first idea was what you might expect: "Let's save the good stuff for last. When people pay the $149, *that's* when we'll give them the best information." **Russ said, "No, no, no. I've been down this road before. You're going to put some of your *best* ideas on that tape, and you're going to give it away free!"** At first they refused, but he finally convinced them that was the way they had to go. Ultimately, more than 8% of their highly targeted market purchased the course, which was much better than they were doing before.

This new company made a small fortune in no time flat, and then continued building it. First, they just worked with people who got their licenses in Washington State, then expanded to Oregon, California, and other states. It was a gold mine! **That shows you what can be done when you give something that's top-quality to a targeted market.**

Russ also helped a friend many years ago at the Sky Blue Water Company in Minnesota. He was selling fishing lures, and Russ talked him into putting together a booklet called *The Bass Fishing Guide*. They used that as a catalyst to sell hundreds of thousands of dollars worth of unique fishing tackle. **Again, it just goes to show you that when you're using free or low-cost offers on the front-end, you can build a mighty powerful business from scratch.** This works with professionals like chiropractors and dentists as well as traditional companies. Russ has to convince them to give away free exams, and they fight him with, "You know this costs money, right? X-rays aren't cheap!"

But you have to realize that while you're going to have to spend money before you make money, that money will be far less than the amount you'd make from an average client. Compare the two figures, and you'll see the value of giving away some of your valuable services free or at a low cost.

As I've noted before, **the key to success here is make your low- or no-cost items extremely valuable.** Here's another example from Russ: he used chopped-up hoagies, 2-3 inch segments of foot-long sandwiches, to help a restaurant called Sonny's draw in clientele even though it was located in what was, at the time, a rough area of San Diego. Just a few blocks away were the big banks and insurance companies of the local financial district. Walking into some of these buildings at 11:30 AM and handing out free food worked wonders. No one said they couldn't; even when someone expressed disapproval, someone else would come along and let them by. **After all, it was free food!** When they came in with those sandwiches, they were absolutely besieged.

Many people were quite willing to walk the four blocks from the high-rent district to the low-rent district to get to Sonny's. Some that didn't come that day came the next, or a day or two later, because Russ had Sonny's personnel give them coupons along with their free sandwich bites. **All of these tactics work—I don't care what kind of business you have, large or small.** You can use this strategy to compete effectively even with the big guys in your market.

You know, when Wal-Mart comes into an area, some of the local variety stores just say, "We'll, we're going to close up now. We're dead. We're done." That's just plain stupid (let's call a spade a spade here). As Sam Walton himself pointed out, "You can do things we can't do. Sure, you may have a smaller store, so you're not going to be able to work with our volume; but you can provide individualized services that we can't, and you can have unique products, and lots of them."

Sadly, the average businessperson doesn't understand that philosophy. **The more *you* do, the more prosperous you'll be.**

Here at M.O.R.E., Inc., we have a strategy we use to blow people away and make them doubly appreciate the value of our seminars. Other providers in our field felt that this tactic was remarkable and dangerous when we first started using it, but now quite a few have followed where we've led. **I tell the people who've spent hundreds or thousands to attend our seminars,**

"You're going to love this—I guarantee it. We've got some wonderful experts here who are going to teach you some great stuff. But if you're unhappy with what you've seen after attending the first day of the seminar, if you don't feel 100% enthusiastic about the information you're receiving, all you have to do is go to one of our personnel and tell them, 'I'd like my money back.' **On the spot, we'll write you a check for the full amount you paid for the seminar."**

That takes away the anxiety people have about spending a large sum of money. So use techniques like these; because when you do, you'll discover that you can beat the boys who have the most money. These marketing ideas will help you overcome the advantages they enjoy based on the size of their bank accounts.

Sharpening Your Marketing Tools

There are really only a few ways you can grow your business. One of those ways, of course, is to get more customers. Another way is to increase the average purchase size; e.g., instead of somebody buying $100 worth of product, you get them to add on a few more things and pay you $200. **Finally, you can get people to buy more often.** If you're up against a wall in terms of people making larger purchases or buying more often, then you're left with acquiring more customers as your only choice.

I've already shared the problems that marketers like Russ von Hoelscher and I face when we suggest that our clients give away something valuable for free. It amazes me how much people fight us on that form of lead generation, especially professionals like doctors. These are people who would charge you for the very air you breathe if they could; they don't want to let anyone have anything for free. If you're with them, think about this: **wouldn't you want more customers if you knew those people would, over time, earn you thousands of dollars?**

Let me repeat: **the key is to be willing to think outside the box and start offering something free or for very low-cost.** Be one of the 10% of businesses that doesn't fight this idea—and you'll instantly have a competitive advantage over the 90% who do. **Put your best stuff out there at the very beginning for nothing or next to nothing, and I guarantee you'll attract more customers when they see the little gem you've offered.** If you can get them to stay on for years, making more purchases for more and more money, you'll see a big payoff over time. When the back-end marketing kicks in seriously, that's when you make the real profits.

Retail businesses are especially averse to out-of-the-box thinking. **Most do the same kind of advertising as everyone else, and for the most part they're getting the same poor results.** Yet when you talk to them about these bold concepts, their eyes glaze over and they ignore you. It's outside the realm of their imaginations to even consider non-traditional forms of advertising, so you hit this wall when trying to explain to them, "Hey, this is proven. Other businesses have used these strategies very successfully. **All you have to do is stop thinking like everybody else, and you'll stop getting the same results everybody else is getting.** Then you can take your business to the stratosphere."

One of the problems, I think, is that these people are taking their cues from the government and its economists—and the economic ideas our government pushes tend to be bad ones, endlessly repeated among their pet scientists. It really doesn't matter who's in Congress or the White House; the economists running the country are simply on the wrong track, and won't admit it. You'd think that after trying the same things for 100 years, they'd have some idea of what works and what doesn't; but they've repeatedly shown they don't have a clue, and aren't willing to try anything else.

If you're in business, I'd make the same argument to you: if you're frustrated with the results of your marketing, don't just keep doing what everybody else is doing... or you'll keep getting the same results you've always gotten. Isn't that one definition of insanity—doing the same things repeatedly but expecting different results each time? Try something different, especially if your business is struggling. **Step out of the normal flow of advertising as practiced in your market.** I realize that if you just can't grasp that what you're doing isn't working, and that you need to try something different, you'll always have an aversion to new ideas; but if that were the case, would you even be reading this now? *If you want different results, you have to try something you haven't tried before.* It's as simple as that—and at some level, I think you know it.

Some of these ideas I've been talking about here may sound strange to you, especially when it comes to generating leads by giving away things you normally would only sell. But these concepts are based on proven models that have worked for all kinds of companies in all kinds of industries. **If you're feeling reluctant to stick your neck out, then study the results other people are getting with these out-of-the-box type strategies.** The proof is in the pudding, as the old saying goes. The proof is in the results that other companies have achieved when they've moved ahead with the strategies I've outlined in this module. They can work for you just like they've worked for countless others.

One of the smartest people I've ever met used to chant, "If you're always thinking the way you've always thought, you're always going to get what you've always got." That's the bottom line here. If you're looking for new results, you're going to have to do some things differently. Unlock your mindset here, especially if you're stuck on the old "I refuse to lose any money!" chant. **You *have* to spend money to make money, though not necessarily very much!**

First, you can test things on a very limited basis. If a particular strategy does turn out to be a disaster for some reason, you'll only lose a little money. That's true even if you test aggressively, as long as you test in a small way; for example, by mailing just a few hundred pieces to your best clients, or running small ads that have an expiration date. There are lots of things you can do to limit your losses, so that you don't have to worry about losing your shirt. **Second, there's a lifetime value to a good customer who keeps coming back and buying from you. *That's* how your marketing mindset must be oriented.**

Remember the fellow I discussed at the beginning of the chapter, who was losing five dollars on every book he gave away for free? That's just one way of thinking about it. **I prefer to take the stance that each of those five-dollar "losses" was an investment towards future profits.** They represent the cost of doing business—the cost of generating a high quality lead, someone who will ultimately become one of your best customers.

I won't tell you that the things you're afraid of won't happen. No, you'll get burned sometimes. You'll run into the occasional deadbeat who takes advantage of your free offer and never becomes a long-term customer. So what? **All that matters are the prospects you'll attract who *will* ultimately become**

long-term customers. Don't let the fear that you'll be ripped off stop you. Of course it's going to happen—but in the mix you'll have plenty of great customers who'll stay with you for years.

It's terrible risky to remain stuck in the old way of thinking. Russ von Hoelscher once offered to help a wonderful printer get more business, even though that person wasn't paying him anything. Russ was simply impressed by the excellent work the printer had done for him. So he told him, "I'm going to give you a list of things you can do that will be easy, that won't cost much money, but will result in a great influx of business for your printing company." Well, the man looked at Russ and said, "Listen, I've got a sign out there. If people don't know that I'm in the printing business, there's something wrong with them. If they want me, and they want printing, by God they'll come to me. I'm not going to them."

That put an end to that. Russ didn't try to help him anymore, because he saw that the gentleman was set in his ways. Well, even though he was probably the best printer in El Cajon, California, he was out of business less than two years later. **His attitude was prehistoric—and it killed him when more flexible (but less proficient) printers took his business away.** That same attitude still afflicts many small businesspeople, though they may not express it in that way. This fellow was more honest and forthright about it than most... and he was bankrupt before long.

This idea of "build it, and they will come" works in Hollywood movies, but not in reality. It's something we wish was true, but it just isn't. So don't adopt that mindset. Of *course* we would all love not to have to advertise or be aggressive marketers. We would love to do only what we do in our businesses, and not have to attract and retain customers. But that's not how the world works. If you don't advertise except by word of mouth, you're taking the lazy way—and it's a road that leads to bankruptcy. Period.

Half of the One-Two Punch

Back in Chapter 3, I outlined the two-step process of front-end/ back-end marketing. **Lead generation is just the front-end of that two-step marketing process.** In fact, for direct marketers, lead generation is the more critical of the two, because if you don't have leads, you're not going to have any customers.

Admittedly, if you have leads but don't convert them, then those leads are worthless. **I'd still argue, however, that lead generation is the more important part of the process, because if you don't have new prospects coming into your business, then your business will eventually die.** You can only resell to existing customers for so long without bringing in new customers, because customers pass away, leave the market, move, or their financial circumstances change. As I've pointed out before, there's always a "hole in the bucket." There's no escaping that.

When you think about lead generation, it's always important to remember who you're trying to sell to—or, more importantly perhaps, who you want your customer to be. Who do you feel represents the kind of person who will provide long-term profits for your business? If you don't give this a lot of thought, and deeply consider the best way not just to reach out to them but to help them pre-qualify themselves, then your plans may misfire. As I pointed out with one of Russ's stories earlier in this chapter, it's one thing to bring in a large quantity of prospects, but something else again to convert enough of them to keep your business in the black. **Russ attracted 12,000+ with his**

Parade **offer—and converted fewer than one in one thousand.**
You can bet he never made that mistake again.

If you don't think through who you want your best customer
to be, and what it's going to take to attract them, then you'll either
end up with no leads or a whole stack of leads you can't
convert—and both issues are seriously problematic for your
business. **You have to begin with the end in mind.** What does
your ideal customer look like? Who are they? What are they
concerned about? What are their daily problems? What pains do
they experience? What solutions can you offer? What will they
respond to the most?

In addition to helping you attract the right kind of people,
these questions help you repel the wrong kind. Bringing in the
wrong leads just isn't productive towards your goal. **The kind of
person you're looking for will ultimately determine what kind
of offer you make to them.** Consider the sport of fishing, where
it's important to use the right kind of bait to catch the right kind
of fish. A tiny hook and a smidgen of shrimp isn't likely to catch
you a big mackerel or shark; you need a massive hook and a big
chunk of bait fish for those. Some fish prefer live bait to cut bait,
and others respond more readily to artificial lures fished a certain
way. Which bait you offer depends on the fish you're after. The
gear's important, too. If you're going after the big fish, you don't
fish with an ultralight rod-and-reel combo. You need something
that can handle the big fish, and can get your bait far enough out
to reach them. You'll have more luck if you go to them rather
than forcing them to come to you.

If you keep your lure or your bait just a few feet off the
surface, you're going to catch a certain kind of fish; if you use a
sinker that takes it straight to the bottom, you'll catch different

kinds of fish. All these factors go into the fishing equation, and you can learn exactly how to attract a specific type of fish if you study up on that particular species. The same is true when dealing with your marketplace. Of course, people aren't fish and we're not using bait *per se*, but I think you get the point. **How you present a lead generation offer and what you include in it largely determines who you'll attract.** Do you want tons of "bait-stealers" who readily go for the freebies but will never become long-term customers, or would you rather land a few "whales" instead?

If you don't match the right offer to the right person, you'll attract the wrong people. Going back to my ocean analogy: if you'd like to avoid catching stingrays and sharks, avoid the kinds of bait they prefer so you don't have to deal with them and end up stung or minus a finger. Just leave them in the ocean. **Ditto for lead generation; you want to attract the right kinds of customers but leave everyone else out there.** When you do little things like charging a dollar here or $7 for S&H there, you're setting up your rig with the kind of bait that attracts the right people, while repelling the wrong ones—which is just as important, if not more so. **The specific offers you make, based on your knowledge of who your best customers are, will ultimately determine your success or failure.**

So in addition to asking yourself what your ideal customer wants, ask yourself what they don't want. **You have to be clear on both points if you want to generate the best leads, because it's impossible to be all things to all people.** Some people want discounts, low cost, and payment plans. Others are happy to pay higher prices for great service. The permutations are endless; so it's important to understand not only who you want to attract, but who you don't—and then to create your offers so they accomplish both objectives.

Some marketers simply don't want to deal with bargain shoppers or those looking for payment plans. So they offer neither, and rarely talk about price. **Instead, they push their level of service, and talk about how they go above and beyond everyone else in the marketplace.** I've heard of a dentist who doesn't talk about price in his marketing; instead, he focuses on the great service you get during your teeth whitening or oral surgery. The price is never mentioned—and it's quite a high one. Nonetheless, because of this great service, they have very few issues with their customers. Other companies in the exact same market have payment plans, low-cost options, discounts, and coupons, and they attract their own target audience.

Now, there are exceptions to this rule; if you have a local restaurant or a shoe repair store or you're a plumber, you'll take all comers as long as they have enough money to pay. But if you have a specialty business, then you may end up charging more money than the average guy would charge—so you then want to emphasize what makes you special. **Never base your unique selling proposition on price.** Let K-Mart or Wal-Mart have that market segment. You want to show your clients that what you have is superior, and therefore, it costs more—but it's worth every cent.

Another Great Example

I'm going to let you in on a very simple lead generation technique that's been worth a fortune to us here at M.O.R.E., Inc. It's something that can help you take dirt-cheap ads or postcards and leverage them for tremendous selling power. Now, the good thing about these items is the fact that they *are* dirt-cheap; the bad thing is that you can't do much of a selling job with them. There just isn't enough space for the copy; usually, the more you tell the more you sell, but the reverse is also true. **So what you do is run little ads or send out postcards that contain the main benefit of whatever you're offering, and direct them to a special hotline with a recorded message that discusses the offer in more detail.**

You let people know it's a recording, so they feel less intimidated. If it's just a phone number, they might worry about getting a super salesperson on the phone, which might drive them away. After all, nobody wants to be sold, even though they typically like to buy. They want it to be their choice, and they want to make their choices cautiously, so they don't appreciate someone trying to push them too forcefully toward a decision. They often reject such offers, **so you're better off carefully leading them toward the deal with a gentle lead generation message.** That's what we've done with our small ads and postcards. People uninterested in our message ignore them; only those interested choose to listen to the messages. They often forget that we invited them to make that decision in the first place.

We've made millions of dollars over the years by using this technique, first drawing people in with a low-cost deal and then following up with new offers, ultimately doing plenty of business with those people once they came aboard. **Once they've made the choice to hear you out, you can really be aggressive in going for their business.**

That's how my wife and I got started in DRM. **We ran very small display ads in two national magazines, directing our prospects to call and listen to a recorded message.** This was back in the summer of 1988; we were brand-new to the business, living in a rented farmhouse out in the country near Goessel, Kansas. We used our home phone number in the ad, and it rang right in our house, so people could listen to the recorded message on our answering machine. If we wanted, we could turn up the machine to listen to the callers, and hear them leaving their names and addresses, requesting the information our ad offered.

That was a transformational experience in my life. There I was, just a small town boy from Kansas in my late 20s, and we'd sit out on our front porch in the heat of the summer with our answering machine turned up, listening to people listen to and respond to our message. Once those ads came out in the magazines, the phone started ringing off the hook. We received hundreds of calls from people who patiently listened to the little message I'd recorded myself, then left their contact information.

We heard from people from all over the country, with all kinds of different accents: people from down South, people from up North, people you could barely understand sometimes, people who could barely speak English... some of it was so garbled we never could figure out where to send our information. Later, we transcribed those recordings and sent the people whose contact info we could understand an initial package of sales material that pitched our very first offer. **Then we followed up and made additional sales.** That led to millions of dollars for us—even though it cost us only a few hundred to get started.

We couldn't afford much, but by using the answering machine, we were able to amplify that. That gave our little ads super selling power. Since then, we've done similar things dozens of times, though of course we've transferred the technique to voicemail technology, since no one uses answering machines anymore.

We've sold a $3,000 seminar by using postcards that drove interested prospects to a 10-15 minute recorded message, figuring that anybody who would listen to me hyping something up for that long *had* to be a serious prospect. **During that recording, I said several times, "This opportunity will cost you about the same amount of money that you'd spend on a long four-day weekend to Las Vegas." I told them, "If you don't have that kind of money, then please don't waste your time here."**

I didn't mean that in a negative way; **the idea was to pre-qualify the listener, and it worked very well.** Those who left their name and address knew this was something that was going to cost them. **We didn't give them an exact price, but we did give them an idea that it wasn't free, and wasn't even remotely cheap.**

We've used recorded messages as much as an hour long — yes, 60 full minutes — to pre-qualify prospects for high-end products and services. Only people who were genuinely excited about the offer were willing to listen to that whole recording and then take the next step, which was to send us money. **So as you can see, this is a superb way for you to pre-qualify prospective buyers, and all it takes is a small initial effort to get things rolling downhill and snowballing into immense profits.** Small ads can offer huge selling power when handled properly.

Wrapping It Up

Please realize that the strategy I've outlined above can work for any business, not just the DRM field where I've made my fortune. It's effective even for traditional Main Street businesses — though the resistance to using this strategy tends to be very strong among brick-and-mortar merchants. Still, if you're willing to break through that resistance, if you're amenable to innovation, you can make it work. **I recommend that you try it, along with a few other techniques I've outlined in this module and those preceding it.** Unless you're happy with the results you're already getting, you've *got* to start doing things differently.

Will everything I've revealed here work for you and your business? Probably not, but will many of these techniques and strategies bring tremendous results? Yes! There's no doubt about it. **So break out of your old mold, and try some of these techniques in your business.** Whether you're national, regional, or local, you're going to find that these techniques *will* work, and you'll be amazed at the breakthroughs that you experience.

I want to encourage you in particular to commit yourself to the art of direct response marketing, DRM. It works wonders for self-qualifying lead generation, and that's just a small part of its charm. Now, I hear a lot of protest when I recommend this strategy. I've heard people repeatedly say things along the lines of, "Yeah, I tried that and it didn't work." Usually what that means is that they ran one ad or mailed a few postcards *once* and didn't quite get it right. But that doesn't invalidate the strategy, and it certainly doesn't represent commitment. The results weren't what they were looking for right away, and so they gave up on it. **Instead, I would encourage you to become committed to DRM, and give it a serious chance.**

DRM can include things like the small print ads and postcards I mentioned earlier, or TV and radio spots. You goal should be to get people to raise their hands and express interest, proving they're predisposed to buy. This is no guarantee they will, but they're much more likely to do so than most people.

Capture their contact info, follow up with them, and make them a compelling offer in an attempt to get them to do business with you. Later on, you can put the back-end aggressively into play in an attempt to convert them to lifetime customers, continuing to test new ideas the whole way. This is something that, in most businesses, can take up just as much time as doing your actual business—especially if you offer a local service like plumbing or electrical repair.

If you find yourself doing that much marketing, maybe it's time to start letting other people do the actual work, so you can focus on attracting and retaining customers. **As much as you may love your work, the marketing is what brings in the money, so that's where you should be focusing your efforts—especially if you're great at it.**

The key here is to *not* be one of those people who tried it once and gave up when it didn't work as you expected. Get serious. Become committed to this form of marketing. It's a better way... and it's an easier way, when done correctly, and can be a lot more profitable. **Make the decision to stick to it until you find the success that you've been looking for.** Do so, and you'll end up in absolute control of your marketing. Your leads will become much easier to convert, because they've already qualified themselves.

And don't fall into the "Everything's got to be online nowadays" trap. That's just not true! **The recorded message combo starting out with a small print ad, postcard, or even a flyer still works wonders,** especially since just about everyone carries around a phone nowadays. This makes it even more incredibly effective. Other businesses than mine have built themselves up by using this recorded message concept logically.

So brainstorm how you can use it for yourself. I think you'll find it a great tool for generating lots of prospects using an automated system.

Lead generation is incredible important as the first step of a multi-stage process that ultimately leads to happy customers who continue to do business with you for life. So do everything you can to implement a simple, self-sustaining lead generation process that pulls in prospects ready to do business with you, right on the spot.

To learn more Ruthless Marketing strategies, turn the page to Module #7.

CHAPTER EIGHT:

Module #7: Website and Internet Marketing

It seems that the businesspeople I meet either love the Internet, or they hate it. I've never met anyone yet who has a truly moderate attitude towards it. Either they think it's going to be the savior of their business— that it's going to revolutionize everything— or they hate it and have nothing but terrible things to say about it. Hopefully, by the time you've completed this module, you'll have a more balanced view of the topic.

As you know, the Internet has changed the entire business world. That's not an overly dramatic statement in any sense: it's destroyed some markets, and given rise to a whole slew of new ones. Many wonderful things have happened as a result of the rise of the Internet... and many not-so-wonderful have happened, too. **But ultimately, the Internet is a business tool, just like your cash register or your advertising; so in this module, I'll offer you a series of Internet tips, tricks, and strategies that you can use to increase your sales and profits if you put them into play properly.**

Let's start by discussing how you can take the direct marketing methods I've outlined in previous modules and amplify them on the Internet—especially the process of acquiring leads. Previously, I've talked about the power of information in marketing your business. You position yourself as an expert when you create a booklet, a pamphlet, a checklist, or a tips sheet that helps your potential clients, in an effort to attract them to you and, ultimately, to get them to buy something from you. **In this chapter, I'll show you how to use this exact same type of content to get a ton of free advertising and marketing on Internet search engines, delivered directly to the right people.** You get to connect with them right at the point when they're ready to buy—which is a very powerful thing.

King of the 'Net

On the Internet, high-quality content is king. Here's why: Most people who are looking for something on the Internet start by going to one of the major search engines—Google, Yahoo, or Bing—and typing in a description of what they're after. **The search engine then tries to connect the user with the best possible example of whatever they're looking for, because they know if they can do that, the user's more likely to come back to them again and again.** The search engines use various methods to sort their traffic; one way they do it is by offering users access to the pay-per-click advertising they sell to businesses. That's one way they ensure their profits.

But the best thing about search engines is that no matter what, they deliver a ton of free information—information that the user then has to wade through to pick the best fit. **Well, those who can optimize their content so that it shows up on the first page of the search results are the people who'll make the most money.** Now, there are plenty of huge courses on how to do "search engine optimization," or SEO, of a website in order to game the search engines... but for most business owners, that's simply not doable. You've got your hands full already. You need a simple way to generate high-quality leads on the search engines based on content; you don't have time to become an

Internet expert.

The first thing you should do is set up your own blog. "Blog" is short for "weblog," which is simply a type of website you can easily update with news, content, and basic information about your business, products, and services. You can post text, pictures, or videos; blogs are usually very easy to update. They're easy to set up, too, using services like WordPress. If you prefer to create a stand-alone blog on your existing website, that's no problem either—even if you're not a particularly technical person.

If you don't already have a person working on your website or doing Internet marketing for you, then log onto a freelancer jobs site like Elance.com. Sign up as a buyer and collect bids from website designers who can create your blog for you. You can provide the content and company contact information, and they'll program the HTML code and upload the content. **You can get a well-designed blog set up for just a few hundred dollars—and suddenly, you have a valuable piece of website real estate you can use to build your business.**

Once you've set up your blog, it's time to write high quality and helpful content aimed at your target market. Here's where you go into copywriter mode and ask yourself things like, "Okay, who are my best clients? What's going to interest them most? What words might they type into their search engine when they're looking for someone who provides my type of services and products?" **It's more important than ever to get into their mindset, to understand what it is they really want right at that very moment.** For example, if they live in Dallas and need a painter for their den, they might type in, "Dallas indoor painter reviews." Or, they might be looking for "Wichita's best pool cleaning service," or "Phoenix plumbing prices."

These are called keyword phrases. **Once you've determined which keyword phrases seem most likely, build your web content around these phrases.** By content, I mean the copy that you create to sell whatever you're selling—short articles, or possibly a checklist or collection of tips for somebody who's looking for a pool cleaning service or the best plumber. Use your imagination when creating this content, making sure you include your keyword terms in that content as naturally as you can, both in the headlines and throughout the body of the text. Then post it on your blog.

One advantage of blogs is that they're not much different from word processing software like Microsoft Word. In fact, you can create your text in a word processing program first, if you like, then just plug it into the blog. What you see is what you get. **Then you review it, publish it, and instantaneously, it's live on your blog.** And here's the best thing: search engines love fresh, new content. **They all have little programs called "spiders" that constantly "crawl" the Internet, looking for brand-new content.** They'll find your blog soon after you've posted it, and they'll put it in their directory. After that, when people type "Dallas house painters" or "Phoenix plumbing reviews" into the search engine (or whatever your subject may be), your blog will appear in their results.

The more often you update your blog, and the fresher the content is, the more authority your blog has—and the more often it will appear in search engine results. All the major search engines love high quality, frequently updated blogs, so you need to make sure you're constantly adding to them with new, useful material. The more often you post on your blog, the more web pages you're going to have in all the search engines—and the more chances you'll have to connect with people in a buying mode. If you have 100 articles on your blog and each is a separate webpage, that's 100 different opportunities per search engine for those highly qualified leads to connect with you.

Needless to say, to be truly successful with this, you've got to write on a fixed schedule. **I recommend that you post a new entry at least once a week, and more often would be better.** Just make sure you're not posting the same old stuff over and over. **The fresher the content, the more the search engines like you.** If you have trouble sticking with your schedule, set yourself a reminder online, or an alarm on your smartphone or watch to keep yourself in line. You can use a specialty reminder service; my colleague Jeff Gardner uses NOZBE.com online. That dings him either once a week or once a month, depending on his schedule for the different things he wants to accomplish.

The point is, with a reminder, you don't have to waste energy trying to remember to do your writing. You'll get your "ding," you'll get it done, and then you'll go on about your other business until it dings again. If you just try to remember it on your own, you're likely to let it go... and then you're going to end up with a dead blog with just a few entries on it. **Well, search engines don't like dead blogs.**

While you can pay other people to provide your blog content (and many do, via Elance and similar sites), you don't have to. You can do this yourself. Your content doesn't even have to be 100% brand new; **you can adapt for the Internet the same content you're using off-line to attract high-quality leads, presenting it free to literally millions of people in your market.** People have gotten used to going online to search for products or services, so be sure that you tap into this particular market segment. **Just be sure you collect contact information from anyone who visits.**

Once you've finished reading (and rereading) this chapter, do a little research on your own. **You'll discover that business blogging is very easy... even easier if you're already doing it for fun. Just transfer those skills to a business site.** There are plenty of people who can help you get your blog up and going for a reasonable fee. They can even walk you through the process of updating it—and very quickly you can have an online presence driving free traffic to your business.

I've always been amazed at how inexpensively you can accomplish all this, especially through the people who work for surprisingly low fees on places like Elance or Craigslist. All you have to do is go to one of these sites, post your project, and let people bid on it. I don't recommend that you always take the lowest bidder, because personally I'm afraid that if someone is *that* cheap, I can't trust them to do a good job. **Instead, select someone in the middle of the bid range who looks like they do decent work.**

Static Can Be Good

You can easily attach a blog to an existing website that includes static items like a photo gallery of your products and services, your hours, a map and directions to your location, and similar information. **If you've already got a site like that in place, in fact, then a blog can draw attention to it and help you drive sales.** You not only want to attract people with your new information, you want to make it easy for them to find the static info they need in order to do business with you. If you *don't* have a website and you set up a blog, then it's easy to create blog pages with that static information right on the blog. Your first page can be the constantly updated content, but then at the top there can be a menu that says: About, Directions, Locations, Contact Us, etc. to allow people access to your static information.

So if you've already got the website, add a blog. If you don't have a website, all you'll need is a blog, since you can add static pages as necessary. **The blog will be the focal point of your site, because it's search engine friendly.**

In fact, blogs have largely replaced the standard website as the online presence of choice. They're a lot less boring than static websites, they let you communicate regularly with your marketplace, and they offer everything you need to get your message across. Many marketers and business owners don't even bother with traditional websites these days; they just fire up WordPress, TypePad, or Blogger. You just have to be sure to refresh it with news, information, and content on a regular basis, so the web spiders keep adding your blog their directories, consistently bringing it to the attention of people conducting online searches. **The price is very affordable—just a few dollars a month (at most) for a robust, dynamic way to communicate with your prospects and customers.**

Tapping Outside Expertise

Another cool thing about blogs—which I think are probably underutilized in the small business world—**is that you can not only post original content, you can also link to other people's content as well.** For example, if you provide a specific service to your community, you can post links to existing blog entries on other sites if you don't want to do the content creation yourself.

Of course, if you *do* create your own articles, you'll be seen as an expert in your field—an important tactic I'll go into in more detail later on. But still, you can also post things like, "Hey, I saw this video on YouTube, and thought you might be interested in it." Now, I'd warn against doing this too often, especially with local competitors. It's one thing if you're in Dallas and link to an expert in Florida; that's probably not going to hurt your business. **But don't link to experts in your area, or your prospects might decide to contact them instead.**

There's also the option of posting "vlogs"—video weblogs. It's so easy that many people do just that, and never have to write a word. **You simply sit in front of a video camera and talk, sharing your experiences or providing information on a specific process.** You might say, "Today, I'm going to show you the five steps of fixing a flat tire" (or whatever the case may be. You can easily upload that video and integrate it into your blog, or post it on YouTube, Facebook or whatever other Internet format you're using.

As you can see, it's relatively easy to create or otherwise link to fresh blog content—**so if you're a small business owner who's serious about tackling Internet marketing, you need to be blogging.** Take advantage of the tools available to you; many are free or inexpensive. A few hours of effort per month can put you ahead of the game and position you to dominate your market.

Instant Expert

Here's another important point to consider: when you're blogging, you're establishing yourself as an expert. **All prospects prefer to do business with someone they perceive as an expert**—someone who really "knows their onions," as they used to say in the old days. Blogs offer a dirt-cheap way to prove that you *do* know your onions, and that gives people more reason to choose you over everybody else.

Blogging is cheap, it's easy, and it sets you up as an expert in your field. **So why won't more small business people do this?**

I think the biggest reason is that there's a learning curve involved, especially for older folks who haven't yet adjusted to the new information technology. Many people think you have to be a trained technician to set up a website or blog; they have no idea how easy it is these days. Admittedly, it might very well have been very difficult or expensive the last time they checked in on the technology 10 years ago; but things have advanced rapidly since, and it's only going to get easier and cheaper. Once somebody bites the bullet and says, "Look, I know I've got to do this. I really want to generate quality leads from the Internet," **then they finally realize there's not that much to it.** You can go out and start stomping around on the Internet without worrying too much, because there's really nothing you can break online, and it's just so simple. That's when they start seriously using the medium in their marketing... but they do have to get there first.

Excuses for not expanding into the online market tend to be technical and monetary. Many of your competitors are still stuck in this concept of, "I've got to hire someone for $5,000 or $10,000 to do a website, and I don't have that kind of money right now." Oftentimes, even those who do have websites are using the ones their nephews set up for them in 1999, and those sites *look* like pre-millennial—because they haven't been updated since. **If you'll dive in with both feet, you'll find yourself ahead of the majority of small business owners.**

Get online and start doing some research, and you'll soon realize their excuses for staying stuck in the electronic hinterlands just don't hold water anymore. **It shouldn't take you long to discover that you have a real opportunity here to build a fast, easy blog that you can update within minutes a day, to provide a truly productive online presence.**

I don't pretend to be an Internet expert, but all this is obvious to me, and it should be to you as well. The growth of the Internet is one of the biggest things that's happened in my lifetime, and it's only getting bigger. **Over one *billion* people are connected to the Internet—about one sixth of the world's entire population.** Now realize that getting on the Internet can be a tremendous advantage for your business, but that it can also be detrimental in some cases. There are all kinds of crazy things happening on the Internet, both good and bad. You have to be on the lookout for criminals there, just like everywhere else. No matter what, though, we marketers simply *have* to take advantage of this medium, because it's so powerful. Ignore the Internet at your peril.

On, Not In

Most small business people get too enraptured with working *in* their businesses to work *on* them—to focus on the marketing that absolutely has to be done if they expect to survive. So in addition to blogs, **I've got a few 'Net-based ideas that I think will help the quiet guy who just works at his business and doesn't take the time to market it.**

I'm sure that wherever you live, there are people who offer Information Technology (IT) services besides those who are on Craigslist and Elance. **They can also set up a blog for you fairly**

inexpensively. Check with your local college; I know quite a few entrepreneurs who have done that. And some newspapers, like the San Diego *Union Tribune*, have set up their own huge websites where you can claim your own little niche. They've broken businesses down by categories, and let you use a free page to describe your business and what you've got in a few hundred words. You can update it easily.

Plus, there's a company called Angie's List (www.angieslist.com) that rates local businesses. I've sure you've heard of it, or seen it advertised on TV; they've got branches of the site for every major metropolitan area. They rank businesses by grades of A, B, C, D and below, based on the reviews that people post about them on the site. **You can take advantage of this by asking for reviews from your best customers, because a high ranking will automatically get people to take you more seriously.** If they're happy with your work, most people won't mind taking the time to give you a nice review.

Those testimonials can be used in all kinds of media, by the way—print advertising, your blog, on TV and radio ads, etc. Millions of people are using Angie's List nowadays to search for local businesses when they need a product or service, and it's a trusted source of information. The best thing is, for business owners, it's absolutely free to use! The members pay to use the site, and even then the monthly fee is cheap. But the fact that they've paid to use the service means that these are very high-quality prospects who have already pre-qualified themselves.

You can create your own account, and use it to manage your reputation. You might find that people have already gone on to Angie's List to report on the service you provided them. If you're unable to respond to that—especially if somebody had a problem that wasn't resolved—that's going to cost you money. **But there's a link on each review page that says "Business Owners Click Here," so you can use that to claim your business site, set up your account, and become active in managing your reputation.** You'll actually get an e-mail alert letting you know whenever someone posts about you, so you can immediately check it out and respond to it if need be.

They offer other benefits as well. **You can create a storefront where you can offer special services or package deals to other members.** You can download reports and other useful data, all for free. If blogging sounds difficult to you—and honestly, it's even easier than I've made it sound—**then Angie's List may be a better option. It's a fairly "lazy" way to drum up extra business at no cost.** Immediately, you're in front of people who have spent good money to become members, people already looking for service providers. If they find you and discover you've got a good rating and respond to all issues, you have a higher likelihood of getting that business than someone who hasn't claimed their account.

Encouraging Words

There are all kinds of ways to make the Internet work for you, if you choose to do so—and you should. If you're too over-worked to blog, then at least look for some of the simpler things you can do. **And know this: you're going to have to deal with the Internet one way or the other.** So it's best to face it head on. **Even if you don't make a major move, you can soon make your presence felt by doing even a few of these small things I've mentioned.** If you don't want to deal with Angie's List, there's a handful of other useful review sites you should check out, such as Yelp.

These can be good tools for small business owners, if you can feed off those reviews and testimonials. **And I'd suggest that you actively request testimonials from satisfied customers,** because a good testimonial is always valuable to your business. Unfortunately, just as with any valuable asset, there usually aren't a lot to be had—if only because happy customers aren't very vocal. Sure, most people will share their good experiences to an extent... but when a customer is riled up, *that's* when they're likely to post a review, and you can be sure it won't be a positive one.

Recently, my Marketing Director, Chris Lakey, returned from vacation. He stayed in a particular hotel during his trip; and while he's never one to talk to a hotel about his experience there, he actually had a pretty bad one this time. It wasn't terrible, it just wasn't what he expected it to be. They always e-mail him later asking him to fill out their survey form... and normally he doesn't, because he has better things to do with his time.

But this time he was upset, and filled out the survey. So as you can see, Chris was more apt to communicate with them when he'd had a bad experience; and sure enough, a few days after he filled out the survey, he got a phone call from the manager of that hotel. They asked some more questions about his experience, did some follow-ups, and offered him a discount on his next stay. **So they tried to make it right with him, because his anger and frustration led him to an action that he wouldn't have taken if he'd been satisfied.**

This is a good example of how bad news travels a lot faster than good news. Unprompted, people are simply more likely to talk about a bad customer experience than a good one. **This is especially true with an online presence, where most people are unafraid to say what they think in an open**

forum, since they can't be easily identified. A forum like this might result in more bad reviews than good ones, simply because the **happy people never take the time to go online and post about their experiences.** They'll just quietly go on using your products or services.

That being the case, you definitely need some good reviews to offset any negative ones; so you have to think of a way to get your happy customers to post such reviews. One thing you can do is offer some kind of a reward to your customers if they'll post on the review sites. **You can say something like, "We'd love to have your thoughts, so please review our service on Angie's List or Yelp.** We're not trying to coax you into making an untrue statement, just asking you to go say something about us, using your own words. **In exchange for your thoughts, we'll give you a discount on your next visit/service... "** What you offer is up to you; the point is to reward the customer for taking positive action, because most of the time happy customers *may* spread the news about their experience with you, but they won't spread it like the people who are upset.

You can't please everybody. You *will* have unhappy customers, and on the Internet, it's just too easy for people to talk about their negative experiences. You need your prospects to hear about the positive ones, too. By and large, I'm sure most of your customers are very satisfied with your product or services. Get those people to say so by actively soliciting their testimonials. **If you do that, you'll find interactive social media to be advantageous, because it passively and inexpensively attracts new business for you.**

Chris tells me that back in the early days of the Internet, he was looking for information on a minivan he was considering purchasing for his family. Among others, he looked at the Ford Windstar. Well, during the process he found Fordwindstar.com, which was actually owned by a disgruntled Windstar owner. The site was very detailed, listing all his Windstar's service records and every single problem he'd ever had, why the Windstar was the worst vehicle ever, and all the reasons he believed that you should never buy one. Today, Ford would probably sue him just to own that website; but back then, they didn't regulate the 'Net like they do now—so you could own a website with another business's name in it. You can see how damaging a site like that might be.

Remember: though it's wise for you to do your best to control your image on the Internet, people can say whatever they want. They feel protected and anonymous, and often they're aggressive with their criticisms. **So you'll need to be aggressive in promoting your good name, and do whatever you can to get people to speak positively about you.** Like blogs and other social media, Angie's List, Yelp, and similar sites are very search engine friendly. If you've got lots of good reviews, with plenty of people actively talking about your business and the high quality of your products and services, rest assured the search engines will pick up on that.

If someone types "Carpet Cleaning Business" into the search engine, actively looking for carpet cleaners in your town, they're likely to come upon the Angie's List or Yelp page for *your* carpet cleaning business—and they're going to see all the good things people are saying, and how they enjoy interacting with your business. **They're probably going to find your blog, where you're giving away tips and other information—and all those things are going to cause people to want to contact you.**

As a result, you're seen as an expert in your field — which is another reason you need to solicit good testimonials. Never forget that happy people are less inclined to talk than unhappy ones. There's no reason to complain; they got what they wanted from you, everything is good, and they're back to their daily lives. **But if you ask them for testimonials, they're generally happy to provide them if you provided good value and they had a pleasant experience doing business with you.** Keep that in mind as you tackle this brave, new Internet world. Keep encouraging your happy customers to talk about you. Reward them for their testimonials, if you must. Offer them something you know they want: a discount or special bonus on their next order, or maybe a gift card for Applebee's.

Let me re-emphasize that you absolutely *have* to have those positive reviews to act as testimonials, because again, people are much more likely to gripe than praise you. That's one of the terrible things about the Internet, as you probably already know — but the elephant's there in the room anyway, so it makes sense to acknowledge it. Understand that the customer is no longer king. **No, the average modern customer is a child dictator, quite aware of his or her power.** They're spoiled rotten, demanding as hell, and have to get everything precisely their way. They like to get on the Internet and complain when they don't, even if you're committed to doing extremely high-quality work. Sometimes they just expect things that can never happen, no matter how hard you try to please them.

Here's a good example. My best friend owns a pest control company in Wichita, and they do nothing but superior work — admittedly for premium prices. And yet people have gone on Angie's List and similar sites and slammed them. They wouldn't think about calling up her company and complaining face-to-face, but the 'Net offers anonymity—and so they're willing to say all kinds of nasty things there, because no one knows who they are. **You have to counter that *every single time* it happens, fighting fire with fire.** Don't be rude about it, but do rebut the critic's comments firmly. Thank God you can actually dispute the claims that people make against you on sites like Angie's List! You can't do that on all sites.

Negative news spreads better than positive news. Print out that statement and tack it on the wall in front of your desk, if necessary. **It's just a basic reality of human nature.** If I go out and see a movie and like it, I might tell a few friends, "Oh, it was pretty good." But if I felt I wasted my money, I'd probably tell more people that. And these days, negative reviews get more press than they ever could have, even just ten years ago. People love to get on their blogs and express their thoughts and feelings about every little thing—and some of them have huge readerships.

Some people even try to make the good look bad by skewing the perspective, if they're really determined to smear a person, company, or institution. Consider Mitt Romney, the Republican presidential candidate for 2012 as I write this. Whether you love or hate him is your business, but there are certain facts you can't ignore. You can, however, manipulate those facts to your benefit. One such fact is that Romney is very good at turning around failing businesses; 82% of those he took on became quite successful, including some well-known businesses like Sports Authority. But 18% of those failing businesses actually failed.

If you're a blogger and have that fact in hand, what do you do now? If you believe in capitalism, you might say, "A lot more than 20% of all businesses are going to fail in the first few years anyhow. So Romney did a great job." But if you're a Socialist, you might say, "Forget about all those successes. What about poor Jesse and Martha, who lost everything they had when Bain Capital failed? Romney's to blame."

I think you get my point. **There are people out there who will bitch and moan and bellyache no matter what you do.** Some have legitimate gripes; some just do it to abuse the little bit of power they have, because the Internet empowers people like never before. No matter their motives, you have to counter them.

Web 2.0

If you've tried using the Internet before and given up on it as either too difficult or too limited, it's about time you gave it another shot. **The Internet has transformed itself in recent years.** In the early days, you just put up a static website with basic information, and it was more or less fixed like that—though with some effort, you could go back and modify it later. Then it would be static again. There was no easy way to add dynamic, rapidly changing information that would pull the web spiders in repeatedly and maximize your listings in the search engine directories. **The advent of blogs, RSS feeds, and similar tools has changed all that.**

These days, we've moved on to what people call Web 2.0. **It's a new age of online interaction, where websites are no longer static and boring, instead offering users better ways to find and share information, often in real time.** Faster Internet speeds have made video and audio so much more practical they've become an integral part of the typical user's experience. Then blogs came about, and suddenly everybody could become an author online, with their own audience. That was followed by social media like Facebook and Twitter, where people began interacting even more on a one-to-one basis.

While a blog regularly offers new articles people can comment on, the new social media make it even easier and simpler to share information on the fly. With Twitter, you get 144 characters for your messages, the ideal length for a text message on a Smartphone. **It's easy to share little snippets of information with people—including your customers.** You know how important it is to stay in contact with your customer base, so they'll remember you're there and think of you first when they're ready to buy what you sell. Well, Twitter, Facebook, and the like make this incredible easy. They weren't initially intended for that purpose, but they can be used for it if you know how to.

And just think: at last count, over *800 million users* were interacting with each other on Facebook alone. Oh, there are limitations: these days you can have only up to 5000 "friends," which can be limiting if you're trying to communicate to a large database. But you can also create a Fan page. **Many businesses and celebrities—entities with lots of people interested in what they have to say—create Fan pages that allow them to have as many people following them as they want.** Some people have tens or hundreds of thousands of users getting updates and information via those Fan pages.

For example, Chris Lakey follows certain musicians he likes on Facebook, and he can see from the information they share on their Fan pages when they're going to be in concert near him. Recently, he learned that the tour bus of one of his bands had caught fire—because they posted a picture of it. It was completely engulfed in flames and was a total loss: all their equipment, computers, everything they had with them on the tour bus was completely destroyed. Before Facebook, before social media, Chris would probably never have learned about that. Word might have gotten out eventually... but in the post-Facebook era, the knowledge spread within minutes of the event to their entire network of followers, all over the world. Chris and his fellow fans also knew that they were all safe, that no one got injured even though they lost all their equipment and instruments.

Many of us have come to use social media as a way to acquire news and information that's important to us. We guard that information, and have ways to access it on our home computers and smartphones alike. The recent expansion of the Internet to cell phones has let us keep our specialized information right at our fingertips. **Who needs the Yellow Pages anymore, when you can tap into not just directories but actual provider websites on your phone?** That's another reason why it's so important for small business owners to utilize these interrelated media.

In addition to Facebook and Twitter, **there are also things like Pinterest, a goofy little website where businesses post items of interest to their marketplace.** It's something like having your own big bulletin board you can pin stuff to—photos, drawings, and the like. You can categorize the items and do all sorts of useful things... and Pinterest is signing up lots of businesses whose owners have realized they can use their walls to share information with their customers.

That's the great thing about social media, whatever the type or brand: **it lets you stay in touch with customers and prospects constantly, and all basically for free.** Imagine that: once upon a time this was something that wasn't available at any cost, and now it costs nothing. **This segment of the Internet offers a very** effective way to create and maintain a presence on the 'Net, especially for small and local business owners who may not otherwise have the funds to do much advertising.

And then there are specialty business-to-business sites like LinkedIn, where you can network with like-minded professionals, and a variety of niche sites that are even more focused or specialized. There are only a relative handful of these right now, but the numbers will surely grow. Eventually, there will be something for everyone!

Lead, and They'll Follow

Here's what I consider the biggest takeaway regarding Internet marketing: the realization that the Internet isn't some big, scary, confusing thing you need to avoid. **It's just another tool, and using it can be fairly simple. Don't be afraid of it; you can use it to make a lot of money.** But you do need to know how to use it right. So get involved, and take what you learn to leverage the blogs and social media for your profit. Build a list of people who know, like, and trust you because of the relationship you've established, and share information with them.

Marketers have been doing this for decades already with newsletters, first solely in print and now both in print and online. **If you write a newsletter, you're building a relationship with customers by sharing helpful information with them on an on-going basis.** You're also keeping in touch, reminding them you're still around and they ought to do business with you. After all, you're a known quantity; they know they can trust you, and they appreciate that you're trying to help them. So why not help you, too?

This triggers the old reciprocity instinct, which is when we feel we owe something to someone who does something for us; and people prefer to do business with friends anyway. Social media harnesses the old newsletter methodology in such a way that you can easily keep up with a large list of "followers" or "fans" that may number into the tens or hundreds of thousands — and it's a darn sight cheaper than direct mail!

Some of the biggest Twitter users have over *1 million people* following what they say. Those followers receive an alert whenever a person they're following Tweets, ensuring that they stay in contact and communication with that person. **So as you can see, social media outlets can help you do things like notify your entire list of a special sale, or an event or discount intended only for your Twitter followers.**

But it's important to remember that these are *not* places to overtly sell your products or services. They're more useful for you simply as a way to stay in touch with your list. In fact, in many cases if you try to actively sell, you'll get kicked off the site — or the people you're trying to sell to will click one button and completely ignore you. So be careful in how you implement your social media communications, or you may find that no one is listening, no matter how much you're talking.

Do it the right way: share lots of interesting stories and useful information. Do the same thing you would in print or in person. There's no difference, except that now you're also using these social media outlets to build a connection with your customers. As I've pointed out previously, that's ultimately the goal here: **to build relationships with customers and prospects that let them get to know you, trust you, and want to do business with you.** This will serve you well, and as long as you maintain and carefully cultivate those relationships, you can build a nice list of people you can turn to immediately with your new products and services, so you can build your business and make more money.

Grab and Hold On!

Since decades before the Internet, we marketers have advised our students to reach out and capture as much information about a potential customer as possible. You've got to record each person's name and address, phone number, fax number, cell phone number, and now their Facebook and Twitter addresses if you can get them. **Grab and hold onto everything you can; store it in an expandable computer database, such as an Excel spreadsheet.** You never know what kind of medium will develop and become popular in the future; look at how Pinterest is spreading. **You need to find every possible way to stay in touch—and you need to update this contact information on a regular basis.**

This brings us to email. **If you've got a relatively small list of only a few hundred customers or prospects, you can use your own e-mail program to send them notices directly from your own computer.** These days, a lot of people are getting Gmail accounts for that, because you can have separate Gmail accounts for business and personal e-mail. Hotmail and Yahoo! are also fine; or perhaps you have your own domain through your local Internet service provider. Whatever the case, you're not going to have a problem sending out a few hundred e-mails at a time.

I recommend that you remember to use the Blind Carbon Copy (BCC) option so you don't expose all of your customer

---

addresses to everybody else. It's easy to forget this, but there are lots of good reasons for striving to keep it in mind. When you use the BCC field, the individual people who receive the email won't see the addresses of everyone else who sees the email. The BCC field hides them. So if you've got 500 customers and you put their addresses all in the BCC field, it will e-mail all 500—but the individual recipients won't know who else got the message. **They'll only see that** *they* **got it. If nothing else, this makes it seem as if you're contacting them alone, that they're special to you—and they should be, since they help pay your bills!**

Also, you don't want them all to see each other's e-mail addresses because, first of all, that's private information. Each person gave you that e-mail address in confidence. Even more to the point, if you put the addresses in the CC field and someone replies by hitting the "Reply All" button, EVERYBODY gets their reply... and it starts getting annoying as you receive replies from people you don't know, and wonder why you're getting all this mail. Well, it's because the person who sent you the message didn't BCC their original message. **So be sure to use the BCC field when emailing to your list.**

Now, suppose you have far more than a few hundred emails to send, and you want to do so easily and in a professional way. **There are several options, like getresponse.com and awebber.com. There are even services like Constant Contact that will manage your e-mail list for you, and help you get set up to send regular newsletters.** But unless you have thousands of e-mail customers, generally speaking that's not going to be necessary.

I will say this: if you have a lot of fans on Facebook, for example, you can send messages directly to their email addresses via Facebook (and the emails will appear in the Facebook message feature, too). **But again, one of the things you have to be cautious about these days is that people are getting tons of spam; they have much more e-mail than they can pay attention to.** A few years ago, the government enacted the so-called "Canned Spam Act" that was supposed to decrease spam... but it only increased it as the spammers found ways around the filters and penalties. So we're all getting hammered by e-mail.

Oftentimes, users have to be expecting and looking for an e-mail for it to get through and be read. **Therefore, if you're marketing via e-mail, you should build an "opt-in" list of people who *want* to get e-mails from you.** Don't just slam them with e-mails they don't want to read; you won't get anywhere. Even if they've given you permission to send them e-mails, keep your messages short and pertinent, and you'll find they get read more thoroughly and more often. And speaking of Facebook and other social media, people are more likely to view those emails favorably, because they're coming from people they consider friends or fans, someone they want to hear from.

On Facebook, you can drive people to your "Fan" page and get them to "Like" you by offering them something. So instead of just putting a banner up that says, "Like us on Facebook," as some businesses do, give them a reason why they should. Tell them something like, "We have exclusive offers for our Fans. Go to our Fan page and Like us, and we'll start sending you those offers." All they have to do is click a button; they don't have to opt into anything, they just Like you.

You can run contests, too. I've heard of one Bed and Breakfast that had a contest in which the person who got the most of their friends to Like that page won a free three-night stay.

That's an effective strategy, and it's a great way to interact with your fans—i.e., your customers and prospective customers. **Give them a reason to Like you. Make sure you stay in contact, run contests, interact with them, answer questions and issues, ask questions, upload videos.** Make it a lively Fan page, so people constantly want to see what you're uploading instead of "Unliking" you later on.

Get Used to It!

The Internet is here to stay—despite the negative things some people have to say about it. And I'll be honest: I've had a lot of negative things to say about it myself. Yet despite my strong feelings about it, I know there's no point in burying my head in the sand and pretending it doesn't exist. **The Internet is here, it's reshaped our lives, and it's certainly reshaped how we do marketing.** Business owners who ignore it or refuse to adapt to the Internet world are screwing themselves and killing their business.

On the other hand, a lot of people think the Internet is EVERYTHING. That's not true either. The reality is somewhere between the two extremes. **The 'Net provides a versatile way for you to establish, solidify, and maintain long-term relationships with customers,** whether through the use of blogging, social media, a static website, or the claiming of your site on Angie's List and similar sites (and never assume you don't have one). All these are good ways to attract new prospective buyers.

So make the Internet a part of your overall marketing mix, and balance out your Internet marketing with other forms of marketing—direct response marketing, space ads, broadcast ads, and the like, whatever mix seems workable

and affordable to you.

My wife runs a pet boutique that Chris Lakey and I have had a hand in getting up and running. They do dog grooming, and sell pet food and specialty items to affluent pet owners who are willing to spend lots of money on their furry "children." I think they're doing a pretty good job of it, and one secret of their success is that they hold a huge number of events in order to stay in touch with their customers—three or four a month. Most of their customers never show up for these events, and that's fine. But some do, and both sides of the equation benefit greatly. If nothing else, it's a part of the boutique's USP—one way they differentiate themselves from similar businesses (See Chapter 2).

For most businesses, any communication they have with their customer is all about selling, selling, selling. The problem with that approach is that after a while, the customers can build up an immunity towards it, and just tune it out. They don't want to hear about your next sale, because they just don't care. This is where one of the Internet's strengths can really serve you. **The Internet works best for indirect selling, and I think that's where your focus needs to be.** Do things that promote your business in more of an altruistic fashion, whether that means establishing yourself as an expert, writing articles for publication on the web, or publicizing your events, as my wife is doing. They come up with all kinds of crazy, goofy reasons to host these events, to get people into their store and exposed to their products and services. You can also use the 'Net to promote a wide variety of informational products I'll discuss in more detail in the next chapter.

Incidentally, hosting events like my wife's store does can easily spill over to media outside the Internet. **The local newspaper always gives them free advertising, since part of**

the newspaper's role is to tell their readers about any upcoming events. It's all fine and altruistic, less sales than service, but free events can also serve you in an indirect way by making people like you.

Again, the Internet's here to stay—so even if you're cynical and bitter about the Internet, don't let that screw up your chances of profiting from it. **If you refuse to move forward with the rest of the world, you're just shooting yourself in the foot.** Even if you hate the Internet, you've got to get your arms around it and stay on top of all of the new stuff as it comes out, the new Angie's List or Facebook or Twitter or Google+.

Five or ten years from now, other services will probably have replaced or superseded all of the specific websites I've talked about in this chapter; but the principle remains the same. **You've got to stay current, and take advantage of everything those new services happen to do—whatever that may be.** Read and reread this chapter multiple times, and think carefully about this. If you're not using social media, blogs, email, and whatever else is going to be invented five years from now and flash through the Internet like wildfire... well, if you're not keeping up with it, you really are hurting your business.

CHAPTER NINE:

Module #8: Using Information to Build Your Business

I believe this module, #8, is the most exciting in this book. I absolutely love information marketing, as do most of my colleagues—and I'm convinced that you'll love it too. It's infinitely versatile, fun, creative, extremely profitable, and highly addictive. **The key here is that when you mix information marketing with the strategies in the other nine Modules in this program, you make it virtually impossible for anyone to successfully compete with you.**

I know that sounds like hype, but it's not: if you really catch the vision here (assuming I do a good enough job of explaining it!), you'll become the competitor that everyone fears and envies the most. They'll be powerless to stop you, because this truly is your edge in the marketplace— an almost unfair advantage for those who really know how to cash in on information. The only problem here is that I could do a full book just on information marketing (and I have!) and still not cover all that my colleagues and I have learned about it over the years.

A Winning Formula

Top-notch information marketing is crucial for virtually any business these days, because as I've pointed out before, modern consumers are skeptical about everything they hear. They have good reason to be. They're afraid of getting scammed, and they're afraid of making the wrong choice when going to *any* business.

When you provide them with compelling, useful information, you help them more easily choose you, since providing that information positions you as an expert in your field. Most business owners miss out on this aspect of marketing, because they tend to focus on whatever it is they're doing to make a living: heating and air conditioning, real estate, landscaping, bookselling, or whatever it may be. They home in on actually providing the product or service, rather than combining it with information marketing. That's understandable, but the truth is that developing an information product that helps people in your target market, and educates them on how to select a provider or how to do something related to whatever you're selling, can benefit you greatly because it *does* position you as an expert. **You instantly have more credibility than your competitors, so prospects feel more comfortable selecting you to buy the product or service from.**

That said, let's start with a simple but very effective formula for writing compelling information that will attract the best prospects in your market. **Begin with a formulaic headline that starts with a number; for example, 3, 7, or 10.** I personally like the number 7. So it might be X Mistakes To Avoid When Doing Y (or Buying Y), where X is your number and Y is the category of product or service the customer's looking for. **It's a simple fill-in-the-blank formula, but you can use it to write some really amazing and compelling information products.** Here are a few headline examples using the Number 7:

- 7 Mistakes to Avoid When Planning Your Wedding

- 7 Mistakes to Avoid When Landscaping Your Lawn

- 7 Mistakes to Avoid When Buying a New Home

- 7 Mistakes to Avoid When Selling Your Home

If somebody's planning a wedding and spending tens of thousands of dollars on it, don't you think they'd like to know the seven costly mistakes they need to avoid? Absolutely! It's compelling. It's like you're holding out a secret they've *got* to know, otherwise they'll make mistakes that might cause problems on their wedding day. As you can see from the other examples, the headline is compelling in just about any form.

Of course, you can beef this up with a few modifiers. For example, you might write the third example as "7 Killer Mistakes to Avoid That Could Cost You Thousands of Dollars When Buying A New Home." **The key here is understanding that we human beings fear loss much more than we desire gain.** If you give somebody the opportunity to choose between a) gambling $100 for the chance of gaining $100 more, or b) holding onto $100 they already have, in most cases they'll choose the second option.

Therefore, what you have to do is create information that hits that hot button of loss—their fear of making a costly mistake. **People are compelled to learn more about these mistakes just so they won't make them.** If someone's planning a wedding or intends to spend a lot of money landscaping their lawn or even more money buying or selling a home, believe me—they want to know what costly mistakes they might potentially make.

Here's another secret that will help make your "Mistake Information" product even more compelling. **One of the mistakes to avoid (of however many you choose) should be**

How To Avoid Scam Artists In Your Industry. Going back to the wedding planning, you could have something like, "How To Avoid Wedding Planner Scams." With the other examples, it should be "How To Avoid Being Scammed by Landscapers," or "How To Avoid Being Scammed By Realtors" (the last one works for both buyers and sellers). So you've got another little fill-in-the-blank formula there: "How to Avoid Being Scammed by Z", where Z is a category of service provider in your industry.

Here's why this is so crucial: **If you're revealing the secrets that scam artists use, then you've just positioned yourself as somebody who is obviously *not* a scam artist, right?** A scam artist wouldn't reveal the secrets of being a scammer, would they? So you've additionally proven to the prospect that you're trustworthy. You're the person who protects them from scammers by showing them how to avoid those unscrupulous people. Simply by including that information, you've ramped up your credibility another notch, making your prospect more likely to want to do business with you above and beyond anybody else.

Using that template, you can craft killer information products that people will feel they absolutely must have before they spend any money buying the product or service you've discussed; and many will then be compelled to do business with you, because immediately, they feel like they're dealing with an expert. **Everyone wants to do business with an expert, and this is a simple way to establish yourself as one.**

One of the reasons I like information marketing so much is because you can create formulas like this to guide your copywriting and other business essentials, or otherwise adopt or adapt one of the many existing formulas out there. These are proven models; and as you become more aware of this marketing strategy, you'll start to see, **whenever you look around, that many of the smartest, most successful marketers are using formulas like this one.** These are the perceived experts in their particular marketplaces.

As I've discussed previously, both in this module and others, it's crucial that you do everything you can to be seen as an expert in your industry. This is one way to get there... or at least to serve as a beacon that helps your prospects navigate toward you. **They'll be attracted to your business because you've already provided value to them, before they even paid you a cent.** Simple reports and information products, provided at no cost, can quickly set you apart from all those competitors who do nothing more than offer them something for sale, however cleverly done. **This is a great way to build relationships with your customers—to get them to like you, trust you, and realize that you're the expert you are.**

The ultimate purpose of your free information product should be to point them to you. Ostensibly, your information product may educate them on how to do something, or it might warn them away from specific mistakes; but in reality, what you're doing is showing them hard it is to go it alone, and why they should trust you to take care of it for them. **So you do a little education, you do a little selling, and you use that information to attract people to you and, ultimately, to get them to do business with you.** The great thing about it is that it's so formulaic, just about anyone can do it. All you have to do is come up with a list of 3, 5, 7, or 10 things. It's just that simple—and it gets simpler the more often you do it.

Plus, this is a way for you to sell things to people without them feeling like they're being sold. Remember: people love to buy things, but they hate to be *sold* anything. What's the difference? Simply this: **when people make the choice to buy, they feel empowered.** They feel they're coming to you—that it's their choice to buy. When they feel they're being sold to, they feel you're chasing them, and that just makes them want to run.

And here's another point I'd like to emphasize: when you put a product like "7 Mistakes To Avoid When Buying New Carpet" together, the only people who are going to respond to it—and I do mean the *only* people—are the ones who are looking for new carpet. Period; case closed. If your report is titled "7 Mistakes To Avoid When Hiring A Plumber," then only people thinking about hiring a plumber are likely to read it. **By targeting your market so specifically, you're bringing qualified prospective buyers to you, educating them on why you're the best choice, and thereby separating yourself from your competitors.** This is the first stage in building that all-important relationship with the prospect. Do this right, and your competitors can't touch you. You become the competitor they fear or envy the most—or both.

So; having told you that, you may be thinking, "Well, what's the fastest and easiest way I can do this?" **In my opinion, it's to record the information in audio format and have it transcribed.** This method obviates one of the most common objections I hear when I tell business owners they should provide written information products for their customers: "But I'm not a writer... I'm a plumber," or "I do heating and AC."

I respond, "Make it simple. You know the most common mistakes, so outline them. If you're an expert in your industry, then you can probably list dozens. Just take the top 7 or 10, create a list, and then talk about them into a tape recorder." **Once you've**

got that recording, you can have it transcribed fairly inexpensively. You can find transcriptionists on a global jobs site like Elance, or you can hire a local transcriptionist if you know where to find one. Then have that transcribed information edited to take out the "ums" and "ahs." There are plenty of editors who can smooth your transcriptions out, and they're everywhere on the Internet. **Once they're done, you have an information product you didn't have to sit down in front of your computer to write, but one that's still filled with your expertise.** So don't let the "I'm not a writer" excuse stop you. You can record your information, have it transcribed and edited, and still provide the same high quality information product that people want—and it's fast, simple, and easy.

My mentor, Russ von Hoelscher, is an expert at teaching people how to do certain things and avoid others by providing useful information products. He's been involved in information marketing for decades, and has written some very detailed work on this topic, including books like *How To Get Rich Selling Information By Mail*, *How To Get Rich Buying and Selling Real Estate*, *How To Make $500 a Day Selling Information*, and *How To Make A Fortune on the Information Super-Highway: An Internet Opportunity Course*. As you can see, in addition to teaching people which mistakes to avoid, he also specializes in "How To" subjects.

People love learning "How To" secrets, which makes this type of information product very powerful in terms of leading into the information you're selling. Russ has used this method to develop information products for clients as well as himself. For example, he once wrote a product called "10 Simple Ways To Get The Most Money When You Sell Your Home" that a realtor gave away free in a booklet form, ultimately to get more clients to list and sell their homes with them. Other examples include "How To Quickly Erase Bad Credit" for a credit repair agency, and "A Smart Investor's Gold and Silver Buying Guide" for a coin dealer Russ worked with many years ago, along with "How To Sell Your Gold and Silver Coins at the Highest Price."

Regardless of the field you're in, you can tailor this formula to your needs. **It works for local markets as well as national ones; so whatever you do, realize that there are ways to tailor-make a "How-To" product to your needs.** It may be just a simple booklet or report, but it shows people you're an expert in your field—and you'll give them the best possible experience when they buy from you. Almost any business can do this, though you may have to think and plan for a while to determine your best approach.

Again: if you don't feel you can do it yourself, then record it, then go onto Elance or Craigslist and hire someone to transcribe and edit it. Each step may cost as little as $50-200, which is very cheap for this type of service—and very much worth the cost, since you're tapping the transcriptionist's or writer's expertise, as certainly as your customers tap yours. It's a remarkably easy way to boost your credibility as someone who possesses great knowledge, a person whom they want to do business with. **You don't have to specialize in selling information to make money with information; you can use it as a giveaway, to draw customers to the services that earn you your real money.**

Your information products don't have to be huge, as long as they provide good, useful information. Even a four-fold brochure or a 12-page booklet can still rev up your business. **Just tell the truth, be very open with people, and they'll realize you're telling them something that's to their benefit.** Give them the best information you've got, and that will sell them on your other products or services.

Profiting on "How To"

"How To" information always makes the best information products, because people are very interested in learning how to do things. And it doesn't always have to be free; this applies equally to information products you can sell. I know of a copywriter who spent months writing an entire course on how to write sales copy to sell your product or service. He went into great detail on each step, providing examples of every psychological tactic he used and precisely how he achieved that step. He spent dozens of pages just discussing how to create a headline—and went to the same level of detail on guarantees, testimonials, and everything else. He then put it into a three-ring binder and sold it for $297 to business owners and entrepreneurs.

Well, that product was incredibly complex, and he painted a vivid picture of how the process of writing killer copy is incredibly time-consuming, and how you *really* only get good after decades of consistent writing. **It turns out that the $297 product was really a lead-in to his own copywriting services— that is, it convinced his customers that the process was so hard they needed him to do it for them.** He'd realized that oftentimes, people who need a good sales letter written would say to themselves, "Well, I'm sure I can do this myself. How hard can it be?" So they'd pay him $300 for his step-by-step course, they would get it, and it would land on their doorstep with a big thud.

Then they'd go through it, and see how absolutely complicated writing awesome copy was. He included his contact information with the book, of course, and it wouldn't be long before some of them would call him up and say, "What would it cost to have you write the sales letter for me?" He'd tell them it would cost $15,000; and the person would ask himself, "Am I going to spend 10 or 20 years learning to write the copy myself, or am I going to give this guy $15,000?" **Well, a significant percentage of everybody who bought the course chose the latter.**

So think about that when creating your "How-To" information. Don't hold anything back for fear that people are going to learn all your secrets. **Instead, over-explain. Give them more information than they want.** Tell them exactly what you're doing and how you learned and polished these skills over time. Emphasize that it's taken you years to get things just right, and that it's very easy to make a mistake if you don't know exactly what you're doing. **Go into minute detail—and what ultimately might happen is that your "How-To" information might convince the reader that instead of doing it themselves, they should just hire you instead.** Obviously, you're an expert who knows every detail by heart. They don't have time to learn it all; they just want it done for them. If you angle it right, your "How-To" info product can push people to hire you instead.

After all, you *are* an expert in your field. I think you need to focus on that reality when you're putting together your information product. **To succeed in any business, you have to be an expert; not just at the particular product or service, but in the biggest benefits your prospects are looking for.** What kind of pain are they in? What kind of solutions do they need to ease that pain? What kind of problems do they have that you can help them solve?

Start by answering those questions to the best of your

ability, and let those answers guide you as you develop your information products. If you're in the financial industry and sell a product or service that helps people develop better portfolios, then you're probably dealing with people who are trying to get their 401(k) or investment account to perform better than the market has been doing lately. They're looking to make more money with their investments, or they're worried about losing their nest eggs. In such a case, you might come up with information products that address those concerns, such as "How To Safeguard Your Portfolio," "How To Out-Perform the Market by 13%" or whatever the case may be—depending upon whether their concern is making more money with an aggressive investment stance, or safeguarding their retirement accounts against disaster.

Use your information product to answer or address your marketplace's biggest fears, challenges, obsessions, and worries—the concerns that keep them up at night. That's the kind of information they find most valuable. You can give that information away, or you can sell it; the direction you take depends on your ultimate goal. In either case, you've got to start by figuring out what they're afraid of, and what their biggest questions and challenges are. From that knowledge will come the ideas for the information products they'll be interested in. **Once you start down this path, you'll find that there are endless ways you can deliver the information they're desperate for.** I'll go over a few of those in more detail later on.

Fishing for Whales

Chris Lakey and I once helped a financial advisor with his marketing, and he kept telling us that he was looking for the "whales" in his marketplace. By "whales" he meant people who had a lot of money to invest and were, in fact, actively investing—but who suffered from the delusion that they knew best, and could do it all themselves. So Chris suggested that he develop some information products that taught them all his greatest secrets in vast detail—just like the earlier marketer did with his $297 copywriting course. **The idea was to shock them, thus educating them on the fact that he *really* knows his stuff.** Then, after exhausting them with that huge information overload, he could offer them a "Done For You" service.

He was already doing live workshops and seminars, so we told him, "Record your next one. Give the audience all of your greatest secrets; hold nothing back. Blow them away with detail, demonstrating that you know a hell of a lot more about the field than they do, and that they should be giving you their money. Then offer them a follow-up service. *That's* how to catch the whales." Otherwise, you see, they're going to keep thinking they know better than you, the real expert, and can do it all themselves.

If it works for a financial advisor or a freelance copywriter, there's no reason that method can't work for you, too.

People tend to fall into certain habits, and then want to stay within the comfort zone they've created. Entrepreneurs and other small business owners are no different, and while some of our habits are good and productive, we often end up not pushing ourselves hard enough. To really make your business wake up and become exciting to you, and to become more profitable than ever, you have to break that everyday routine. **You have to get excited again about what you're doing. If you do that, then great things will happen.**

So step out of your comfort zone and move forward in a positive way, looking for new opportunities every single day. Those opportunities are out there; it's just that they fly by so quickly, and often we don't seem willing to capture the moment. **If we expect to maximize profits, we have to do more of that— and setting yourself up as an expert by selling people information is just one way to accomplish that.**

Selling information is thrilling! I've been doing it for more than 20 years; Russ von Hoelscher has been doing it for going on 40 years, and it's still exciting to him. Sometimes when you're working on a project, the hours fly by and you barely even notice. But you've enjoyed yourself. We have to break the routine of watching too much TV or spending too much idle time being passive and letting someone else entertain us. **We have to think, "What can I do that will benefit me and my business? What will pay big rewards?" And most of all, "What can I do that's** *fun* **to do?"**

When you're having fun with your work, it isn't long before the money follows. We all want to be entertained, and information products can help entertain your customers because you're making the subject exciting, sharing your passion for what you do. **So don't just sit back and be entertained; be the one TO entertain.** Sometimes that translates into giving the information away; in other cases it means packaging that information and selling it. Here at M.O.R.E., Inc, we've done all kinds of things with the information we've produced for our prospects and clients. **Most of the time when we give information away, it's because we're trying to use that information to build a relationship with a customer or prospect, hoping the giveaway gets us closer to making a sale.**

Incidentally, I hope it's not lost on you that this very product you're reading right now is an information product that we developed in order to share these strategies with you—one of many we've produced and sold in various forms over the years. **In fact, this book started out as an audio product before we had it transcribed and edited.**

Forty Options

Next, I want to share with you a list of 40 types of information products you can create—because I don't want you to think there's only one way to do it. **Information can take many formats; so hopefully this section will be something of an idea-starter for you.** You can get moving very quickly on some of these formats. One of the information products we produced in the past was titled something along the lines of *How To Create A Hot-Selling Information Product In One Day or Less*. In some cases, you can do it in as little as an hour, depending on the type of product and what you're trying to accomplish with it. We've done it ourselves; and later in this section, I'll discuss how you can do it.

I'm going to cover most of these topics very briefly—because the truth is, I could spend a whole book discussing them. At the very least, I want to get them on the record for your consideration. You can then chew on them a little, and explore the possibilities. **Think about how they might appeal to the people you're trying to attract; that should help you incorporate at least some of them into your marketing.**

Now, I want to give credit where credit is due, and explain that I'm actually reading a list out of a book by Robert Scrobe called *The Official Get-Rich Guide to Information Marketing*.

Robert has put together a good book on general information marketing and why it's such a great industry to be in—which is one of the reasons we're excited about being information marketers ourselves. So with no further ado, here are the 40 types of information products listed in his book.

THE FIRST CATEGORY IS PAPER AND INK:

1. **Reports**. Small documents, usually 1-8 pages long, addressing specific topics.

2. **Tip Sheets**. Usually these are one page long. Sometimes "How-To"; no fluff, just specific details on how to do something.

3. **Manuals.**

4. **Books.**

5. **A Boxed Set of Books**. Several books packaged together.

6. **Home-Study Course.** This could include several kinds of the information I'm talking about here, including any or all of the ones on this list.

7. **Tests and Quizzes**. In certain cases, tests and quizzes might interest your target market.

8. **Seminar or Speech Transcripts**. One way to turn an audio product into a paper-based one.

9. **Newsletters.**

10 **Back Issues of Newsletters.**

11. **Other Continuity Products**, like a Book-of-the-Month club.

12 **Sets of Cards**. These could be reminder cards, recipe cards, game cards, or anything else you could print on a card and sell by the package.

13. **Forms**. For example, time management systems or step-by-step processes.

14. **Posters.**

15. **Multi-Author Publications**. These are books or reports where several authors come together and produce a package of paper-and-ink products.

OUR NEXT SECTION IS AUDIO AND VIDEO. Most of the items I'll list here you can produce in either format. I'll start with audio.

16. **Live Recorded Speeches, Seminars, or Consultations**.

17. **How-To Instructions**, usually studio recorded.

18. **Interviews, Conversations, and Roundtable Discussions** (something very similar to what this book grew out of).

19. **A Collection of Radio Broadcasts**. You must own the rights to these.

20. **Interactive Audio with a Workbook**, similar to a home-study course.

21. **Subliminal/Self-Hypnosis**. For example, to help people

stop smoking or lose weight.

Items 22-25 consist of repeats of Items 16-19 for the "Video" category. For instance, you could have an audio CD of "How-To" topics, and you could also have a DVD of the same topics.

THE NEXT SECTION IS INTERNET PRODUCTS:

26. E-books.

27. Downloaded Information, whether written manuals, audio or video.

28. Membership Sites.

29. Structured Lessons. Simply a series of lessons delivered online or by email.

The last category is Miscellaneous Things:

30. Training Kits, used in the classroom.

31. Membership Sites.

32. Devices. Things like stress cards, concierge service cards, or other items that have specific purposes.

33. Plaques. Information products that say something like, "Congratulations—You Won an Award!"

34. Computer Software.

35. Packages containing a bunch of different information products.

36. Continuity Programs involving multiple information

products.

37. **Services**. Memberships attached to some kind of information-based service.

38. **Customized Information**. Information items created specifically for certain marketplaces.

39. **Private Label**. Information products privately labeled for others, so they can purchase a branded or a licensed version of that information to sell to their own customers.

40. **Licensed Information**. Proprietary information products that people must buy licenses for before they can republish them.

Personally, one of my favorite classes of information product is audio, mostly because audio can be converted to print very easily. Oh, you can go in the opposite direction too, but audio is easier to produce from scratch—because you can just talk. That's always easier than typing. There's much more work involved in writing a book from scratch than there is in just audibly discussing important things you're passionate about. In fact, you can talk for a long time if you're not careful; so when you're subject to a limited timeframe, you have to make sure you limit your discussions, in order to make sure you discuss everything you need to.

It's so easy to record audio these days. Handheld digital recorders are everywhere, and you can even record straight into your computer sometimes. The Apple operating system actually has spoken-word integration built into it, so that you can transcribe audio directly into a Microsoft Word document. This lets you record an audio product and at least the first steps of a written one simultaneously. **The document would probably have to be edited a little to make it more readable, but in many cases, you can sell the unedited transcript exactly as is, word for word.**

Whether you prefer audio, video, or the written word, consider those 40 different types of information products and think about how to apply at least a few of them to your marketplace. Some may be easier than others for you to adapt to your needs, depending on what you're trying to accomplish. **Remember, start with the biggest benefits your prospects are looking for, based on their biggest problems and greatest challenges, then create applicable products you can either sell or give away as lead generation items.**

I've provided such a wide variety of examples here because I don't want you to assume that all I'm talking about are brochures and reports. **There are so many ways you can get information into the hands of the people you want to do business with.** You might even come up with a few I haven't mentioned here. For example, you can do a recorded hotline or tele-seminar where you train people on the benefits of Lasik, copywriting, plumbing, or whatever you happen to sell. You could do blog posts, as I've emphasized before. You can post PDFs and online audios on your company website. **The information marketing industry is massive, and there are many different ways to disseminate information to your particular market.** You can easily advertise multiple information products generating leads on the Internet, in the newspaper, in magazines, from newsletters, and more. **The more tools you use—that is, the more information products you put into the marketplace—the more leads you'll get.**

Shock Tactics

If you really want to shock the people in your marketplace, I suggest creating multiple information products and publishing them using multiple media, so you dwarf your nearest competitor in terms of all the leads and clients you generate. It's not all that hard to do, since most business owners do little more than hang up a shingle and wait for customers to find them.

This is what most restaurateurs do, for example. Now, if they have a great location, they may do well in spite of themselves. Otherwise, they're likely to flop, because the restaurant business is highly competitive. Ah, but some restaurants have started going beyond using websites to post their menus; they're also adding video inserts where they display all the elements of a multi-course meal. When you do something like that to make the food look extra enticing, you're inevitably going to draw in customers. **And don't assume that this works just for restaurants; you can (and should) use your website in any type of business to entice people to come do business with you.**

So while you may prefer to use print media, billboards, and the like in your marketing strategy, realize that the Internet is too big to ignore (see Chapter 8). **Use as many elements of it as you can; if you use them wisely, it's not going to cost you much money to project your business to your prospects in a concentrated way.** Don't let the list of 40 information products I presented a few pages back overwhelm you.

Instead, think of the list as the marketing equivalent of a dinner buffet. One quick look demonstrates that there's a whole spread of options for you; and obviously, you can't sample them all. **So you don't try; you pick out your favorites, and maybe you choose a few things that you've never tried before** to see how they taste. You might grab a steak and fried chicken, add some French fries and corn, maybe some asparagus spears or artichoke hearts. Then there are all those desserts to choose from. You take what you like and eat the rest, and hope your eyes aren't bigger than your stomach.

Well, our buffet consists of more than 40 different types of information products. Most people won't use all of them; so why should you? **Don't be overwhelmed by the enormity of the options available. Just pick the things that you like best—the things you think (or know) you could get excited about.** Maybe paper-and-ink products excite you. Maybe audio information turns your crank. Maybe making DVDs interests you most. **Whatever the case, choose something you can wrap your mind around and think your customers and prospects would be interested in.** Realize that our list isn't even exhaustive. There are all kinds of other ways to delivery information to your customers and prospects, whether you're selling it or giving it away. Just find one that sounds good to you; the others will be waiting in case you ever want to try them. You may not; it doesn't really matter.

All this choice is what makes information marketing so great. You've don't have to just pick one way to market. You don't have to pick the way everybody else is doing it, because then you'll get the same results as everybody else, which usually aren't very good. **Look over the choices, pick one thing you can get excited about, and get moving.**

Superstar

Some of my fellow marketers may disagree with my next point, but I think you need to set out to be a celebrity in your field. **Do whatever you can to be the hero, the rock star, of whatever you do.** Become the talking head that radio and TV stations go to automatically. If you pay close attention, you'll realize that there are business people who are always on the TV news, on the radio, or in the newspaper. The media goes to them because those people have stuck their necks out and said, "I'm the expert!"

Information products let you do this like nothing else. In fact, they can be self-reinforcing, because whenever you have an event like a live seminar or workshop, the newspapers, radio, and TV stations will often be glad to give you free publicity. They're looking for news, so send them a written press release that, if they're a print or Web publication, they can use as is, or if they're a broadcast station, alerts them to the event. They're looking for content, and this makes their job easier. **You're not asking them for anything, really; you can't take that position at all.** You've got to realize you're doing those media outlets a service, no matter what medium you're dealing with.

You've got to make yourself into the local hero, the hometown celebrity everyone looks to as an authority. **Take the best of the ideas I hope I've sparked in you with this module and put them in play.** Do some seminars or workshops, deliver a good presentation where you teach people something, create audio CDs (those are easy), or make some DVDs. You could record panel sessions with other business owners outside of your market area, and form productive alliances.

Let's say you've got a pet boutique; that's one of the

businesses Chris and I are involved with. Well, you could develop an information product with other pet boutique owners from all over the country, and share that product. You might be one of 9 or 10 different experts putting it together, making your job very easy. Depending on your market, you may even be able to do joint venture marketing with experts outside your marketing area.

Let's face it—there's a ton of written stuff already on the Internet. **It's loaded with research material. You can take all this material and synthesize it into something new by taking a fact from this source, adapting another from that one, and so on, as long as you put it all into your own words and present it your own way.** That's another fast, simple and relatively easy way for you to develop information products bearing your name and face, thereby becoming a hero of the marketplace. Now, I realize some people are going to have problems with that, because they don't *want* to stick their necks out. We've been raised since we were little children not to be too proud, and not to put ourselves ahead of other people. Well, I say that's nonsense!

As a marketer, you've got to learn how to get beyond that. Hey, somebody's got to do it! If it's not you, it's going to be somebody else. **There's nothing wrong with sharing your expertise; and it's up to you to decide that you have that expertise.** No one's going to magically fly in and anoint you as an expert. *You* have to tell people you're an expert, and then you have to prove it. Sometimes you do it through your actions, and sometimes you do it through a direct self-identification—where you tell people, without hesitation, that you're the expert in your specialty. Because you are. **If you know more than the average person in any field, you have expertise. If you have expertise, you're an expert, period.**

Now, this doesn't mean you have to be perfect. Too many people mistakenly believe they have to know everything there is to know about an entire industry before they can call themselves an expert, and that's not the case. **People want to know what you know if you know even a little more than they do in a particular field. Give them the benefit of that information.** Don't worry about being the world's greatest expert; you just have to have some expertise that other people want.

Most people don't know very much about most things, you see. That's not intended as a put-down; it's just reality. Many people know a lot of general information, but when it comes to being an expert in most subjects, they can't claim the title. **So if you're a little more knowledgeable than they, you're an expert from their perspective.**

Take advantage of that. **You can't make a living as a timid salesperson or a shy marketer; you have to be aggressive.** If you're not, someone else will be—and they'll claim your market share. **To maintain or, better yet, increase your slice of the pie, you need to go out there and use every single advantage you can.** So why not be the celebrity? Why not go position yourself as an expert?

You might have seen doctors field questions on various TV shows. Well, those doctors probably have the same expertise as many other doctors—but all of a sudden those TV doctors are elevated as celebrities, for no more reason that they shared their expertise in a popular medium. Similarly, certain gardeners are elevated to celebrity status by their little segments on TV shows. So if you're looking to plant a garden or want to have the best lawn in town, you turn to such a person—because you know they're an expert. How do you know that? Well, they're on TV, so they *must* be an expert. **That perception brings more business to their nurseries.**

You can do similar things in your own marketplace to give yourself celebrity status. You don't have to get on the TV or radio to do that; you can position yourself as an expert in other media as well. Those free information booklets I discussed earlier are a good way to do it, or you can contribute a column to your local newspaper or create and distribute a newsletter to position yourself in the prospect's mind as the one to turn to.

Make it known that you're happy to do radio interviews or go on TV shows. Make it known that you're available for print interviews. Let people know they can contact you if they have any questions about your field. **Start positioning yourself that way, and people will come to know you as the expert in your industry. Again, don't feel you have to know it all.** Just start calling yourself an expert, start acting like an expert, start carrying yourself like expert—and people will realize that you are, in fact, an expert.

If you can't see yourself speaking before a group or appearing on radio or TV, then you're not likely to succeed in this effort. So if you can, become a member of a local Toastmaster group. **Toastmasters is the best tool you can use to become comfortable with appearing and speaking in public.** There are 1,000+ Toastmaster groups in the U.S. alone, so there's probably one in a city or town near you. It's an inexpensive organization to join.

Basically, you practice public speaking. And that's a great thing, because public speaking scares the hell out of people; according to polls, about 98% of us are deathly afraid to do it. In Toastmasters, you speak, people critique your performances, and you critique theirs. **I've seen people absolutely bloom in this environment.** People who couldn't put three words together at the beginning, who were shaking when they found themselves standing at a microphone in front of a group of 30 people—six months later, they were accomplished speakers, ready to appear on TV or radio. So think about joining Toastmasters. If you can acquire some expertise at public speaking, and combine that with your expertise in your particular field, then nothing's stopping you!

Personally, it took me about 10 years to get over my fear of public speaking—and even now, I sometimes feel nervous during the first few minutes of a talk. Well, let's be honest—sometimes I'm frozen stiff. But I soon loosen up, because I know that to succeed at a profitable yet scary field like information marketing, you have to push through your fear, step outside your comfort zone, and take risks. Becoming the local celebrity in your field is a stretch for most people. **So approach it from an altruistic direction; do your best to serve the people in your field. Let that be your primary focus;** you're not just out there strutting your stuff, trying to show off. That's not the right way to handle it.

Tighten your focus to a narrow beam, and address, in the best way you can, the main problems your prospects have— the things that keep them awake at night and cause them to seek out companies like yours. What are their biggest fears, failures, and frustrations? How can you help them the most? When you get right down to it, that's what an information product really does, and that's what it's for. It's all about them, not you.

So it's somewhat ironic that on one hand, if you develop a bunch of information products, you'll end up as a celebrity in your marketplace. But on the other hand, it's not really about you flaunting your ego. **Celebrity is a useful tool that lets you help people, thereby giving them as much as you can of what they need.** The more altruistically you can do this, the more your prospects will think, "Man, I want to do business with this person." This works like a charm—but few of your competitors will ever do it. Those who do typically just scratch the surface of what's possible.

But if you do this right, you can get very, very wealthy indeed. You can become the leader of your marketplace by simply throwing yourself into it. **Get on the Internet and start searching on information marketing.** There's a wealth of information out there. **Let yourself get excited, work on positioning yourself as an expert—and you'll have a tremendous advantage over your competitors.** It's as simple as that.

CHAPTER 10:

Module #9: Work *On* Your Business, Not *In* It

We've all heard the business buzz-phrase that goes, "Work smarter, not harder." **Well, true business success comes from working both smarter *and* harder, not one or the other. To accomplish this, you have to focus on the most important aspects of your business, the ones that only you can do or that you do best, while delegating everything else.** This is the heart of the principle of working *on*, rather than *in*, your business. The world's most successful business people are all great delegators. They've trained themselves to work effectively through other people. You can't let brushfires or little things that other people can do more cheaply steal your precious time away.

If you handle this principle right, you'll end up working fewer hours and making more money. You'll wield enormous leverage, allowing you to take your business to the next level. You'll jump ahead of your competition, simply because most business owners suffer under a tremendous disadvantage: they're technicians, not entrepreneurs. They actually *do* the work in their business. If they own a bakery, they're baking cupcakes. If they own an accounting firm, they're doing the client's books; and if they own a restaurant, they're doing the cooking or running the front.

Unfortunately, none of those activities is scalable, and that's where they run into trouble. **When you're a technician, your**

business's potential growth is limited by the number of hours you can put into your business. You can do the best marketing in the world, but you'll never be able to serve more than a few people at a time.

Once upon a time, a salesman named Ray Kroc bought a little restaurant called McDonald's and, over time, built it into a huge corporation. Now, what if Ray Kroc had run that restaurant himself? What if he was the one behind the grill flipping the burgers, or taking orders up front, or sweeping, or even just managing his employees as they did all those things? If that had been the case, he probably never would have opened up another restaurant. He wouldn't have had the time. However, in this reality, there are over 31,000 McDonald's restaurants worldwide, with 1.5 million employees.

The only way Ray Kroc was able to accomplish that was because he created systems where he personally never had to be in any individual restaurant for it to work properly. He created such easy-to-use systems that even teenagers—and in some cases really unexcited teenagers—can run restaurants that produce millions of dollars in sales annually. **With the systems he perfected, he had the ability to duplicate that first restaurant over and over, tens of thousands of times.**

That's a prime example of what it means to work *on* your business instead of *in* it. **You have to build robust business systems that work so well you don't need to tend them constantly.** Eventually, all the little systems you create fit together to form an overall system that generates profits. It may include a marketing system to consistently draw in prospects and convert them to buyers, joined with a product/service delivery system that gives each customer the same high-quality experience every time they do business with you, regardless of who they deal with. Add in a customer service system, an accounting system, a training system, and systems for everything else that needs to be done in your business, and they'll add up to the one big, conglomerate system which *is* your business.

Now it becomes scalable; now you can document all your systems, put that documentation into a binder, and hand it off to somebody to learn. After a while, they'll be able to run your business for you, or even start a new one that looks exactly like the one you're running right now. This idea was popularized by a fellow named Michael Gerber, who wrote a book all business owners should read: *The E-Myth*. **In his book, Gerber argues that most businesses should be systematized like a franchise, even if you don't plan on franchising.**

Here's why: first, it alleviates stress. When you systematize all parts of your business, you'll start getting more predictable results, instead of suffering through the roller-coaster ride of peaks and valleys so common to the small business. **Once everything is smoothed out, you won't have to worry about where customers are coming from and what's happening day-to-day.** You can then remove yourself from the business, which also alleviates stress, since your systems allow others to run the company for you.

Systematizing allows you to grow your business more easily, because you have more time to think about marketing and product/service development. You can more easily duplicate that successful business in additional locations, too. Then, if your business model proves successful, you can franchise. Every major mega-franchise success story started out as one business where the owner perfected their systems. Once they had it down pat, they

---

started to franchise it to other business owners.

There's an interesting example of this in the Dallas, Texas area, where my colleague Jeff Gardner lives. He recently moved from a place called Uptown, where there was a frozen yogurt place called Yummylicious. The gentleman who owned it really perfected his systems, and that business began making a lot of money. So he thought, "Maybe I should open a second location." He did, using his perfected system, and it too started making a lot of money. Then he had somebody come to him and say, "I really love your business. Are you franchising? Is there a way for me to buy into it?"

That opened up the owner's eyes to the franchise model. Now he owns quite a few Yummylicious shops, but he's also franchising them out to other people. They're happy and profitable because it's easy to translate his business model into reality. **He's making money, they're making money—it's a win-win situation.** So never just dismiss the idea of franchising your business, because after you systematize everything so that it can all run without you, you might realize how wonderfully it works and decide that you want to try your system in multiple locations.

It's important to understand, however, that it's not going to happen by magic. **You've got to work hard on the right things, avoiding everything else so that you free up enough time to focus on what matters.** If you spend all your time doing low-value tasks and handling all the brushfires, you're never going to find the time to spend on perfecting your systems. Instead of being a technician, pull yourself out of the mundane and focus on ways you can make it easy for anyone to do the daily work. **Your job is to step back, look at the big picture, and perfect and maintain the workflow process.** Tighten up everything so that you can hand the business off to someone else, who can then take the same steps repeatedly and get the same, predictable results each time.

The System Formula

Here's a quick strategy to help you move into this process of systematizing your business. **Step 1: outline everything that happens in your business.** That is, take your routines out of your head and put them down on paper. One way to simplify this effort is to ask yourself, "If I had to hand my business over to someone else in six months, what would they need to know to run it successfully?" Then start writing it down, dividing it up into different categories: marketing, product/service delivery, customer service, and all the other pieces required. You're going to be creating a manual of how to run your business. **That way, if you do have to hand it off to a manager, they're going to be able to handle it on their own without having to bug you constantly, and without you having to actually be there.**

Step #2: Once everything is down on paper, review it carefully and look for sticking points, problems, and other issues that repeatedly crop up. You'll note places where things slip through the cracks or slow you down. It's important that you identify those as you're creating this system, because you need your systems to run as smoothly as possible from the very beginning. **So actively search for issues, questioning your assumptions as you go, and look for solutions to those challenges.** Ultimately, your system has to be as perfect as possible, because think of it this way: as a business owner you have the ability to solve problems on the fly, but your employees aren't going to be able to do that. They're going to be looking for answers, and if you don't want them bothering you all the time asking for those answers, you've got to make sure you solve all the obvious problems from the very beginning.

Step 3: Test it out. Give your system to your employees; get their feedback. Ask them if you missed anything. Does something need to be added or reworked? **If so, get to work on it, and keep tweaking the system until your business is humming along without you.** Then you might even make the ultimate test: you might hire someone to replace you, to make absolutely sure that your employees are running through the system properly.

If that's too daunting for you right at the beginning, start slowly, decreasing the time you're working in the business. You might decide, "Instead of being here seven days a week, I'll take Sundays off." Once you've proved that works, you can take the whole weekend off, then three days a week off, and so on. Give it a little time and don't push too hard. **You can tell your managers you're still available by phone; this will help you discover where the breakdowns are in your system, while still allowing you to pull back.** Once you've rigorously tested the system and everything seems to be working, you'll have some scalability—the ability to really grow that business. This lets you focus on crushing the competition, which is a foundational principle of Ruthless Marketing.

The sad reality is that most businesses just don't have systems in place to allow the owner/operator to step out when he needs to. **So if you can do it, your competition is going to suffer as you take their market share—which you must do in order to take your business to the next level.** Stop wearing all the hats like everyone else does! Even if you enjoy it, it's just going to stifle you, because you don't have enough time in your day to even think about growing. I see this over and over in the businesses I deal with daily, especially service industries like gardening, lawn maintenance, plumbing, and the like.

Most of these people are working really hard in their businesses, but they're not working at all on making their businesses as productive as they can possibly be. Sometimes I'll strike up a casual conversation with these folks, and when they find out I'm a marketer they'll tell me, "I don't really need to do any marketing, because I'm busy all the time." They've got plenty of business and can't handle any additional clients... in fact, some already have a huge waiting list.

Well, it might seem good, at first glance, for a fencing contractor to have a three-month backlog—but it can also hurt his business if people don't want to wait. If he'd hire some more workmen, he could expand his business and make even more money, while being no more busy than before—and possibly even less so. **All he'd have to do was invest a little time in developing and testing some systems.** Surely he can shake loose an hour or two here and there in the evening, after it's too dark to work.

As someone who knows how much better such businesses could be doing if they would just implement the strategies I outline in this book, I often feel a sense of frustration when I talk to these people. They just don't get it. Yes, you can have what appears to be a very successful small business—and yet you can be working like a dog, be tired all the time, and have a backlog of work you just can't catch up on. Successful or not, the burnout rate for such businesses is high. **There *are* ways to work smarter, and they're the key to working on, rather than in, your business. Delegation is one of the most important,** because it allows you to have other people run all the daily functions while spending more time administrating and entrepreneuring.

That's how Eileen and I ran our business for the first 12 years or so. We were the perfect partners: she was excellent at day-to-day operations, while I handled the creative and marketing aspects. I didn't know just how good a job she was doing until I tried to take over for her after she stepped down due to health reasons. You see, I'd always thought, deep down, that I could do a better job at managing the business than she had; and boy, was I ever wrong. **For 2½ years, I tried everything I could to run the day-to-day operations at M.O.R.E., Inc.—and finally concluded I was the world's worst manager.**

I made every mistake in the book, no matter how hard I tried. I would come home from work every day absolutely exhausted. That's when I started getting all my gray hair, and when my hair started falling out. The worst part was, Eileen would ask me, "What did you do today?" and I couldn't think of a damn thing I'd done that was worthwhile, because I was putting out brushfires all day long. I was dealing with measly little crises from the minute I got there to the minute I left; it was just one thing after another. **I didn't enjoy the work; it was killing me. I wasn't doing the kind of work that I needed to do, either, which is the kind of work that only I can do—the kind that makes the biggest impact on our sales.** Eventually, I put an end to that by hiring a general manager.

The bottom line is, I know what I'm talking about. I see so many businesspeople doing the same thing. So let me emphasize this point: **just because you CAN do something doesn't mean that you SHOULD do it.** This applies to all levels of business life. **Other people can probably do it better than you for a lower cost, so delegate everything out so you can work *on* the**

business rather than *in* it. Do only the high-dollar things that only you can do, and systematize everything else so anyone can do the basics. That's a simple recipe for turning your business into a money machine.

So why don't more business owners do this? I think it's because they just don't think of it. I've heard this story from others; Jeff Gardner, for example. He'd been running his own small business for years before somebody recommended that he read *The E-Myth* by Gerber. That's when he realized that he wasn't the entrepreneur he thought he was, but only a technician of sorts. He was doing it all himself—all the copywriting, design, marketing, and all the little office tasks—and thinking of himself as entrepreneur just because he owned his own business. Then he realized that if he were to pass away or become disabled, there would *be* no business, because it wasn't systematized—as opposed to someone like Ray Kroc, whose business lives on decades after his death.

Just knowing this can be done is enough to shock some people out of the "many hats" syndrome. In fact, it can be completely mind-blowing for an owner who's been running their business for 20 or 30 years to realize, **"Oooh, so I should be treating this as something that I can walk away from—more like an asset than a job!"** And I think a lot of business owners do treat their businesses as jobs, rather than as stand-alone assets that can make them money regardless of whether they're tending them constantly or not.

True Intelligence

One of my hobbies—and forms of self-education, really—is to read biographies and autobiographies of great entrepreneurs, managers, and business owners. One of them was the late Henry Ford. Now, Ford wasn't a very well-educated man in classroom terms, but he was passionate about making automobiles and innovating new processes that made them inexpensive enough for the average American to afford... which, of course, expanded his personal fortune greatly. **He was a tremendous man who did a great deal for America.**

But because he was uneducated, spoke slowly, and wasn't a good speaker, some of the media people of the day considered him a backward hick. **His employees knew better, but he occasionally he made a slip that the press vilified him for.** Once he was talking to a reporter from *The Detroit News*, who asked him about certain car parts. He said something like, "Oh, we get those from North Dakota." And the guy asked him, "Do you know what the capital of North Dakota is?" (As if most Americans would know that!)

Ford said, "I think we get those parts from Fargo. Is that the capital?" The newsman said, "Bismarck is the capital!" He made a big deal of it, and asked Ford to name the capitols of all of the states in the Union. Ford said, "Well, I know Michigan's capital and a few others. New York City, I know..."

The newsman said, "New York City isn't the capitol of New York!" By then, he was convinced that Ford was damn stupid— completely forgetting that he'd built a huge company out of nothing, which a stupid man could never accomplish. Ford told the man and his colleagues, "Look here, I've had enough of this! I've got about a dozen college graduates on the floor below us. I'll bring a couple of them out and they'll tell you what the capitol of every state in the Union is. **I know how to build cars. I have people in place to take care of all the things that I *don't* know.**"

It's quite amazing that we often prejudge people as unintelligent because they don't pay attention to current events or to historical questions that are of no concern to them. But many of us who should know better make the same mistake. My mentor, Russ von Hoelscher, has told me of his experience with a man named Jay Greenstein, who ran the Minnesota News Corp. They distributed books, magazines, candy, and sundry items to bookstores and drug stores, liquor stores, and newsstands in the Minneapolis-St. Paul area. Russ got to know him pretty well, and says he was a nice, fun guy to be around... but Russ didn't consider him very smart.

Part of that was because Greenstein was interested in things like professional wrestling, and even gave the impression that he thought it was on the level, not just entertainment. That and other things caught Russ's attention and caused him to think, "This guy's making a ton of money—and I don't know how he's doing it!" **But as Russ got to know him better, he realized that Jay's true talent lay in surrounding himself with all kinds of sharp people: managers, accountants, and others who took care of the nuts and bolts that kept the company together.** It just goes to show that to be truly successful, you've got to have the right people on your team.

I've told you I'm one of the world's worst managers, and Russ says the same about himself. **On the other hand, we're both very good marketers.** But not being good managers has been a hindrance for both of us, because even though we've been successful and made tons of money, there's no question that we could have been far more successful if we'd been good managers, too.

But frankly, you can't do everything. To be super-successful, you really do have to have good people around you who can fill in the voids in your abilities. If you try to do it all, you're likely to louse up everything, or at least dull your own ability to profit. **Think of it this way: When you hire people who are smarter than you are, you're proving that at some level, you're smarter than *they* are.** That's what working on your business and not in it is all about: delegating as many of your weaknesses as you possibly can.

Skills Leverage

Most entrepreneurial types find it hard to delegate, because we have a hard time relinquishing control. When we're faced with something that needs doing, we tend to want to do it ourselves. There are practical reasons for that, including the old "if you want something done right you have to do it yourself" attitude.

But even if you *can* do the best job of it, you may be better off entrusting that job to someone else. Sure, you'll probably have to train them first, so there may be some time involved in delegating the task. Then, once they know how to do it, you'll have to trust that they'll do it correctly, and then you have to verify that they're doing so. There has to be some accountability process in place, which is one reason why we often avoid delegating. And yet, to be most productive, we have to look at the big picture.

Sure, there are advantages to doing it all yourself; yet in most cases, the advantages of delegation far outweigh those, because they allow you to spend more time working on your business. **Chances are that if you're doing too much in your business—if you're wearing all the hats yourself—you're probably not making as much money as you should be.**

The Dangers of Not Delegating

Jeff Gardner tells me he used to have the hardest time delegating things... until he took a closer look at his books. He hadn't taken the time to do so before because he was constantly busy, literally doing everything from creating the products to writing sales copy to doing the customer service on the phone, going to the copy center and getting products copied, packaging them up, and taking them to the post office. When he did look at the books, **he realized that he was making about a quarter-million dollars a year no matter what he did—and no matter how much marketing he managed to put out there.**

He realized then that he wasn't doing as good a job as he'd thought he was doing, and decided that if he ever wanted to break through a quarter-million a year, he needed to learn to delegate... whether he wanted to or not. **So he pushed himself to do so by creating duplicable systems.**

You need to do that with your own business. **Create robust systems for everything, systems that thrive with less than stellar effort.** Tell me: how many times have you gone into a McDonald's or a Subway, and thought that the person behind the counter was a superstar at their job, great at what they did and constantly smiling and attentive, almost like they owned the place? Not very often, I suspect, because people like that don't last long up front. They're soon in the back managing the crew, or even up higher, moving up through the ranks of the company. That's because the ordering, cashiering, and food preparation processes have been so highly systematized that disaffected youths can run them and still give people their food in a timely manner.

Delegation is crucial, especially if you're comfortable that you've put together systems that can thrive with less than the 110% effort that you would give them. Let's be honest: nobody is going to love your business like you do. To make real money, you have to be willing to let that worry go and create systems that anyone can use to produce positive, productive results.

Now, depending on your business type, some of this may not apply to you. You might have no choice about wearing most or all of the hats. But this isn't always the case. One of your family members might have an incredible financial sense and handle the basic day-to-day efforts far better than you can. My wife Eileen is an excellent example; she ran M.O.R.E., Inc. with precision and style without exhausting herself, which I couldn't do to save my life. I almost ran the company into the ground a number of times.

But now I've got some great people working for me, picking up the slack and covering for me where I'm weak. I'm a marketer, plain and simple. I can bring in the business like gangbusters, but I need help when it comes to the managing and customer service. I feel no shame in that; I understand my limits and know what I need to do to work around them. If you're in the same boat, I recommend you try to get as much help as you can—because God knows, you'll need it.

There's enormous power in working through other people; if not employees, then partners, temps, or even online contractors from sites like Elance. com. That's been one of our great hiring secrets here at M.O.R.E., Inc. They say you're supposed to hire slowly and fire quickly... but that usually doesn't happen. We use a lot of temporary helpers, and only 1 out of 10-15 is any good. Those are the folks we hire on full-time or go back to again and again.

Getting it Right

Earlier, I told you not to work either smarter or harder, but to do both. However, this won't get you far if you're not working on the right things. **Sometimes it's hard to separate what comprises working on the business rather than in it, and I believe that trips up a lot of us.** This is especially true in smaller, service-oriented businesses.

Here's a good example: Chris Lakey, my marketing director, has a man who mows his yard; with six kids at home, Chris finds it hard to mow himself. Now, this fellow does the job consistently, faithfully, and well; but he sometimes goes for weeks on end without getting paid. Chris is usually at the office when he mows, which on average is four times a month during mowing season. But if the lawn man doesn't catch Chris or his wife at home, he just shrugs and goes on about his business — because he's not only the guy who mows, he's also the guy who collects the money.

If Chris doesn't stay on top of him, he'll go a long time without billing. He's one of the people I look at and think, "Man, you could do so much better." **He could have a whole team of people all over the city doing yardwork for him, while he managed the business and took orders instead of doing the mowing, trimming, and all the other things no one else likes to do.** He could definitely benefit from this concept. He's working really hard, but he's working hard on the wrong things.

The same is true of the man who does Chris's landscaping. **He's really hard to get ahold of, because he's trying to do everything himself.** He's very good at what he does, too, so he's always overworked — and again, he's working hard on the wrong things. He could be working a lot smarter by putting all that energy into something more productive in the long-term, in terms of building and growing his business.

That's how it is with a lot of small business owners. No one would ever doubt their work ethic, but it's misapplied. Maybe this is where you are—and you're probably working harder than you'd work if you actually worked for somebody else. Maybe your family never sees you, you never go on vacation, or you never get to enjoy life because you're working too hard. If that's the case, the sad truth is that you've probably been working hard at things that aren't the most productive for your business. **So you have to change gears, which means you have to delegate—and give up some of that control.**

I also feel that entrepreneurs tend to be loners. Maybe we're a little eccentric; we tend to work best on our own, and don't mind doing it all ourselves. More often than not, we don't directly interact with many people. **We're often reluctant to ask for or seek help.** As a result, we end up wearing all the hats—and then we just keep doing it because that's how we've always done it.

Many small business owners start their businesses because they used to do the same kind of work for someone else, and they thought, "I've been making money for them; I might as well be making money for myself." So they get started and stay busy constantly, never realizing they could do even better, because it feels like the business is thriving. The calendar is booked for weeks, they have more business than they can handle, and enough money is rolling in. **But when you find yourself in this situation, you've essentially maxed out your capacity for making money. It's all time-based.** If you're not working, you're not making money. You've only got so many hours in the day you can work on or in the business; once your time is up, you have to wait until the next day. You've got to tell new prospects that you can only get them in three weeks from now, because you don't have any appointments available until then.

Whereas if you just changed your concept a little and had other people doing all that work for you, you might say, "I can have a team there next week," or "We're ending a project in the next 24 to 48 hours, so we can be there this Thursday. Would that work for you?" **At that point you're managing the company rather than trying to do it all. That's one example of maximizing your time by working on your business instead of working in it.**

It does requires you to engage in a little conceptual thinking, to look at your business model closely and decide how you can best implement some of these ideas; you may even have to retool your business model from the ground up. That said, **if you'll implement this principle and keep moving forward with it, I guarantee you'll find yourself making more money and with more free time and greater productivity.**

The Exception

There's one caveat to the delegation rule: **I would encourage you *not* to delegate your marketing.** You might be inclined to think, "What I really need to do is turn over all my marketing to an agency, or let the Yellow Pages or a local TV station handle it all for me. I'll keep doing my work and innovate on the side." **The problem here is not only are you *not* getting away from working in your business, the people who market for you are going to be stuck in the same groove they're used to.** The local Yellow Pages representative will offer you the same old advertising and not much else. The local TV station will put together the same kind of boring commercials they always do. **They don't have your best interests at heart; they don't know your business well, or have any idea of the best way to attract customers to your type of business.**

So delegate just about everything else; build a team of people to be the worker bees in your business, while *you* focus on the marketing. Let that be the thing you're the expert in, if nothing else, while your team handles the rest. If you delegate your marketing, then ultimately you will lose. Keep it in-house and keep it to yourself.

That's why when people ask me, "What should I be learning how to do?" I tell them, "Marketing!" You can find a lot of people who can follow a recipe, or keep track of the books, or actually work in a business—**but there are so few good marketers.** Sometimes little retail businesses and mom-and-pop shops fork over thousands or tens of thousands of dollars to ad agencies and individuals who claim they can take the marketing burden off their shoulders; and they accept that, because marketing is such a mysterious thing to them. **They haven't been trained in it, so they're willing to hand it over to others, because they know they need to bring in customers to grow their business.**

But you have to do the exact opposite to truly succeed. **If you want to control something in your business, control the marketing; because if you know marketing, you can do that for *any* business.** You can market your bakery or your accounting service and grow it to the next level, because once you've systematized the delivery of the product or service, your marketing can then help you scale above and beyond your competition. You can serve more clients and customers, you can create more products and services, and you can handle more business. **If you know marketing, you will always, always outperform the competition.** Go ahead and give up the day-to-day operations that employees can handle, but think twice about delegating your marketing.

Managing is important, but if you don't have anything to manage, things aren't going to work out very well. If you want to have something to manage, you'd better have some good marketing. **The greatest thing you can do for yourself is to focus tightly on the marketing and then, when the money starts coming in, start thinking about hiring people to help with the management.** And realize this: for every great marketer you might hire to help you in your business, there are thousands or tens of thousands of people who can be good managers. Good managers are much easier to find than good marketers.

The late, great Peter Drucker once said, "Everything you do within your business is an expense, except for innovation and marketing." The two are closely linked in any case; and since they actually make money, shouldn't you focus on them almost exclusively, and let other people do everything else as soon as it becomes possible? Now, I'll add my two cents to Drucker's idea: **I believe that good managers will ultimately make you money rather than costing you. So will good salespeople;** so while Drucker makes a good point, I don't necessarily agree with everything he said.

The Voice of Experience

I started my first business in December 1985. At the time, I cleaned carpets for another man, and I thought I could do it better for myself. So basically, I told him to take a hike, went out and got my own equipment, and started my own carpet cleaning business. **I ended up wearing all the hats. I had a few friends helping me now and then, but basically I was running the show.** That's about the time I met my wife. A couple of years later, my whole life changed.

Here's what happened: we had a couple of guys who were working on the truck with me, kids fresh out of high school, and we had a big carpet cleaning job that I'd booked myself. Then Eileen said, "Why don't you just let them do it?" By then, our employees had already been working with me for a couple of months, so they knew how to clean carpets. Not that you have to be a rocket scientist, believe me! Anybody with a bad brain and a strong back can clean carpets.

So I said okay. It was a big job and it was going to take them all day to do... so Eileen and I had a nice lunch and went to the movies. The whole time, I felt torn. Part of me was elated because of the freedom; these other guys were making me money, and it felt really good. Another part of me felt guilty, like I was doing something wrong. Well, when we came back into town and checked in, they were just finishing up. I went in and inspected the job, praised them for a job well done, and then collected the money from the customer. **Now, *that* felt great. I never thought that business could feel like that.**

That experience changed my life. It opened doors for me, and I started thinking that this delegation thing was pretty cool.

About a year later, Eileen and I started our little mail order business. We hired employees almost immediately, because I didn't want to transcribe names off an answering machine; you see, we ran little lead generation ads and people were calling in and leaving their messages. **Then we hired more people as the business started taking off, and were able to delegate most of our work out to them while Eileen ran the business.** We took a lot of vacations back then, because we had the time to do so.

This was before the days of cell phones. We were worried all the time, so whenever we vacationed, we'd end up stopping three or four times a day at a payphone to call back to the office, frantic: "Is everything OK? Is everything OK!?" They always told us everything was fine. Then one time, we went all the way to South Padre Island in Texas; it took us three days of leisurely driving to get there, and we had just checked into our hotel to stay for the week when we called in. **Well, this time everything wasn't OK; there had been an emergency.** Today I'd just blow it off and deal with it when I got back; little things that used to bother me horribly don't even faze me now. Back then, though, it seemed like a big emergency—though I don't even remember what it was now.

But oh my God—we had to get back! So we spent one night in South Padre and then drove home. It took us less than a day, because we *had* to handle that emergency personally. **I laugh when I think about it now, because that's just not the way I operate today. I've realized there are very few real emergencies.** Things that used to bother me for a day bother me for an hour, and things that used to bother me for an hour don't even bother me at all; I just don't care anymore. **I don't sweat the small stuff.**

I've learned that good people are a major asset. They are *not* a liability, which is why I disagree with Drucker when he says that only marketing and innovation make you money. I'll add a third—**really great employees.** Because if you have a well-trained staff of honest, talented, and highly skilled people who possess all the qualities you lack or are weak in, they'll never cost you. They'll always make you money.

That's why I've surrounded myself with such people. While they run the business, I get to enjoy working on it and not in it. I find this empowering. I became self-employed because I wanted freedom, and I know that you probably feel the same way. You want to call the shots and to do your own thing... but when most of us actually take action and start our own businesses, we end up working harder than we ever did when we were working at a regular job.

The Right Priorities

As a business owner, you achieve true freedom only when you work through other people and spend your personal time focusing on marketing. Only then. What we think is so important often isn't; and conversely, what we think *isn't* very important can be vital to our success. So it's good to reflect on what you're doing in business and in life, and to try to solidly define your priorities. Oh, you can go for a while without priorities, drifting along, like it's not a big deal... but when you do that, you're just killing time. That's rarely a good thing.

When it comes to life and business, what are your priorities? **We've been told for years by people in the motivational field that we *have* to have a plan to succeed. Well, I'd say that 99% of business people don't.** Sometimes I have a specific plan for this or that and sometimes I don't, so at those times I'm no better than anyone else; but if nothing else, I do have overarching goals for my business as a whole.

Now, realize that while it's good to have a plan, it shouldn't be so rigid that you have to follow it every single hour of every single day. **A plan is there to guide you, not to dictate your every action.** The idea is to understand where you are now, to visualize the future, and to determine how to most profitably get from Point A to Point B—not just in business, but in all aspects of your life. So look around and consider the people who are important to you, the people you love in your life, the people who are working with you or helping you while you're helping them; and then start thinking about where you want to be next year at this time, or even next *week* at this time. **You can define short-range plans as well as long-range ones.** Also, look at five years from now, and so on.

My point here is that you need to give it all some thought rather than just let things come to you and deal with them passively and reactively. I hate to use a business buzzword, but you really do have to be proactive and anticipate what's coming. **Move forward in a direction that makes you feel good, and know what you're likely to face the further you go along that path.**

I'd like to re-emphasize that this is about feeling good. If you don't feel good, then what are you fighting for? People go into business for specific reasons: they want to look out for themselves, they want to control their day, and they want to be in charge of their life. So they start their own business, and after a while, they realize they're stuck in it. The business becomes like a jail sentence, where they've got to work 60 or 80 hours a week. They're stressed out of their minds, they're missing valuable time with their friends and family, they're not taking vacations— they're just working themselves to death. **Their whole dream of being an entrepreneur has become a nightmare.**

Plainly put, systematizing your business lets you avoid that. It gives you the opportunity to find real freedom, in terms of both money *and* time. Look: the benefits of owning a business aren't dying young from stress, no matter how much money you make. The true benefits of owning a business are having free time and a lot more money, and being able to travel and achieve at least some of the dreams you had when you started it.

So look at this as a way for you to break free of the self-employment nightmare so many business owners are stuck in. **Leverage it to open up the door to the fulfilling life of owning a business, but not having it own you—so that it's a moneymaking asset that funds the lifestyle you want.** This can truly transform your life, offering up some amazing opportunities you may not have experienced since first starting your business.

Dream into Nightmare

The dream of starting your own business turns into a nightmare for many people, simply because **they never learn to delegate well enough that they can start working *on* the business rather than *in* it.** Most small business owners get stuck wearing all the hats, doing the little daily stuff and handling all the brushfires. **All of a sudden years pass, and they realize that all the benefits they were looking never materialized.**

When that's the case, they probably would have been better off working for somebody else—because at least when you work for somebody else, you don't have all the added stresses and responsibilities of being your own boss. **Running your own business is supposed to be a reward, not a punishment!** You have to set yourself up for success; you have to go in knowing precisely what you're trying to accomplish, and create an action

---

plan to achieve those things. **You want to be able to enjoy the lifestyle and freedoms that come with being your own boss.** You can do it; you *can* get there. If you've been stuck and frustrated in a business, it's not too late to change course.

Use these strategies I've outlined here and elsewhere in this book, in addition to any other resources you can take advantage of. **You *can* succeed, if you're truly committed to it.** It may mean some changes in the way you do things, and you may end up working just as hard as before; **but you'll be working on the smart things, the right things that will get you where you want to be, instead of just spinning your wheels.**

Here's a new habit you should think about acquiring: get up an hour earlier than you normally do, and adjust your bedtime accordingly. **Take that hour and devote it to thinking about ways to improve your business.** Consider how you can attract and retain more customers. Write down ideas and brainstorm with yourself in the beginning; then, when you have a team of people to work with, brainstorm with them as well, because the best ideas will come to you as you discipline yourself to look for them. That's really essentially what it's all about. **Just ask yourself and your team what you can do to make more money for the company.** I make sure I tap into the knowledge of my sales team, because they're on the front lines all day long with our clients. They come up with great ideas all the time.

During your brainstorming sessions, ask questions like, "What's going to turn our customers on? What are they looking for? What aren't we giving them? What are we doing wrong? What are we doing *right*?" Toss out ideas a mile a minute, open up your filters, and be receptive. **Over time, your ideas will get better, and remember: all it takes is one great idea to make**

you a fortune.

One of my favorite stories about Henry Ford took place when he brought in an efficiency expert who claimed he could make any company more productive and profitable. After the man had snooped around for a couple of hours, Ford asked him, "How are you doing?" And he said, "Well, it's going to take me a while to figure all this out, but I can tell you one thing—that guy in the office four doors down? Get rid of him."

Ford asked, "What do you mean?" And the expert said, "I've only been here a few hours, but every time I've walked by he's had his feet up on the desk and his eyes closed. He's been asleep at his desk the whole time. Get rid of him—he's no good." Henry Ford just looked at him and said, "You don't know what you're talking about, mister. The man is *thinking*. Last year, just two of his ideas made us millions of dollars."

I love that story, because it tells me all kinds of things—much more than its brevity might suggest—and it should tell you those things, too. **If nothing else, it's clear that this was a man who knew how to work *on* the business and not *in* it, and Henry Ford was smart enough to recognize that...** even if the efficiency expert wasn't. Henry Ford did the same thing. **Study the lives of the world's greatest, most successful entrepreneurs, and you'll find that they all worked *on* their businesses and not *in* them.** Reread this chapter, as many times as it takes, and learn to emulate them.

Now let's go on to the final Marketing Module, #10.

CHAPTER 11

Module #10:
Building Relationships

One of my favorite films is *Jerry McGuire*, starring Tom Cruise. There's a scene in the movie when his mentor is imparting his wisdom to young Jerry McGuire and he says, "It's all about relationships." That statement holds true for every single business in the world. ***It's all about relationships.*** Relationships with your customers, your prospective customers, your staff members, your suppliers, your joint venture partners, your banker, your accountant, your lawyer—**all the relationships in your working life.**

The most successful people in any business surround themselves with the very best people they can possibly find, and do everything they can to solidify those relationships. Those are the people who experience the greatest success in business. Those who fail at relationship building never make the money that could be theirs; so in this module, I'll reveal secrets on how to maximize your relationship-building skills. Investing a little effort into this aspect of your life—and it *is* an investment— can transform your business like nothing else. **You can start doing it very quickly, too; all you have to do is connect or reconnect to clients and start building a strong bond.**

Again, relationship- building is imperative in any business you can name. Even if you've already done everything else I've outlined in this book to build your business, **you won't achieve**

maximum success until you add relationship building to the recipe. Without it, you'll just be going through the motions. With it, you'll bridge the gap between you and your clients, and you'll end up having them spreading the word about your products and services. That helps you hook additional long-term customers — and that's the secret of long-term success. So let me tell you a little story about someone who did phenomenally well at relationship building, and got some great results in return.

Back in Chapter 3, I told you that a car salesman named Joe Girard is listed in the *Guinness Book of World Records* as the world's greatest salesman — and that covers every business there is. He still holds that record to this day. Now, most people don't trust car salesmen — for good reason. But Joe Girard became the world's greatest salesman in that or any other industry. How did he do it? **By focusing on building relationships. Over and over, he pointed out that he wasn't selling cars, he was selling Joe Girard. He was selling his relationship with each individual customer.**

He did this a lot of different ways, but one of the tools he used was greeting cards. Every time he sold a car to a new customer, he'd send that customer a greeting card every single month, January through December, and then again on their birthday. Those cards were very simple: on the front they said, "I Like You," and on the inside they might say, "Happy Fourth of July" or "Happy St. Patrick's Day." At one point he had so many customers and referrals that he was sending out *13,000* greeting cards per month; he had to hire two assistants to help him. **The result was that he sold an average of six cars a day, every single day.** Now, did he work every single day? No, he had days off. But some days he sold 18 cars, so it did average out to six cars a day.

The Guinness Book of World Records recognized Joe Girard as the world's greatest salesman not because he sold cars, but because he sold *himself*. **He built long-lasting relationships with his clients that profited him (and them) immensely over the lifetimes of those relationships.**

I want to give you a shortcut for doing the same thing. I'm not going to guarantee that your name will replace Girard's in Guinness, but there's no reason you shouldn't try. I want to give you *one* idea, *one* concept that will help you build incredibly strong relationships that are certain to pay off in multiple ways year after year. Here's the strategy: **start caring about your clients.**

It's Just Common Sense

Now, I know you've already heard all about relationship building, and no doubt you practice many of the tips that I and other experts have taught you so you can get your prospects to know, like, and trust you. That's great; there are many different directions to take with this effort, and many work. **But the key is to honestly care about your clients.**

Care about their experience with your company. If you provide a service in which you go into their home, care about their home and be respectful of it. **When you deal with customers one-on-one, care about their feelings.** That means you have to make sure your employees also care about your clients and your customers. **You need to care about whether or not the customer will come back and do more business with you. You need to care about whether or not they're going to recommend you to somebody else.** You simply have to start caring, because a lot of business owners don't. They care about the books and whether they're making money or not, and about how they're managing their employees and working on the business... but they just don't care about their clients.

Let's look at two quick stories: one about a business that cares about its customers, and one about a business that doesn't. I tell this first story a lot, because it really had an impact on the person it happened to—my colleague Jeff Gardner—and it's a perfect illustration of how important caring is. A few years ago, Jeff had a clogged garbage disposal, so he called a random plumber from the Yellow Pages because he was in a new house and didn't know the area well. When that fellow arrived, Jeff could tell just by looking that this was a person that cared, because he looked very professional. He had on a pristine white shirt: no smudges, no smears, nicely pressed. He also wore dark slacks and dress shoes, and carried an organized clipboard, not just a wad of papers.

He was very respectful, and even told Jeff who he was and showed him identification (which is rare). When Jeff invited him in, he said, "Wait just a moment," and slipped on some blue shoe covers. They're inexpensive—about a nickel each—but that made an impression on Jeff, because he'd had all sorts of service people at his house working on things, and you know how they are: most just tromp dirt into the house without even caring about your carpet or floors. By contrast, this person actually seemed to care about Jeff's home.

He came in and checked over the garbage disposal, then told Jeff exactly what the problem was, what he was going to do to fix it, and what the cost was going to be. **He fixed it quickly at a reasonable price, and he left with a handshake and a smile— and Jeff was phenomenally impressed.** As a result, Jeff used that company a number of times over the years, and recommended them to his friends in the area. **They got a lot of business from him just because they made a positive first impression.**

Now here's a story about a company that *doesn't* care. Jeff has a friend who had been going to a Mexican restaurant in Fort Worth, Texas for years. She ordered the same thing for Sunday brunch every single week. Well, not long ago she ordered the same plate that she normally gets, but it looked like a child's portion — about half its regular size. Since she's been going there for years ordering the same thing, she knows exactly what the portions should look like. So she called over the waiter, and he didn't seem to care; basically he said, "Yeah, whatever. This is what you get."

So she said, "OK, then, I need to talk to the manager," hoping the manager would care. Well, he didn't; he actually argued with her that yes, this was the correct portion size, and **he didn't care that she had been going there for years and that she noticed a difference. He refused to do anything about it.** When she left, she recognized the owner standing by the cash register and mentioned the issue to him. Guess what? He didn't care either. He mumbled something and went into the back, and that was it.

The result was that the restaurant lost a long-term customer because of shoddy customer service, and now she's boycotting that restaurant. She posted on Facebook that she's never going back. Well, she's got hundreds of Facebook friends, and many of her friends said that they've put up with the bad service there, too. But when they saw her post, they said enough was enough. They decided to show some solidarity, and now they're boycotting that place as well. By not caring, that restaurant ultimately lost about a dozen long-term customers just because of that one situation.

You can tell from her experience that it's a top-down situation. The business owner doesn't care, so the manager doesn't care, so the waiter doesn't care. If nobody cares, your customers get bad experiences. **If nobody cares, you lose those customers, creating situations where your unhappy customers tell dozens or hundreds of other people... and you lose some of that business, too.**

It's very important to care. **If you care, you'll keep the clients you attract and those clients will refer more clients to you—simply because they sense that you** *do* **care, and that you're willing to go above and beyond in your efforts.** If you don't care, you're not only going to lose clients you already have, you're going to turn off more prospects as those angry clients tell others. And believe me, people love to spread news about bad experiences—much more than they like to spread news about good experiences. So start caring more about your clients and their experiences with your customer service, product delivery, and any other ways you interact with them.

If you do this one simple thing and train your employees to do the same, you create a situation where people can more easily come to know, like, and trust you. They'll do more business with you because it's obvious you care. That's how you build strong, long-term relationships that have them coming back to you for years, while referring you to friends, family, and neighbors. This can create a phenomenal burst of business for your company, without any additional payments or cost. All you have to do is care. **If you can't care about the people you're supposed to serve, how can you expect to stay in business long?**

Chris Lakey has also experienced something like Jeff's restaurant story. Once he, his wife, and several other couples all decided to try a new restaurant they'd heard good things about. The waitress told them about a particular special, and most of them ordered it. Sure enough, the food was wonderful and they had a very pleasant meal—until the checks arrived. Suddenly they were all in a state of shock, because the special was considerably more expensive than the price the waitress had quoted; apparently she had made a mistake. So Chris and his friends questioned her about it without being rude, pointing out that she had inadvertently misled them.

After talking it over for a while, she went back and out came the owner—who was very rude, and made it all too clear that she would lose money if she let them pay the quoted price. The deal was *too* good, she didn't know why they'd been quoted that price in the first place—and she was very matter-of-fact in saying that there was no way that she could honor the price. Now, sometimes people do say the wrong thing, and when that happens, the smart business owner just sucks it up and moves on. **This owner should have honored the price quoted, but she handled the situation badly.** Despite the pleasant, delicious meal, they all left in a foul mood. That was more than ten years ago.

If the owner hadn't been so rude, and had in fact owned up to the waitress's mistake, Chris and his friends might have gone there many times in the future, spending tons of money. **But most of them never returned... so the owner lost far more money in the long run that she would have if she'd accepted the mistake and moved on.** Chris and his wife did go back once, but only because a client wanted to meet them there. That story always comes to the top of my mind whenever a negative experience like that arises in a discussion about relationships or customer service. All it took was that episode at the end of the meal to sour eight or ten people on the whole experience — and you can bet they told everyone they knew that story. Chris and his wife lived in a relatively small town then, so the restaurant could definitely have used the business.

Ironically, she probably doesn't remember Chris and his friends, because most of them never went back; and she probably wouldn't understand that she had hurt her own business by treating them that way in the first place. **But she has no chance of gaining their trust again, because she severed it so thoroughly when she acted like they were trying to get one over on her on that first visit.**

People Want to Feel Important!

Relationships are relatively easy to build; but if you ruin one, even one of long standing, it's very hard to go back. So you've got to strive from the beginning to handle things well, and keep striving to treat those involved right every time thereafter — so you never have to go back and try to rebuild.

Right about now you may be shaking your head, thinking, "Okay, this is just too damn simple to be real." And yet it *is* real. This is a huge mistake that many business owners are making, simply because they don't realize one key thing about every person they meet — customer, joint venture partner, supplier, whatever. **It's almost as if all these people have flashing signs on their forehead saying, "MAKE ME FEEL IMPORTANT!" That's your main job if you want to make money.** Make everybody you come in contact with feel they're important, because that's what they desperately want.

It's all about *them*, not you. If you just can't comprehend that, then go ahead and pretend that sign is there. Fake it until you make it. All your customers want and need to feel important to some extent. Everyone does; it's part of human nature. Because here's the deal: to us, we *are* important. It's all about us! Even the best of us are self-centered, selfish beings constantly thinking about ourselves first. That may not sound so nice, but it's the truth, even if many of us refuse to admit it.

You've got to treat your customers like Kings and Queens, because in their minds they are; and they're vital to your business. **So they deserve to be #1, because without them, you wouldn't *have* a business.**

Sadly, so many business people develop this attitude of "us vs. them," and end up feeling contemptuous toward their customers. Yes, customer relations can become strained, and people can get burned out sometimes. That's reality. But it's equally true that consumers nowadays have more choices than ever before, and all it takes is one unpleasant situation like the one that Jeff's friend or Chris Lakey experienced, and BOOM! You not only lose a customer forever, but they'll probably tell a whole bunch of other people about their bad experience.

That's just common sense, folks. You *should* care about your customers or clients, but I'd say a majority of companies don't. And it makes *such* a big difference. Just recently, for example, Jeff Gardner went with a friend who was looking for a dog to adopt. In their city there's the local pound, which is flush with cash, and right across the street there's the SPCA of Texas. The buildings are the same size and age, and both deal with animals on a daily basis. Jeff found it interesting that the very first time they went to the pound, nobody even said hello; there

---

were plenty of people around, but they were all doing their own thing, mostly text messaging.

They never said one word to Jeff and his friend, so they followed the signs to the back and checked out the cages where the animals were—and the place was dirty. There were hand sanitizer dispensers on the wall, but they were all empty, and there was trash everywhere; it just looked horrible. Jeff figured the place was like that because it must be very depressing and sad to work with lost animals.

But then they went to the SPCA of Texas, literally across the street—and the place was sparkling. The moment they set foot through the door they were greeted politely by the smiling, well-dressed person at the counter. The employees they passed were friendly and told Jeff and his friend, "If you're interested in adopting a pet, make sure you sign in!" The cages were clean, the animals were clean and healthy, and all the hand sanitizers were filled. **It was a beautiful place with beautiful energy inside, and that was essentially the only difference between them and the pound. The people at the pound were going through the motions; those at the SPCA cared very much.**

Here's another quick story from Jeff: he knows of two bakeries located next door to each other. One has really great lunches, and the other's a gluten-free place. Jeff's been to both of them, and the difference is interesting to observe. At the first bakery, the owner is right there at the cash register smiling, talking, chatting—she really cares about the food, and if anything ever goes wrong, she takes care of it (though rarely does anything go wrong). When you go next door to the gluten-free place, you deal with employees who aren't really interested in doing anything. They obviously don't care about the customers as much as the owner of the other place does.

My colleagues and I see that kind of thing repeatedly. Two places might otherwise be identical; but if you add caring to one and leave it out of the other, the caring place is the one that will prosper. After all, how many times have you been to a store or a restaurant where the employees' actions made you think, **"These people really just don't care about me or my experience, and they don't respect me"?**

Aiming for that caring attitude and good customer service seems like common sense... but you don't often encounter it, do you? Some of the big, popular fast-food chains manage it, because they deliberately train their workers in customer service schools. I honestly think that gives them an edge, even when their food isn't the best ever. Add good customer service to the convenience, though, and you have yourself a winner. In fact, some of the national chains do a much better job than local restaurants where the food is top-notch but the customer service leaves something to be desired.

If this brand of common sense really were common, then everyone would be doing it. That would force even better customer service as businesses competed for this facet of the mercantile experience; you'd have to step it up in order to be better than the next guy. This does happen occasionally, when a specific industry changes overnight because someone has a special touch, and everyone else decides they have to go above and beyond suddenly. The cell phone industry is a great example; competition has driven the technology extremely far in just a few years.

Chris Lakey recently did some research while preparing to

buy a new smartphone for his daughter, and realized that while most of the companies have their individual ways of doing things, they also tend to follow each other. One company will innovate and do something creative, and the others will find a way to innovate beyond that, and on it goes. This benefits both the industry and the people in the marketplace hugely. Every time someone takes a big step forward, everyone else scrambles to catch up. It may take six months or a year, but soon they're all back even again. Now, *that's* common sense.

The one thing you can almost always do better than the other guy is building a positive relationship. You're the only you out there; there's nobody quite like you, so the relationship you build with a customer or client represents something they can't get from anybody else but you. If you do a better job at relationship building than your competition, the other business factors in play will take a backseat to the growing relationship. They may be a part of your success, especially your products and services, but the relationship will be the focal point of your business, the real reason people choose to do business with you.

High-Trust, Low-Trust

Chris Lakey is part of a nonprofit organization that works with Chinese orphans, so he's currently working through a course on relationships with people in other countries. One of the reasons he's doing so is to gain a better understanding of how he and the people he works with can come across as a little less over-the-top. For better or worse, many Americans have a kind of superiority complex, an attitude of "we're right and you're wrong."

This can get in the way when dealing with people from other countries. **Often, cultural differences can negatively impact**

your relationship; so you have to realize that just because they're doing something differently, that doesn't necessarily mean that it's wrong. It's just different. Even if you think you have a better way, you still have to be careful when dealing with people from other cultures, especially in the area of nonprofit work. **You need to work with them on an equal footing, which requires careful relationship building.**

While working through this material, Chris read a chapter from Stephen Covey's book *The Speed of Trust*. Covey has some really good things to say about relationship building; **his central point is that as trust develops in a relationship, it will ultimately lead to either increased trust or decreased trust.** In a low-trust relationship, there's decreased speed and increased cost. On the flip side is the high-trust relationship, characterized by high speed and low cost. **Your goal should be to develop the highest level of trust possible in your business relationships,** which is appropriate to what I'm outlining in this final module. **The less people trust you, the harder and more expensive it is to do business.**

A low-trust relationship may form either when you're working with a brand new customer, or when you've done something to damage an existing relationship. That slows you down. It takes longer to make a sale, and you have to get through greater difficulties along the way. **A high-trust relationship greases the tracks.** Let's say you already have a relationship in place, where the customer knows, likes, and trusts you, and you come to them with a new product similar to one you've already sold them. In a case like that, they can quickly see the value and make a decision to purchase—as opposed to when a customer is new and doesn't yet trust you,

We do direct mail here at M.O.R.E., so it's not uncommon for us to mail an offer to a client and then follow up with them 10-20 times. If we have a high-trust relationship with a client, we may not even need to mail them anything. We can just talk to them on the phone, explain our offer, and they'll see that what we're saying is true. **They can evaluate the offer based on their trust and needs and make a decision to get involved.** A new client may require the slower process and greater cost of multiple follow-ups before saying yes.

Covey equates this to a low-trust tax or a high-trust dividend. That's an easy way to understand the value of building relationships, and I think you definitely should put a lot of thought into the concept. Covey estimates that in the mid-2000s, low-trust situations cost businesses $1.1 trillion a year. The cost has probably increased substantially since then.

The Purchasing Power of Trust

People will buy when they trust. There are two different business models that seem to work best when you're dealing with almost any type of customer. **The first model is that they trust you, they like you, and they feel that you're a kindred spirit.** People tend to have a high regard of themselves; so if they feel you're enough like them to understand their problems and their aspirations, they're much more likely to buy from you.

The second model also has to be based on trust, but it takes advantage of the human tendency to gravitate toward an expert in a particular field. In the case of business, the prospect is already active in that field or wants to enter it. If they find themselves dealing with what they consider to be a first-class company with a highly regarded expert as the president or CEO, they're going to love dealing with that company.

In a previous module, I discussed positioning yourself as an expert by means of information products. This helps people perceive you as an authority in the field, if not THE authority, so they'll want to do business with you. **The key here is to make sure you live up to your word and never, ever break that trust.** You need to have an unassailable level of integrity; you need to do exactly what you've said or promised you'll do. If you do that consistently, then you're going to develop such a high level of trust that the customers will come back to you repeatedly, even to the point of ignoring your competitors' specials, one-time deals, or lower prices. They'll have such loyalty because they know they can trust you.

In the earlier restaurateur examples, those business owners ruined their customer relationships because they violated their customers' trust. They didn't deliver on their promises, and when confronted about it, argued with their customers instead of giving in gracefully. Trust could have been built even on the waiter/waitress level if they'd just done what they should have. **The employee is the spokesperson for the business owner;** so when an employee says that the special is a certain price and then it gets rung up at a higher price, you don't want to present them with that higher price if you want to build trust.

What you do is have the manager or owner apologize and say, "You know what? The price is normally this, but we always make sure that we honor what the employee says; and even though she misspoke, we're going to let you have it for this price. We'll take care of you." **Just show them you mean what you say, even if what you say is a mistake.**

But in Chris's example, they didn't; and Chris and his friends didn't go back. On top of that, Chris has probably told the story many times to people who then changed their minds about going to that restaurant. In Jeff's example, a long-time customer ended up boycotting the restaurant, and so did her Facebook friends. So as you can see, it's crucial to make sure that even if you have trust at the beginning, you don't allow that trust to break down later through inconsistency. **If you always do what you say you will, you can create long-term, rock-solid trust that can pay you back over many years.**

Your best customers will be the ones who trust you the most and buy from you the most. **That's why whenever I develop a new product or service I want to promote, we always go straight to our best customers and don't even bother sending them expensive sales materials.** We've got the trust established with them, and can quickly make that cash register ring. We're not doing this because we're saints; it's just good for business.

You have to win people's hearts before you win their money. You do that by making them feel special, because that's what they want more than anything else. They want to feel like they're Number One, so your job is to make them feel that way.

There's a saying that goes, "Sincerity is everything. Once you learn how to fake that, you've got it made." While I don't agree with the faking part, the rest is right on the money. And admittedly, some days it's really, really hard to express genuine sincerity in your efforts to win people's hearts and give them that special feeling they're seeking. That's the reason why so many business people give lousy customer service in the first place; they're totally burned out from dealing with problem customers and all the other little issues that grind you down if you take them personally and internalize them. On a really bad day, it can leave you feeling like your spirit is crushed... and that's why business people treat their customers like crap sometimes.

During those moments when sincerity is a struggle, you just have to put a smile on your face and bear with it—and you have to teach your people to do the same, because they have rotten days too. And let's be realistic here; some customers can be very unpleasant to deal with. After a while, that "us vs. them" mentality can develop, yet you can't afford to play that game. **You have to take the high road, keep your mouth shut, and treat your customers like royalty if you want their money.**

The Five Steps

In this section, I'll share five steps to phenomenal success. Relationships represent the foundational premise that these steps are built on, in the sense that **good people don't cost you money, they** *make* **you money.** This holds true for staff, suppliers, accountants, lawyers, joint venture business partners—everyone. The best people aren't always the cheapest, but if the right systems and processes are in place, they'll always make you money in the long run. Here are the steps you need to follow, some of which reflect items I've outlined elsewhere in this book.

Step #1: Seek out the very best people you can find for all aspects of your business. I've already introduced this concept. When you find dishonest people, get rid of them as fast as you can, because a few dishonest people can spoil the bunch.

Step#2: Once you have the very best people in place, let them run the day-to-day aspects of your business.

Step #3: Focus on your core business. You should direct your time, attention, and energy to the marketing, product development, and other profitable aspects of your business. What's going to make you the most money? You have to ask yourself this question over and over. Put your focus there and let other people take care of the rest.

Step #4: Once you have really good people, treat them as assets, never as liabilities. These people make you money, so do everything possible to hold onto them and nurture those relationships.

Step #5: The less you do, the more money you'll make. Write this one down and hang it on your wall. Commit it to memory. Now, when I say less, I'm not necessarily talking about the number of hours you put in; I mean the number of tasks you handle personally. Trim your task list to the few vital activities that produce the maximum amount of sales and profits—and therefore the most money—for your business.

When you have the right relationships in place, you can do that. You need a solid group of people you can count on to run the daily business, loyal suppliers willing to work with you, and superb joint venture business partners. That's when you can focus all your time and energy on those fewer things that produce the most money. Product and service development head the list. Constantly ask yourself, "What are the customers looking for? How can we do that better? What new products and services can we introduce that will be even more exciting to the customers we serve?"

Next comes building and maintaining your marketing systems. Marketing is all the things you do to attract and retain customers, so your marketing systems are the processes you put in place that do that for you as automatically as possible. You should also spend a lot of time strategizing. You can do this in almost any situation, even while sitting in front of the TV half-watching some dumb show, as long as you have a notebook in hand and you keep jotting ideas down as they come to you.

It also helps to have good, capable, competent, talented, and smart people to brainstorm with. Those are relationships too, and they're vital ones. People who really understand your business at an intimate level are best: people you've worked with for a number of years, so that you trust them and they trust you. They all have skills and abilities they bring to the table, so that there's a synergistic effort when you come together and compare notes.

Think deeply about these steps I've given you. Think especially about that fifth and final step: **The less you do, the more money you make.** You can limit your scope to those vital few activities because you've built solid relationships with people who are trustworthy, capable, competent, knowledgeable, and have skills and abilities that free you up so you can then spend more time doing what I discussed in the last module: working *on* your business rather than *in* it. **While doing less can be a recipe for disaster if poorly handled, it can also be a prescription for great success.**

What Truly Matters

One thing I've noticed over the years is that some of the richest people I've ever gotten to know haven't struck me as super-intelligent. I've also noticed that many of them aren't good managers; some are even terrible at marketing. So how did they become so successful in the first place? **Simple: they had at**

---

least one good idea, and they were smart enough to surround themselves with good people who could offset their weaknesses and flaws. Some of these people spend a lot of time at the racetrack or on the golf course, yet they make millions of dollars a year. Well, their talent lies in finding good people who do great work—and holding on to them for all they're worth.

This happens too often to be coincidence. **These people know how to combine their gifts for implementing good ideas or picking a winning business or investment opportunity with the talents of other people.** If you can do that, you can achieve success far beyond what you'd ever ordinarily expect, simply by using this formula.

My colleague Jeff Gardner used to wear all the hats in his business, until he met a gentleman who made a fortune doing just a handful of things. His company was massive, and he served as the idea person, the strategist—the business growth engineer, if you will. He let his employees run the business, while he did the things with such a high return on investment that some of them earned him thousands of dollars an hour. That's one of the reasons he *could* let all the great people he hired do everything else.

Jeff took that to heart and started hiring employees, then learned more about finding good suppliers and dealing with other companies. **One of his biggest lessons learned—and it's one we all eventually learn—is that getting into these type of relationships is almost always easier than getting out of them.** There are occasions when a relationship sours and you try to end it, and realize that it's hard to disconnect because they've burrowed in. They want to stay there because it's comfortable.

The flipside is that it's often challenging to keep great

employees, the ones who really contribute to your success. Because they're so awesome, they're offered other opportunities, so it's important to pay them enough or give them sufficient bonuses and benefits to get them to stay with you. **Interestingly, it's often better to look for someone who already has a job than to advertise for people who don't.**

I have nothing against the unemployed, but those who already have good jobs have those jobs for a reason: they're exemplary employees. **They keep their jobs through good times and bad.** Jeff tells me that the last two people he hired already had full-time employment at the time. In one situation, he was a client at a business and saw the individual at work, and soon realized that the person really cared about what they were doing. You might have thought they were the owner, given how much they cared.

Now, Jeff really didn't have an open position in his own business at the time, but he thought that maybe he could unload some of the stuff he was doing on someone like that, someone who cared as much as he did about his business. Ultimately he interviewed that person, and hired them at a higher rate of pay than they were receiving. They came to his business and did a phenomenal job. Eventually, they got an even higher-paying position with a larger organization. That's what happens with good people: they can and do move on to bigger and better opportunities. **But it was a great experience for Jeff and that employee alike.** Now, whenever Jeff meets great employees in other businesses, he makes a mental note; and if there's a chance to hire that person at some point, he tries to connect with them. If you're always looking for star players, **if you can build a team of people who care as much as you do, you can build a very strong business very fast.**

Lessons Learned

You should always be looking out for and working on relationships—because you never know. Whether it's a great hire or a wonderful vendor, you never know where you're going to come across someone who can provide something valuable to your business. **So cultivate positive relationships with all kinds of people. That will serve you well; and even in the worst-case scenario, you make some good friends.**

I think it's particularly appropriate for small business owners to do this, given that they do often try to do everything. They're pulled in so many different directions they can't do *anything* well. **You really can learn to make more money and have more productive days by doing less, in the sense of focusing on a smaller number of high-value things, or even just one thing you do very well.** That doesn't mean you work fewer hours. You may end up working your normal 8 or 10 or 12 hours, but you're focusing your energy on the things that are the most productive for the business.

It all goes back to my central premise: good people don't *cost* you money, they *make* you money, presuming they're managed properly and the right systems and processes are in place. Otherwise you may as well flush your money down the toilet. **So it's not just good people that matter, it's good people working with good systems and processes that are your biggest assets.** I'm convinced of that, though many small business people just can't seem to get their heads around it. They always look at employees as a cost, rather than an asset. They're trained to. And sure, maybe they *are* a cost if you don't have the right systems and processes in place.

As long as you have good people working with good systems and planning, though, you'll profit. Period. **You need long-term relationships with the right people so you can develop a staff that intimately understands your business.** It can take years before somebody gets to this point. When they do, there's an incredible synergy there. I see this with Chris Lakey constantly. He's been working with us since the early 1990s.

I finished teaching Chris everything I know years ago, and now he teaches me on a daily basis. When he finds a new opportunity that could make us a bunch of money, I say, "Teach me all about it!" The best people are like that. **You give them everything you've got and then they'll reciprocate, and it's absolutely amazing.**

So find good people, cultivate them, build good relationships, and find out what they want. As the late Zig Ziegler taught us, you get what you want by helping others get what *they* want. **Focus on trying to help people, serving them, giving them things they value and that are important to them.** Make your business a fun place not only for your employees, but also for your loyal suppliers, the folks who will bend over backwards for you to give you good service and do things special just for you. Treat your joint venture business partners well, so they continue to want to work with you repeatedly.

I learned all this the hard way. Many years ago, when we first started our business, I'd just come out of the factories working construction and working in the oil field, where management is all about yelling at people and hitting them over the head with clipboards. Once we got started and hired employees, Eileen ran the company while I did the marketing and the other things I was best at. One day, after we'd been in business a few years, she was gone and I was working in my office—and I heard several of the employees out in the hallway laughing. I immediately called Eileen at home and said, "Get your ass over here. Those employees of yours are out in the hall laughing!"

She told me, "TJ, we want some of that. The more fun people have on the job, the more they'll transfer some of that over to the customers when they're talking to them on the phone. **If they're in a friendly, fun environment where they have a good time, some of that will rub off on the customer."**

I never forgot that, because dammit, she was right. Oh, I know it can be carried to extremes, but if you don't overdo it, it becomes the icing on the cake—because ultimately the customers get served even better. **That's where it all reflects back on you: you treat your staff right, and your staff will treat the customers right. It doesn't always happen, but it should and it can.**

Now let's go on to the final chapter, where I'll wrap up this book.

CHAPTER 12:

Ruthless Marketing, Summarized

In this book, I've provided a fairly quick but detailed discussion of ten principles that define the Ruthless Marketing philosophy. After studying the ten modules I've provided, along with this summary and the introductory chapter, you ought to have a good understanding of what Ruthless Marketing is. **It's not about mistreating your customers or ripping them off, though it won't make your competitors happy because it *is* about aggressively going after the largest possible market segment.**

The Golden Key

As I outlined in Module #1 (Chapter 2), it starts with establishing your USP, or your Unique Selling Position. You know, I just got an invoice from the guy who's been mowing our yard, and on the bottom of his invoice it says: "Excellence—One Lawn at a Time." That's supposedly his USP, yet he doesn't realize he's not living up to that at all. I'm ready to fire him. If I could find somebody who could do a better job tomorrow, he'd be gone tomorrow. **Your USP is that one thing that separates you from everybody else, so it needs to be precise.** This landscaper claiming that he's "Excellence—One Lawn at a Time"... that's nonsense. He's doing a crappy job. There's nothing excellent about his company. You have to make sure your USP is based on reality.

Your USP boils down to that one thing that causes people to want to do business with you instead of all of your

competition. Therefore, you have to spend some serious time brainstorming how you're going to position yourself, your product/service, and your business in general so people are automatically attracted to you. That makes everything a lot easier, because you don't have to sell them on doing business with you. **It's worth the amount of thought and effort you put into it if you can find something that instantly sets you apart from the crowd.** Don't just tell people "I'm the best" or claim you exemplify "Excellence," or anything so general. Find specific ways to make yourself unique, and you'll be a lot more attractive to the market you want to attract.

Consider what your customers *really* want. In the landscaping example, they don't just want someone to do landscaping; they want someone to create a new image for their yard. When you ask most businessmen, "What's your specialty?" they say, "We provide quality and service in our field." But those are empty words. So think beyond the pale; determine what your customers really want, and make that part of your USP.

I think it's important to start with the ultimate end in mind, and to constantly keep it in mind. Don't just step into the woods and start cutting a trail in a random direction; **you have to establish your destination *first*.** If you think that's just common sense, great! Because apparently it isn't for many would-be entrepreneurs. Ask yourself: "What am I trying to accomplish with my business? Who do I want my best customer to be?" **Then formulate your USP by figuring out what those best customers want the most.** Your USP should be a big, bold promise, offering a big, bold benefit. What are people going to get when they do business with you? What can you offer that your competitors don't? How can you enhance their positive experience?

That's what your USP should be about. Don't make the mistake my landscaper did, in thinking that a few words are going to make a difference. **You've got to actually fulfill on those words.** *That's* **the one thing that separates you from everybody else.**

The World's Best Marketing Method

In Module #2, I clued you in on Direct Response Marketing, a.k.a. DRM. This is a powerful marketing method that most of your competitors know very little about. You've heard the saying: a little knowledge is a dangerous thing. **You've got to immerse yourself in the field to get it right.** Because of their lack of real knowledge, they're making a tremendous number of mistakes. **The best strategy for DRM is getting the right offer to the right person through the right media.** If you can marry those three factors in the most powerful way possible, you have the foundation for good DRM.

Even better, if you can automate or systematize your DRM so you can get the same results over and over, you have the ability to scale it up. That's how you build a bigger business than your competitors. Most small business owners and entrepreneurs just throw a lot of ad copy out there at random. Because they aren't sure what to do, they invest in limited media like the Yellow Pages, coupons, and online marketing—and they're never sure exactly what the results are. If something actually works, they can't be sure which effort it was.

DRM is a lot more scientific than this willy-nilly, throw-things-against-the-wall technique. **You market in measurable ways, systematizing your ads and your responses, as well as how you and your prospects interact.** You then have the ability to take it to the next level, to place more of the ads that work best, and just blow your competition away without doing much more work than you were doing before—if that much.

Ultimately, marketing comes down to either DRM, which most people don't understand, or image marketing. Or if you're Coca-Cola or Budweiser or Proctor & Gamble, you can do image advertising. You just want to pound your brand names into people's heads with beautiful girls or funny clips, so you use billboards, magazine ads, the sides of buses, and everything else you can to reach them and get into their brains. **But 99% of us aren't in that kind of business, which makes DRM so powerful for you... whereas image advertising will just waste your money.**

I honestly think one of the biggest problems small business owners suffer from is bad advertising. Often, they focus on image advertising they have no way of tracking. If you're doing more than one type of advertising, there's no way to know what works and what doesn't. **DRM is trackable.** You know exactly where every advertising dollar is going, and where every dollar of income is coming from. You know all your costs.

Ad agencies hate that, because when everything is trackable, you can hire or fire them based on performance. If it's not trackable, you can keep paying them the big bucks to do advertising that doesn't really get results... or if it *does* get results, you can't be sure what's working and what isn't. **So switch to Direct Response Marketing. The transition period may be difficult, but it's worth the pain.** In the end you'll be a lot happier with the results, and you can quickly get rid of what doesn't work. **It puts you in direct control of every dollar you spend on marketing.**

Front End, Back End

This leads us to Module #3, Front-End and Back-End Marketing Systems. A decent front-end/back-end combination takes care of every aspect of this marketing process. **It attracts the best prospects to you automatically, and then gets them to come back again to do more business with you.** Once you build these marketing systems, they go to work like a money machine.

While bringing in new business via the front-end is very important, maintaining a decent back-end is critical. This is where I see many businesses fall short. They spend 95% of their time focusing on bringing in new business, forgetting that the real money comes from selling to someone a second, third, fifth, or tenth time—as often as possible over a period of years. **Serious marketers often barely break even or even lose money on the front-end, but that doesn't bother them; they know their true business is built on back-end sales.** Their front-end promotions aren't even designed to make money, because they give away items at cost... or even for less. **When they do that, though, they make sure that people are so satisfied and happy with the product or service that they'll want to come back for more.**

There's a restaurant called Perry's in El Cajon, California, Russ von Hoelscher's stomping grounds, where you can hardly get inside because they treat their customers so well. The waitresses come out and give some of the older guys hugs and ask, "How are you?" The food is good, but the service is fantastic. **If you do that in your business, you'll see the money come pouring in from all the repeat business.**

I think it's best to think of your business model as a huge funnel. You take in a lot of people with your lead generation process, and start winnowing down the crowd by having them qualify themselves. By the time you get to the bottom of the funnel, you have a steady stream of very qualified people who are likely to accept your offer. Once they become customers, they receive back-end offers from you, and many graduate to long-term status. **Meanwhile, you use your front-end process to bring in new customers to replace the old ones who drop out for one reason or another, and to build your business.** As you can see, the front-end and back-end go together like hand and glove.

Tireless Salesmen

Marketing Modules #1-#3 form the foundation of our Ruthless Marketing Program, but there are seven others built on top of that foundation.

The fourth Marketing Module is direct mail. Some people call this junk mail—but that's the last thing those of us in the business would call it. **This type of mail can make you a fortune when you do it right.** Back in Chapter 1, for example, I told you that when Eileen and I first met Russ von Hoelscher, we were bringing in an average of $16,000 a month. **Thanks to the strategies we learned from Russ, we were bringing in almost $100,000 a week within nine months. We did that mostly by learning to use direct mail effectively.** Direct mail made us our fortune—and it can make you a fortune too, *if* you do it right. I showed you how to do that in Module #4.

One point I want to emphasize is that this is only "junk mail" if it doesn't go to the right person at the right time. If somebody gets something in the mail and it's an amazing offer directed towards them at the proper time, then it's not junk mail anymore: it's a valuable offer. **It's crucial that you understand**

that direct mail is incredibly powerful, but that it must be done correctly for it to get you the results you need to grow your business. And here's a little good news for you: if you're a small business and want to attract new customers within a 5-10 mile radius of your business, you can get special rates from the post office and mail at a much lower cost than people who are mailing nationwide!

Now, the reason most people think of direct mail as "junk mail" is because most marketers are doing a crappy job of it. They don't understand its potential, much less what direct mail is really all about. It's often poorly targeted "Occupant" type stuff, completely hit-or-miss. So use the strategies that I've taught you in Chapter 5. **Be sure you understand how to target the right kinds of people—that is, only those who are looking right now for what you have to offer.**

If you do that, direct mail is *money* mail. It's kind of like sending out little salespeople by envelope— salespeople who go out there and make that sale for you. A good salesman (and your little "direct mail salesmen" can be the best) gets prospects to pull out their checkbooks, credit cards, or cash, and place their orders ASAP. **Doing direct mail properly can get you more orders, it can get you more business, and it can help you achieve the results you've been looking for.**

Take-Away Selling

My fifth Marketing Module is based on the old principle of supply and demand. You always want people chasing *you* rather than you chasing *them*, because the more you chase someone, the faster they'll run. Therefore, you have to set up your marketing so they come to you voluntarily, or at least create the perception that they do. **Ultimately, take-away selling is about limiting access to yourself... and when you limit something, there's scarcity involved, so people want it.** It's been scientifically proven that people are wired to want scarce resources more than plentiful ones.

In Chapter 6, I've gone into detail on ways to create that sense of scarcity, so that people want to do business specifically with you rather than your competitors. Now, chasing after clients is understandable in a down economy, or when you're struggling to get your business going. **But one of the worst things you can do for your business in any situation is to let your desperation show.** Instead, use the power of take-away selling to attract prospects. And be sure to set a deadline with your takeaways, or people will put off their response and forget about you. **Many of your promotions should have a deadline of 10 days or even less to force people to respond while they still can.**

You want to create the perception that you've got something very special for them at a very good price, but it's up to them to take immediate action. The worst thing you can do is to delay the sale, because if you can't get the sale today, you're probably not going to get it tomorrow. That's not always true, but in general, you don't want to give people an excuse to wait. **Take-away selling is one of your most powerful tools to get people to make a decision today, because you're taking something away from them if they don't.**

The offer's on the table for a very limited time. They have to get it while it's hot, while the getting's good. **Ultimately, take-away selling is a great tool for getting all the money you can as fast as you can.** *And* it's contrary to what most of your competitors are doing, so it does help to differentiate you from all the rest.

The Importance of Lead Generation

In Marketing Module #6, I discussed methods of lead generation: front-end strategies for getting the very best prospects to come to you pre-sold and ready to buy. For most businesses, that's only a fantasy... but if you'll practice the methods I outlined in Chapter 7, you'll learn how to make it work. **The best prospects to work with are those who raise their hands and show their interest in what you have to offer.**

It's kind of like narrowing the search parameters on an Internet search engine. There are plenty of easy things you can do to generate a huge mailing list with a lot of prospects. If you do that, though, you're going to waste a lot of time, effort, energy, and money following up low-quality prospects. The power of quality lead generation lies in making potential buyers jump through hoops, raise their hands, and qualify themselves. **You'll almost certainly end up with fewer actual buyers, but they'll be of higher quality and more likely to become long-term customers with an excellent lifetime value.** You'll end up with a more robust business where you're not chasing curiosity-seekers.

If you have a high-quality jewelry store where you sell Rolex watches, diamond rings, and emerald tennis bracelets costing thousands of dollars, you don't send advertising to just anyone. If you do, most of it will be wasted on people who can't afford your products. If someone has $10 to spend on costume jewelry, you don't even want them in your store. Not that you're trying to be holier-than-thou, but it just doesn't work. So you want to qualify your customers, and that's what good lead generation does.

The important thing about lead generation is knowing what kind of leads you're looking for, and paying attention to who you ultimately want to do business with. **This goes back to the overall strategy of keeping an eye on your end goals, and knowing who your best customers should be.** Only a tiny percentage of the total number of people in the marketplace are going to become your best customers, and there are all kinds of reasons why that's so. **Never aim to attract everyone in the marketplace; you simply can't please everyone.** The strategies I outlined during Chapter 7 will help you develop the right strategy for attracting the right kinds of prospects and customers.

Online Marketing

In Marketing Module #7, a.k.a. Chapter 8, I explain how to handle website and Internet marketing. So many small business people want to bury their heads in the sand when it comes to the Internet and World Wide Web. They want to pretend we're still living in the late 1980s or early 1990s. On the other end of the scale are the marketers who believe that website and Internet marketing is *everything*. That's just not true for most small businesses...but you can't bury your head in the sand about it, either.

One of the things I emphasized in Chapter 8 was simplified Internet marketing. I think one of the reasons why many business owners don't do online marketing is because they believe it's too technical and difficult to understand. But I went through some very easy ways to market on the Internet, specifically through review sites. **There are sites like Angie's List and Yelp that your best prospects are frequenting.**

When your clients look for a business in their area to provide a product or a service, they very rarely go to the physical Yellow Pages anymore. **Now they're going online and searching for a company like yours—and in many cases they're going to these review sites, because they want to make sure they don't make any mistakes when choosing a business.** That's one reason it's important to be online. I've told you how to use these sites for free or for a low price to advertise to your very best potential clients. If you're not doing any online marketing, review Module #7 and start implementing some of the strategies I've suggested there.

In addition to review sites, nearly every medium-sized to large city has sites run by the local newspaper or television station that you can go onto and plug your business. Then, of course, you should also consider a user-friendly site of your own. It's all part of an image you're creating, proving you've got the best small business on Main Street or your local mall, or wherever you're located—and if people want to get the best service and products, they should come to you.

Don't forget the value of social media. If you've been wondering how to incorporate Facebook into your business, if you've been wondering what Twitter is and whether you need one, and if you've been thinking about Pinterest or Angie's List or Yelp, investigate the possibilities. **If your customers occasionally tell you that they saw a review of your business online and you wondered what that meant and whether you needed to pay attention to it, YES!** You do need to pay attention to it! This and the other secrets I've revealed in Module #7 will tell you how to dominate social media.

Chapter 8 outlines the main strategies you need to master in order to take advantage of this area of marketing—which you can't ignore. **Your competitors are all getting online, and you need to be there too.** I've shown you how to navigate the minefield and avoid the pitfalls, and make sure you do it the right way.

Only the Best

Marketing Module #8 is, in my humble opinion, the best one of them all. **This module covers how to use informational products and services to build your business.** If you decide to get serious about only one of the marketing modules presented in this book, this is the one you should choose. **I guarantee that if you do get serious, and decide to dedicate your life to and learn everything you can about information marketing, your business will be transformed forever.** This is the most fulfilling, challenging, profitable, and exciting marketing module of them all. It's the King of all Kings, the crème de la crème. So I recommend you reread this one religiously, again and again, and study everything you can about information marketing. If it sounds like I'm a convert, well, I am—and you should be, too.

This is truly an amazing "secret strategy" for success, if only because information marketing gives you the ability to position yourself as an expert. **Here's a little secret: no one gives you that title; you give it to yourself and then prove it by producing quality information for people at low or no cost.** It can be a brochure with 10 Tips or Tricks, or a simple checklist. It can be a book, it can be reports, it can be online information, or videos; whatever works for you. **Information really is the primary secret to positioning yourself as an expert.**

All things being equal, people want to do business with experts above and beyond anybody else in the marketplace.

That's especially true when the media starts getting in touch with you for your take on things. Let's say you're the local real estate expert, and you've written a booklet or report called *How To Sell Your Home For The Most Money*, or *Tips and Tricks that Will Make You Thousands of Dollars Extra When Selling Your Home...* well, you'll be the person they call. If you're a jeweler and you tell people *How To Know If Your Diamond Is Really High-Quality,* you'll attract some attention. **Whatever your business is, you can put out a report or book that will make people realize that you're an expert, which you really are.** You can even get a ghostwriter to write for you, while you reap the benefits—because our society loves experts.

Many small business owners don't even realize they can incorporate information products into their businesses. They think, "I'm a plumber," or "I'm a chiropractor," or "I'm a dentist," and have no idea about how they can approach the information aspect from the proper angle (assuming they think about it at all). **Whether or not it puts you into the top-expert category in peoples' minds (and it really can), producing your own information products can help you build your business.**

If you think information products just aren't your thing, I urge you to reconsider. **If nothing else, they can help you increase your sales and profits.** Because again, never forget this: no matter what your business, you really *are* an expert compared to your customers and prospects. Why not prove it in a way that can draw in a phenomenal amount of business?

On, Not In

Speaking of making lots of money: Marketing Module #9, which I covered in Chapter 10, is about working *on* your

business rather than *in* it. Now, that sounds like a play on words, but it's catchy and easy to remember—and it's the #1 thing that the world's richest business people have in common, at least those who've built everything from the ground up (along with the smartest of those born with silver spoons in their mouths).

You see, a business system is really a combination of numerous smaller systems. **What happens with many people is that when they decide to start a business, they approach it like a technician, rather than an entrepreneur.** They start a bakery, for instance, because they want to do the baking. But when that happens, you've just given yourself another job; you don't really have a separate business, and you surely don't have an asset.

Module #9 is all about creating a business as an asset, mostly by having employees who act as the technicians while you focus on building the business systems. Once you've done that and all of the parts are working well together, you have the ability to walk away from it and still make money. That's real freedom, in terms of both money and time. Most of the people who feel stuck in their businesses are missing this one piece.

If that's where you find yourself, sit down and think about what you can do to make your business better. Many of us want to be hands-on all the time—and we're so busy we don't take the time to think about how we can make our businesses more exceptional or profitable without killing ourselves. This really *is* one of the chief secrets of the world's richest and most successful business people. **There's no doubt they know how to work hard—but they achieve and hold onto true success because they have other people doing all of the work while they're working on ways to make more money.**

If you're wearing all the hats in your business, I'd suggest you doff a few and start farming out that work the minute you can afford to. Let accountants and bookkeepers do the fiscal work, including the billing. Hire clerks to sit behind the counter and check folks out. Otherwise, you're not as productive as you could be, although you're doing a heck of a lot of work. So start rethinking how you're working in your business. **Spend more time working on ways to make money and less time doing the actual work.** Usually, there are other people who can do the work for you more profitably, freeing up your time up to do the marketing and all the other things that directly bring in sales and new customers.

Last But Not Least...

Our final module is Module #10, Relationship Marketing. Sounds something like matchmaking, doesn't it? And in a way, I suppose it is: matchmaking between you and your very best prospects. **First you win their hearts, *then* you win their business.** People will do business with you for years, sometimes even for decades, if you do everything you can to build a strong relationship with them.

I believe it's hard to have a solid, successful business without working with great people—not just at the customer level but also as employees, managers, suppliers, and partners. **When you think about it, it makes sense that great relationships with all those people would actually increase your sales, profits, and enjoyment.** When both sides are happy with each other, they want to do more for each other. That's why it's important to focus on the people aspects as well as the technical aspects of building your business.

People want to do business with people they know, like and trust—people they know care about them. But too many business owners don't realize that, or just don't care. They don't spend any time building relationships with anyone, and then wonder why those people have no sense of loyalty. If they just added that one piece to their existing businesses, they would undoubtedly see an increase in profitability.

Recently, Russ told me that he viewed (for the second time) the life-story of Harlan Sanders, the man who created Kentucky Fried Chicken. It was amazing; if you ever get a chance to see it on TV, watch it. Dave Thomas (who went on to create Wendy's) worked for Colonel Sanders opening up Kentucky Fried Chicken outlets all over the country. Sometimes he'd just go to existing restaurants and say, "Hey, we're willing to let you use the Colonel's secret recipe here."

The Colonel treated his people right, so they wanted to do their very best for him. Thomas said that when he was working for Colonel Sanders, "When we'd fail to get enough business in a month, we'd have a big meeting with the Colonel—and we were so sad, because we felt we'd let him down. We loved the Colonel, and if we didn't open up 4-5 new stores each, sometimes within 4 or 5 weeks, we just felt pathetic." Now, *that's* loyalty. **When you really care for someone, you're going to work harder for them. So try to make your employees and customers love you, or at least like you, because it will pay big dividends.**

Relationships are the key to almost all business, traditional or not—all types of relationships. As I outlined in Chapter 10, business guru Stephen Covey has this theory that in a low-trust relationship, there's low-speed and high cost. On the other hand, high trust results in increased speed and lower costs.

You want to set your business model up so that you have high trust in all your relationships. **High trust means you do things more efficiently, your costs go down, and you make more money.**

That's most of what relationship building is about. **It's just being nice, treating people the right way, and building relationships that last.** That's how you get customers to come back to you over and over again. If you go to a restaurant where they treat you great, you're going to want to go back again, even if their food isn't wonderful.

Relationships are at the core of business because, ultimately, it's still all about people selling to people. If you set up your relationships properly, your business will thrive. You'll have increased speed, productivity, and efficiency, with decreased overall costs. **But if there's a *lack* of trust, things get slower and break down more easily, costing more than they should.** Keep your relationship-building skills honed, so your business will thrive.

That's All, Folks

Thank you so much for reading this book. Now I recommend you take a break—and then start reading it again, cover to cover. **It's well worth the time and effort if even one of the ideas I've outlined here works for you; it could even be worth millions of dollars to you over time.** Unless you borrowed this book from the library or a friend, I encourage you to highlight significant passages, do some underlining, write notes in the margin, mark it up with Post-It flags—whatever helps you study and remember what I've taught here. I believe your volume will end up well-thumbed because you refer back to it so often.

Remember: no business ever failed because its sales and profits were too high, unless they were doing something illegal and the government shut them down. You don't have to worry about that if you follow the strategies outlined in these 10 Ruthless Marketing modules, because from our perspective, "ruthless" doesn't mean screwing over people—especially the customers who grant you your living. **It's about relentlessly, aggressively going after as much of your market as you can and serving your prospects in the highest possible way in a purely legal, moral, and ethical manner.**

So become a Ruthless Marketer. Learn and develop the skills I've laid out in these 10 Modules, implement these strategies—and you'll end up light years ahead of your competition.

www.ingramcontent.com/pod-product-compliance
Lightning Source LLC
Chambersburg PA
CBHW031919190326
41519CB00007B/345